Mushrooms

Art by Kim

Garry 'Moonboot' Masters

Mushrooms & Moonboots

An Autobiography

by

Garry "Moonboot" Masters

Foreword...

Growing up in West London in the crazy, hazy 1960's/70's, much like the television sets of the time, progressing from black and white to vivid technicolour, Garry 'Moonboot' Masters served his freakadelic apprenticeship with his fellow adversaries in such exotic locations as London's Portobello Road, among the towering bluestones and surrounding fields of Stonehenge and beyond, elevating from his humble 'white bread' beginnings to a freaky-deakier hippy stoneground wholemeal...

Episode 1:

FROM THE CRADLE TO THE 'GROVE....
(1960 – 1982)

MASTERS OF THE UNIVERSE

My entry into this world and in particular the Masters dynasty was on the 7th February, 1960. Bloody Aquarian rat, head in the clouds and a tendency to gnaw holes in the skirtings. My dear Mum named me after Cary Grant ...she thought his name was Gary Grant! We were very poor in those days, oh lawdy. True story this.. my folks were so poor, they couldn't afford a cot for me right away so they made me a bed in a drawer. They swear that it was out of the chest of drawers at the time, but I dunno... I still now get visions of my two younger sisters Paula and Sonya being in lower drawers. I've heard of 'coming out of the closet', but being in a drawer.. maybe that's why the world has always slightly smelled of mothballs to me..

My earliest years are a bit vague these days (I always remember my childhood in black & white for some reason) but I do seem to remember spending copious amounts of time sitting outside pubs with a bottle of Coke and a packet of cheese and onion crisps... keeping an eye on my little sisters and occasionally peeking through the pub window, waiting for my Dad to get drunk enough to play the piano..

My Mum, Yvonne is from Enfield in Middlesex and my Dad, Roy is an Acton (West London) boy. They met in the late fifties when they were 'Teddy' boy and girl, he had an American car and was a bit of a flash Harry around town, with his drape coat, quiff and drainpipe trousers and my Mum was young and good looking and awop-bop-alooma, there I was!

Dad was the oldest child in his family, with three brothers and two sisters with just my Nan to look after them all. His Dad, my Grandad, had been a victim of the Second World War. The Masters family home was in the 'Vale' flats on the Uxbridge Road in Acton. Stark, dull red three-storey blocks of flats that had been built by German prisoners of war. They were very square and regimented (much like the Germans that built them) and the stairs always smelt really badly of stale piss. It was considered to be one of the rougher areas of Acton and was a breeding ground for a lot of hard nuts, including my Dad and his brothers.

My Dad is a great artist and especially cartoonist, he could absolutely destroy my Mum's self-confidence with one swift flick of his pen. He'd give her a double chin and make her nose longer and her eyes would be reduced to just beady pinholes. We kids would all roar with laughter at this and as soon as I could hold a pen I too learned the art of 'revenge by cartoon'.

Apparently Dad spent a lot of his 'conscription' time with the RAF in their kitchens peeling potatoes and suchlike as a punishment for doing 'derogatory likenesses' of the Sergeant Major.

Dad is also an excellent musician, he brought me up on a healthy diet of Jazz, Rock n' Roll, Blues and Beat Groups. I used to love going to peoples' houses as a kid and noodling through their record collections. The younger ones would always have some Beatles and Rolling Stones but the older ones always seemed to have multiple copies of 'Ray Connif's Hi-Fi Companion', 'Twenty Bawdy Bloody Rugby Songs' and those old 'Top 30 Hits Performed By Someone Who Sounds Not Very Much Like The Original Artists' ones with the topless chick on the cover and a 2/6d sticker placed strategically over the nipples.

Pretty much all of the Masters family are musical, my Nan was the archetypal pub pianist who used to play in pubs all over London's East and West End. My Dad did it too, he also had a

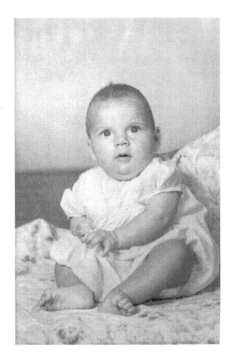

February 7th 1960, a new Moon is born into the Masters dynasty...

Me as Screaming Lord Sutch, fancy dress at a holiday camp. Lucky for my parents that I didn't turn out this way for real... Oops!

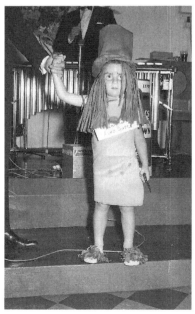

residency at the Acton British Legion club every Friday night, so I got used at an early age to the joys of live performance. The main lesson I learned through it all though, was to not do what my Dad was doing, to go further, write and perform my own stuff. There were times when I felt really sorry for him, seeing him play some great piano, swinging out with the band, but constantly looking over his shoulder at the growing queue of drunks waiting impatiently for a chance to get up on stage and slur through something like 'Love me Tender', dropping down on one knee with the passion of it all.. There had to be more to it than that! He did however always manage to win the talent competition at the 'Sunshine Holiday Camp' on Hayling Island where we went religiously every year for our Summer holidays, 1st prize being a free week's holiday there for two at the end of the season (2nd prize – two weeks! Nah, jus' kidding..) so off they'd go for a cosy seaside romp without us kids, leaving us with a childminder who looked like a blonde Nana Maskouri.. We were all really proud when Dad won though and maybe I liked the sound of the adulation he got while performing and fancied a bit of it myself...

There were a couple of brief brushes with stardom within the family. My Dad's sister Wendy was once going out with a local flashy lout called Terry Nellams. He was a bit of a rebel with attitude and thus highly attractive to the local girlies. He fell head over heels with Wendy and wanted them to get engaged but she blew him out, thinking there was no way someone like that would ever come of anything.. and shortly after that he changed his name to Adam Faith and rocketed to stardom.

My Uncle Eddie was the coolest for me, he was the youngest of them all, so nearer to my age and best of all he was a guitarist, and boy could (and still can) he play! I used to listen to him jamming on his guitar, spellbound, perched on the end of his bed. He was a true inspiration to me. The guitar seemed a natural instrument for me to pick up, I was never going to be a piano player.. my Dad had sent me to piano lessons when I was young and I was taught by this gnarly, moth balled, wrinkled old lady who would whack me on the back of the hands with a knitting needle if I played a bum note. As you can imagine, I would proceed to hit more bum notes and by the end of it I was playing like Les Dawson with my swollen stumps.. kinda put me off the idea.. anyway, back to Uncle Eddie.

He'd been jamming around in his teens with a group made up of local lads. They had a meeting one day where they decided that they'd like to have a go and turn professional. Eddie for some reason didn't pursue it and not long after they changed their name first to The High Numbers and eventually The Who. He later went on to jam with another local band who became (without him) 70's rock band Stray. He's never stopped jamming and gigging though and even as I write is still treading the boards pumping out R&B and blues, only these days on the bass guitar. He also plays a mean piano too (must have had a friendlier teacher!).

THUNDERBIRDS AND BATMAN

My Mum's Dad (my Grandad) was a carpenter and an excellent one at that, he could build anything (and almost did!). He had a wicked sense of humour and a great 'character' face, like a cross between me and Sid James from the 'Carry On' movies. There is Romany Gypsy in me courtesy of that side of my family (so watch ya hubcaps!). He worked for a long time at Elstree Film Studios (when it was owned by ATV) making all the huge wooden stage sets, props and housefronts.
On one particular birthday of mine, he brought me to the studio with him and showed me around all of the film and TV sets that were in production at the time. It blew me away when I discovered that although they would take weeks to build all these amazing sets, as soon as it was 'a wrap' they'd destroy it all! I remember we sat next to Gilbert O'Sullivan in the coffee shop, he was sporting his then famous 'pudding basin' hairstyle and donkey jacket style then (boy, I'll have half of what he was on then, eh? Probably just Guinness tho'...). Another time there was a Xmas party for all the kids of the staff. I can remember

Getting a taste for the custom bike lifestyle early, but why am I riding bitch?

Me and my dad (sporting a splendid 70's moustache) on our way to a Queen's Park Rangers football match.

that vividly.. all of the construction staff were dressed as members of the TV series Thunderbirds, including my Grandad who drove us around the studio floor in a yellow Morris Minor van that had been painted yellow and numbered to look like Thunderbird 4, as we screamed in the back with joy.

I really liked my Mum's brother Brian too, he'd often whisk me off to somewhere great, giving me a break from the concrete playground that me and my friends played in when we lived in a tower block in South Acton. He'd often take me to the West End of London to see a movie, I remember once seeing a huge crowd standing around the windows of a TV retailers, as I fought my way through the crowd, I saw my first colour TV set! Uncle Brian even forgave me for ruining his wardrobe. You see, like all kids in the 60's I was totally obsessed with the Batman TV show, it was a huge phenomena and Batmania was all around. Unfortunately, with the family's finances being as tight as they were, my hopes of dressing myself in the official Batman playsuit were close to zero. I tried to hide my disappointment, but my Mum picked up on it and decided to improvise.. she remembered that my Uncle Brian had an old black suit that he was going to get rid of, so off she went to find it and after much snipping, shaping and sewing presented me with my very own 'one-off' Batman mask and cloak which was really nice, being made from real cloth as opposed to the cheap-ass plastic ones that my wealthier friends at school would taunt me with. I felt special and promptly dashed out of the flat to proudly display my costume to all and sundry. When Brian got home from work I showed him my latest acquisition (daring him to recognise me) but his reaction wasn't quite what I was expecting.. yep, Mum had unwittingly grabbed the wrong suit (his best one!) and cut it up for my Batman outfit and all that was left of it were a few squares of dark material on the kitchen floor with vague 'bat' shapes cut out of them. Uncle Brian emigrated to Australia in the late 'sixties, one of many 'ten pound' emigrants. I was really sad when he left and I can still remember standing at the dock, waving goodbye as his ship sailed away with loads of ticker tape flapping loosely in the sea breeze. Unfortunately for me, he moved back to the UK just before I emigrated here to Australia myself.. I'm sure it wasn't because of the Bat suit... was it????

FAR OUT MAN

I can remember my first experience of 'hippies' quite vividly.. I've personally never really liked being called a 'hippy', to me they were the 60's flower children, granny glasses, flutes and velvet loon pants, but come the dawn of the 70's, the woodwork creaked and out came the 'freaks' which in some way explained better how I felt I was perceived by the straighter citizens (but then, being an old hippy, I WOULD say that..). In this instance tho', it WAS the 60's so they WERE hippies.

I must have been about eight or nine years old and we were on a family holiday at the 'Something-by-the-Sea (mud and dead fish usually)' Caravan Park and as usual there were the archetypal 'thrilling activities' such as ping-pong, darts or rain-bathing.. then there was my Dad's favourite bit.. the clubhouse. Not having to worry about driving home, he'd enjoy more than a few bevvies (and good luck to him, Dad's always been nothing less than good entertainment when lashed). Us kids loved it too, because it meant two things. Yup, Coke and cheese & onion crisps! I suffered really badly from travel sickness when I was little, so our holiday journeys would involve numerous stops for me to leap out of the car and chuck my guts up at the side of the road (if I made it out of the car in time) as well as the usual piss stops, leg stretches, overheated engines, traffic jams, wrong turns and elusive caravan park signs. Always an experience....

Upon arrival and after eventually finding and settling into our caravan, we were all looking forward to that first night at the clubhouse. However, as we approached the dance hall we became aware of a very unusual smell, it was thick and pungent and smelt like burning grass, which in a sense it was, but not the sort of grass that Dad had been cutting in our garden. We entered through the main glass doors and the music just hit me right there in the chest.. it was wild baby, yeah! It was dark in there, but it was light. There were ultraviolet lights glowing and strobes flashing, big blobby, globby slime slithering around the walls in technicolour and the people, wow, the people wore velvet cloaks and big, swingin' bell bottoms and beads and fur and top hats with feathers in. They had stars and wild paintings on their faces and everyone seemed happy and good with the world. There were these weird and wonderful freaks sitting cross-legged on the floor sharing 'cigarettes' (now THAT'S caring and sharing) or leaping about, waving their arms and gyrating to the throbbing, crazy music that was pumping from the DJ console's speakers, this when DJ's played music rather than just beats! I soon found myself (just a kid) walking among the dancers, watching what they were doing and trying to copy them. I was a shakin' and a shimmerin' with the best of 'em, I felt so free and the next thing I know I'm surrounded by all these hippy women with large, pendulous breasts (all their bras had been burned, remember?) who smiled a lot and thought I was 'cute'. I was. I'm sure at one point I looked over to my parents for acknowledgement but instead saw them looking at each other in dismay.

Mum and Dad didn't know what to make of it.. they were dead straight, down the line and psychedelia went waaaay over their heads. Sure, Dad did have pretty boofy hair for a while there and a Sergeant Pepper moustache (but then, so did one of my Aunties) and I remember my Mum in hot pants (but try not to think about it), but they just couldn't get their heads around what was going on.. I'd sensed that much already. It was the start of a crack in the family unit that was to eventually become a (generation) gap. For me it was like a wall had come tumbling down and I'd discovered that I'd been in a small box for all that time. I'd often wondered why I hadn't fitted in with a lot of the 'normal' kids, I wasn't really into sport (much to my Dad's disappointment) or very much of anything really.. I just loved to ride my yellow Raleigh Chopper bicycle, draw cartoons and read comics.. but above all I was just learning to get into my music.

LIVIN' IN THE 70'S

Wot a crazeee era to spend your teens in, eh? My most vivid memories about the 'seventies are the colours orange and brown. Everything was fucking orange and brown, walls, curtains, furniture, cars, Hot Wheels tracks, even if you look at yourselves in photos from that era, they're sure to have that familiar orange and brown tint..

Of course, the Western world was trying to recover from the after effects of the even crazier 'sixties.. ban the bomb, Vietnam, freedom of speech, the commies, Beatle AND Bat mania et al. and added to the ensuing chaos were the humungous amounts of strikes and shortages at the time. Power cuts on an ever-regular basis, mountains of rotting rubbish filling every kerbside courtesy of striking garbage men, bread shortages and, even worse, the 'Great Toilet Paper Shortage'!! With the announcement of the impending shortages, 'panic buying' would ensue leaving only the weird Turkish-style bread that nobody liked and horror of horrors, in the toiletry department the only toilet paper left would be that horrible, nasty, shiny stuff that came in a flat box like they had at school. You know the stuff, you release a sheet from its scabbard and as you wipe it around yer date you realise that it's not porous in the slightest and you are in fact just smearing the shit all around your butt and the back of your balls.. but not before delivering a deft slice into your bum skin courtesy of said paper's razor sharp edges thus exposing said wound to the approaching poo smear.. yowsahs!!

The antidote to all the chaos was to be found in the two colours orange and brown. Their bold shades would fend off the most foulest of evil doings. So, armed with open-crocheted tank tops of that popular hue and shirts with collars wider than themselves, the populace strode garishly into the 'seventies...

I, of course, had to start the decade differently. My friends and I grew up in pretty tough areas around Acton and poncey, noncey paisley shirts with orange and brown flares weren't the go if you didn't want to have the shit kicked out of you at every street corner around your estate. The nearest major soccer ground to Acton was that of Queen's Park Rangers and all the local yobs (including me, do or die!) would converge at the Loftus Road end of the stadium and do yobbish things like spit lots (an art in itself!) and take notes on the emerging skinhead fashions.. I was lucky and suddenly became hip for a while there as my Mum had a good friend who worked at the local Levi's Jeans factory who would 'liberate' the odd article of clothing for me, so I was well sorted for the 'two-tone tonic' trousers and button-down shirts that were the 'duck's guts' at the time. My folks couldn't afford to get me the Dr Marten boots that were just coming 'in' at the time, so I had to make do with 'Monkey' boots which were an acceptable alternative (read – you wouldn't get beaten up) if your family were poor.

As luck (kinda) would have it, I was already sporting a shaved head, something I'd had done to me since I was a toddler... what was that about? Was it a lice thing? Who knows? Of course, you didn't say your head was shaved back then, oh no.. you were sporting a 'crew cut' or 'crop', in my case, courtesy of the dreaded Bert Spires. Bert Spires was the Demon Barber of old South Acton, he was cheap and he did two styles, the aforementioned crew cut or the 'pudding bowl'. Any of you who remember Dwayne Dibbley from the TV series 'Red Dwarf' will know immediately that the pudding bowl was an even worse option, so down I'd go to Bert's on a regular basis throughout my childhood, being dragged by my Dad who somehow always managed to get away with not sporting either style. Bert hurt! That bastard used to shear me like a sheep, grabbing my ears roughly with his leathery hands and rolling my head to one side while he scraped his rusty-toothed torture machine along the side of my head, removing several layers of flesh from the tops of my ears in the process, then, to add insult to injury he'd spray some mystery concoction from a puffer bottle into the open wounds. I was a crap skinhead anyway, I didn't wanna fight anyone, I just wanted to read my comics and listen to music, so as soon as I could muster the courage (through a crack in the door) I said 'No more Bert Spires!!' and my hair finally began its epic journey down my back. That was my only ever foray into fashion and what a vacuous world it is, eh kids??

The first real pop/rock band I ever saw live was Slade. It was 1972, during Noddy Holder's mirrored hat phase and I guess they were at their peak then. I was only twelve years old at the time, but the power of the music just blew me away. It was possible to play your music that loud?... and people would applaud and ask for more? Who-Hoo! They were a great band to be into at the time as far as pop bands go and I still rate their early live album 'Slade Alive' as one of the most kick-ass, dirty mutha-fuckin' records I've ever heard. I understand that Lemmy once offered Noddy the role of vocalist in his fledgling Motorhead ..imagine THAT if you will!

The 'seventies was a popular era for fads or crazes and most of them involved some kind of personal injury risk either at school or at home. Conkers were bad enough, especially when you were in the final heat, playing against Bluto the school bully, size of a cow, brain of a flea, who's Mum has cooked his conker in the oven to secure him a win, thus saving his Mum further embarrassment and giving her a chance to prove to her family that the fat shit was at least good for something other than brutalising people smaller/thinner than himself (make that everyone then..). He probably went on to be a cop, or maybe a politician...

Rapidly superseding the venerable conker though, was a new kid on the block.. the evil menace that were the terrifying 'Clackers'!! If you are anywhere in the vicinity of my age, you too will remember the Clackers and a chill will run down your spine as you recoil in horror at the memory of the pain associated with them.. oh, the pain! To the uneducated, clackers were two hard (and I mean hard, they shoulda built cars out of the stuff..) plastic resin spheres about the size of a plum each, with a string running through them, joined at the top, like two conkers tied together in fact. The idea was that, if you could get the two balls to 'clack' together, eventually they would gain momentum and be violently clacking away above and below your clenched fist as you jiggled about in accelerated upward and downward thrusts. Grown men were known to cry as the inevitable happened and the balls became bored with going in the same direction and decided to change the rules of physics and smashed with great force onto the most painful, pointy bony parts of your knuckles. The school playground was deluged with the cacophony of sound produced by eager Clacker-ettes, clack-clack, clacking away, soon followed by an all too familiar blood-curdling scream. Now, my school was a rough school, but at that moment in time knuckle-dusters were out and knuckle bandages were in...

KUNG POW!!

Of course, the greatest of all 'seventies crazes was Kung Fu. I believe the origin of the name came from when Grasshopper was practising Tai chi one day in the grounds of his temple, when all of a sudden a ferkin' great spear flew past his face. He span 'round to see who the perpetrator was, shouting angrily "Oi! What 'Cung Fu that?". Bruce Lee started the whole craze and his fighting skills are/were legendary. He was the Karate-kickin' aide to the Green Hornet in the TV show of the '60's, but it was his Martial arts movies that hit the right note in the 'seventies. A lot of the appeal, I believe, was courtesy of the recently added wah-wah pedal to the Chinese soundtrack guitarist's inventory and the introduction of a few Afro-haired black dudes who strutted their funky stuff to its chunky, choppy rhythms.. "Listen here, Mr Han MAN!" Then, as is the way of most unexpectedly popular movies, there swiftly followed a TV series. 'Kung Fu' was its name, but our Bruce had been pipped at the post by David Carradine, son of John, a famous cowboy/western actor of earlier times.

Kung Fu the series was amazing, I don't know if the writers thought everybody too dumb to notice, or whether somebody HAD actually put LSD in the water supply, but somehow they managed to make a complete series out of just the one plot. It was the same every week! Silent, mysterious Chinese stranger in dusty clothes turns up at some remote town way out west, everybody tells him to "Fuck Off!" so he proceeds to kick the shit out of them all then leave. And quite how he managed to do so much damage by fighting sooo slooowly, fuck knows.. Those townsfolks sure musta been perty dumb if they didn't read at least a few of those punches, chops and kicks coming.. my Nan could've. Thereafter followed a plethora of t-shirts, bubblegum cards, posters, magazines and before ya knew it nowhere in the playground or street was safe. A seemingly innocent corner or doorway could suddenly see you confronted by a howling, wailing, arm flailing assailant who was hell bent on giving you a sound thrashing, regardless of the fact that he may well be your best friend.

I, like many kids my age (and older!) really dug the 'Nunchucks' that Bruce Lee used in his movies. Basically a 'rice flail' which comprised of two hard wooden handles joined together by a sturdy chain (Uber-Clackers!). Some of the flashier kids at school managed to get a hold of real ones, or at least knew someone who did.. the rest of us had to make do and improvise.. enter my Dad... after warning me about the dangers of inflicting violent acts upon people (yeah, right Dad!) he pottered out to the shed and proceeded to knock up a set for me. Dad's a real handyman, he can build, paint and fix anything.. I can't (but I can write a song about it!). After a sturdy lecture about how they were only 'for show', he presented me with said weapons of self-destruction. He'd got some hard, plastic plumbing pipe and made two handles which he filled with thick, wooden dowling (that'll be two coshes then..) and connected them via a thick, sturdy metal chain fixed to the handles by two large 'eye' hooks. They nearly broke my arms just from the sheer weight of the things as he placed them into my weedy hands, but with several grunts and the odd wheeze I managed to get those suckers spinning.. I couldn't believe it.. I was a weavin' and a bobbin', flipping them around my back and between my legs like the mighty Mr Lee himself.. you know what's coming, don't you? Yep, with an almighty 'CRACK' one of the handles up and smashed me on the back of the head, causing me to see many stars, but at the same time giving me instant cool status as the proud bearer of the biggest, egg-shaped bump on the noggin that I'd ever had. I finally managed to get it down to a fine art (the injuring that is..) and soon added to the collection.

YOU CAN'T STOP THE MUSIC

With my family upbringing, music came very easily to me, but like the rest of the family I can only play 'by ear'. Show me a piece of sheet music and it won't mean shit to me, but play me a tune and I'll eventually work it out.. there might be a few 'jazz' inflictions.. but what the hey?

My first electric guitar was an 'Airstream Deluxe' which if you were partially blind or in a dark room would at a real push of the imagination vaguely resemble a Fender Stratocaster. It was post box red and had one of those 'tortoiseshell-esque' finger plates and a whammy bar, which I think was put on the instrument to give you the option of putting all of the strings out of tune in an instant should you desire that effect (or not). The neck of the guitar was as thick as a telegraph pole and chords had to be held down with a vice-like grip! It came with a tiny practise amplifier that looked like a small television set and it was mine for the princely sum of twelve pounds. By then I had a job delivering newspapers in the mornings and had been saving for ages, getting nowhere fast.. so it was the best I could get at the time..

That was it though.. I was on my way. Other friends at school had also got electric guitars and we became the 'musos' and 'jammed' in turn at each other's houses (so's not to set just the one set of parents off). We'd be plinkin' and plonkin' and making all sorts of rackets but as is the way of rock, once we'd mastered the opening riff to 'Smoke on the Water' that was it.. the discovery of the mighty power chord... KERDOOOINNNG!! After that it was simply a case of wearing an army greatcoat, growing my hair and smoking joints in the playground at school. I used to walk around with one of those 'Bush' portable cassette players in a carrier bag, blaring out albums like 'We're Only in it For the Money' by the Mothers of Invention or 'Led Zeppelin 2'. We couldn't afford to buy guitar leads, so one day we went around to all of the phone boxes in our area and cut off all the curly telephone leads and replaced the headsets back on the phone. It must have been a bit of a shocker for all those people who tried to use them after that.. "Hello? Hello?" Goddammit!!!#**@@!!! One of our friends would solder jack plugs onto the leads for us, enterprising if nuthin' else..

There was a guy in my school year called Neville, sadly no longer with us, he was already a much more advanced guitarist while we were still wrestling with the chords to Black Sabbath's 'Paranoid'. We'd sometimes go out of hours to a school in North Acton on an Industrial Estate where we could rent the hall to practise in and play as loud as we liked! Well, as loud as our puny starter amplifiers would let us, but the hall had that lovely cavernous reverb which upped the sound levels admirably. Neville and his older brother were really hip and had the appropriate freaky hair, bit o' stubble, tatty ol' afghan coats and best of all.. relatively decent guitars. They gave me something to aspire to and introduced me to many kool tunes and bands that I'd never heard before.

Another old school friend of mine, Chris, had a guitar and also played his Dad's drums, in fact, his Dad and mine played in a band together for a while. Chris had a really decent singing voice too, so together we got over the initial obstacles of 7th and minor chords and the mighty F major with our puny, infantile fingers and he tried to help me learn to sing. We formed a duo, calling ourselves 'Toad' (for reasons which escape me now!) and we wrote a lot of songs and performed at a couple of pubs and clubs, harmonising precariously due to imminent breakage of the vocal chords courtesy of impending ball-dropping.. Chris's older brother Gary worked for Bronze Records at the time and he got us heaps of promotional records from bands like Uriah Heep so we wuz rockin' from an early age. His Mum also worked for the McKewans Brewery so we had an endless supply of beer too.. result!

MEET THE NEW SKOOL, JUST LIKE THE OLD SKOOL

It was around that time that I began hanging out at school and beyond with fellow reprobate Steve 'Speed Machine'. We both attended (kinda) Faraday High School which was in our home town of Acton. It was a huge brick and glass construction that housed around 1200 pupils, well over thirty a class I remember.. It was pretty rough at times and you had to have your wits about you. It was then about equal thirds white, black and asian kids and the tension was always around, you could feel it in the air and things would explode violently with the smallest of provocations.. Our school had such a bad reputation that I remember the BBC deciding to do a 'Panorama' documentary about us. The Headmaster had told us about the filming just the day before and had sternly warned us to behave or else, the TV crew however asked us to disregard that.. what would you have done? They got what they wanted, the film crew that is..

I spent a lot of time in detention at school.. a lot, funnily enough my mate Steve did too, the rebellious streak was well and truly implanted by then. In my first year at High School I was part of a committee that decided to organise a huge 'run out' by all the pupils in protest against school uniform, it was an amazing sightseeing a huge mob of kids rush a few heavily outnumbered prefects trying to stop the stampede and spill out into the streets. We were eventually named and shamed and thus began a well-trodden track from my classroom to the Headmaster's office for suitable (to him) punishment.

Another time a few of us had bought flicknives while on the obligatory trip to France. Like most kids I really wanted one because the kool factor was optimum, regardless of the fact that I could have lost a few digits in a matter of seconds. I'd managed to stash mine really well on the way back through customs at Dover and all was looking rosy until one of the kids shouted "Hey Garry, show everyone your flicknife!". I was instantly leapt on by the teachers and forced to hand it over. I had to go see the Headmaster with my Dad the next day (who was none too chuffed about that!) and the situation was explained to him. A further series of detentions was planned and severe beatings duly admonished by both parties. I did eventually discover said flicknife in Dad's fishing tackle box many years later...

The rest of the time I was held back after school or just plain sent home due to what I was wearing. By then it wasn't uncommon for me to turn up in my leather cowboy hat and boots with this big, old Afghan coat that smelt like a damp yak that I'd found down Portobello Road. I'd tried in vain to disguise the smell by splashing patchouli oil (the Brut 33 of the alternative sect!) all over it, but that just produced the even headier whiff of a damp, patchouli-splashed yak. So, back out of the school gates I'd go and straight down the road to the chippy. The only lesson I ever really enjoyed and couldn't bear to miss was the art class. I loved it all, the drawing, the sketching, not so much the painting, but most of all I loved Miss Coop... ah me.. Miss Coop. She was a statuesque Swedish blonde who resembled Ursula Andress in that Bond movie (but without the snorkel, although she gave me a snorkel if you get my drift..). I excelled at that class and (for once) would often hang out after class by choice, fondling my pencil..

By the time I met my mate Steve, I was in the 'not quite top of the class but has us believing he's brighter than he is' class and Steve was in the 'Oh my god, why us?' class. We did share a few classes together, you know, the really useful ones.. er.. Social Science? Economics? (say wha?). We didn't know what any of it meant but we did know that it brought forth a constant supply of bearded, corduroy wearing 'relief' teachers who were sent in like fresh cannon fodder to replace their predecessors who'd had nervous breakdowns, therefore presenting us with the fresh challenge of seeing how long they would last before themselves running screaming from the classrooms.

There were actually a few pretty cool, younger teachers there who encouraged us to express ourselves freely, so they only had themselves to blame, but they stuck with us. One of our English teachers would bring into class albums like 'Dark Side of the Moon' or 'Tubular Bells', play them to us and ask us to write down what we were experiencing while listening to them... kids today don't know what they're missing! Our proper Music teacher had long given up on trying to teach any of us 'La Cucaracha' on his battered, spittle-stained brass instruments and instead opted to let us bring in 45's to play on the school turntable. One of the kids would bring in Judge Dread singles, he was a fat, white guy who sang dirty limericks to a reggae backbeat.

One of the more bohemian teachers asked my friend Chris and I if we'd decorate her flat for her in return for a trip to the cinema followed by a meal. We didn't hesitate and promptly set to the task in hand, not doing too bad a job at the time, although after it had all dried we soon discovered exactly how close her flat was to the neighbouring train tracks because it all cracked and split.. oopsy! When she asked us what movie we'd like to see we both immediately replied "Emmanuelle!". The movie had just come out in the West End and rumour was that it was rather rude and explicit (especially to a permanently-erect sixteen year old). She didn't even bat an eyelid at the suggestion so off we went to the West End of London, saw the movie (yup, it was that good!) and after she took us both to the Hard Rock Café.

There was also a trip organised by some teachers to a gig at

London's Lyceum Ballroom where we saw Kevin Coyne, The Pretty Things and Link Wray perform. We got pretty stoned with those ones that night and there was an after-party back at the teachers' shared house. The music was pumping, there were bongs being stacked on the tables and best of all, water beds, where I got intimate for the first time with a young girlie of my acquaintance.. ahh.. sweet, young Anna...

She used to let me put my hand between her legs in the back row of the Maths class. She always wore long-ish skirts, tights AND knickers so, we'd tip our desks and chairs back against the wall, as all the kool kids did anyway (Sheriff's position, no chance of attack from behind!) and somehow, very slowly and very gingerly I'd snake my right hand under the desk, up her recently opened nylon-clad leg, under her skirt, up to the waist band, down through the front of her tights and knickers and if I had any blood left in my arm by then I'd have a fumble about in the fluffy undergrowth.. she came across to many as shy and timid, but I knew better..

CHICKS, DICKS & HOT LICKS

I tell ya, I don't remember NOT having a boner at that age.. a bit awkward at family gatherings and suchlike! In time I soon came to realise that if I played my guitar lots it would give me something else to do with my hands rather than scuttling off to the toilet with a dog-geared copy of 'Health & Efficiency' magazine every five minutes.. boy that magazine had a weird effect on me and probably lots of other spotty permanently-erect boys too. In those days it was illegal for nudie mags to show pubic hair and especially any sort of fanny lippage for some inexplicable reason, so instead there'd be a sort of airbrushed-out nothingness between their legs.. it freaked the shit out of me when I saw my first picture of how a woman's pussy really looked.. I thought their insides were coming out! Anyway, I digress..(see how easily distracted I was then?) so.. playing the guitar gave me sufficient kool at school (well, no-one wanted to beat me up!) the chicks were suddenly finding us interesting and I felt an intense sense of freedom and joy in letting my hair grow and following a path that was rapidly making itself clear to me as 'my own way', as opposed to any other type of future that may have been planned for me or expected of me. I became me, for better or for worse....

Over time, my friendship with Steve grew through a mutual love of certain bands and associated cultures of that era, many of which happened to have a 'Ladbroke Grove' connection, bands like The Pink Fairies, Hawkwind and especially the newly formed Motorhead. We also shared a fascination with the mind-altering substances that also played an important part in shaping the phenomenon that spawned the afore-mentioned groups. I'd already been in a couple of serious Heavy Rock Bedroom Bands and had a couple of gigs already under my belt and Steve was keen to get together and have a jam, which we did in his Dad's garage (with a view of the neighbouring cemetery – eat ya heart out Black Sabbath!).. I knew there and then that we'd both be in for a very interesting life at the very least... We started going to a Disco every night up at Park Royal, don't worry kids, we didn't have no 'Night Fever', instead we'd break out the speed and chat up the girls (which was kind of self-defeating really!). The Disco music, especially at that time, was atrocious and we'd be propping up the bar watching the budding Travoltas with their medallions swinging to the beat and the chicks dancing around their handbags, but more often than not, we'd be out in the car park puffing on spliffs and doing the business with the eager North Acton Disco Boys.

GET SOME MENTAL ANAESTHESIA

It was Steve that first introduced me to Motorhead (and a lot of other good bands over the years too..). We already shared an interest in other acts like Hendrix, Hawkwind, The Pink Fairies, Stray etc. but when he played me his newly acquired copy of the 'Motorhead' 12" on Chiswick Records, it truly rocked my world and when I discovered that for the 'B' side they'd recorded a version of 'City Kids' by The Pink Fairies (one of my favourite tunes of all time) I realised that here at last was a band that was of OUR time, playing at about the same velocity that we'd just begun living at. Punk was in the air and all around us people were cutting and spiking their hair, wearing safety pins and bondage pants in a desperate attempt to look different, yet somehow ending up looking all the same.. we wanted to keep our freaky roots, we were still getting off on all the good stuff that had gone on before, we liked our long hair and Hendrix and hashish, but at the same time we were bursting with an unstoppable energy and living fast.. partly due to copious amounts of the white stuff, but also because we were on a mission.. "It's ok Ma'm, we're musicians.." so we were freaky-punks or punky-freaks and only one band out there related to us, Motorhead. In no time we became proud owners of shiny bullet belts bought hastily down the Portobello Road before the antique dealers realised their value to all these rabid, leather-bound freakoids. Steve already had a black leather jacket, but, yep, I couldn't afford one but instead had a suede 'bomber' jacket that my Uncle John had brought back from the 'States. I eventually swapped it for a rather more appropriate black leather jacket but it was a real cheapo one that was so stiff it was like it was made out of wood! We'd kick it down the road, jump up and down on it, throw it in front of cars, but to no avail..

At the time, Motorhead's manager had a huge version of their (now iconic) 'Skull' logo painted on the side of a house that overlooked the Shepherd's Bush roundabout, we'd often pass it on our way to, or back from gigs. Lemmy was, and still is, a very affable chap. For such a well-known musician he was/is always accessible and didn't talk down to you while preening his hair. We'd always get to the Motorhead gigs earlier than needed because we'd begun to meet similar, like-minded freaks and with the state of mind that we were often in, we had a whole lotta talking to do. Eventually there began to form what would now be called a 'posse', not always the same people all the time but all part of the tribe.. livin' the life… and you would always bump into at least some of them down the Portobello Road.. especially Lemmy.

THE ADVENTURES OF THE PANCAKE 'LOLL KID

The first time I ever got arrested was a bizarre turn of events. I was seeing a girl at the time called Joyce who lived on the other side of town. I'd always walk home from her place along the same route, alongside the park, past the Chinese takeaway and up along the A40 to my place. The smells that wafted from the Chinese takeaway were soon to entice me in and I was to become a regular there on every return trip, without fail. I soon became a constant source of amusement for the staff as I always ordered the same thing.. one pancake roll. Never having much money, what I did have got spent straight away on records, comix and recreational additives, in no time at all I became known as the 'Pancake 'Loll Kid – har har har!' and sure enough, as soon as I walked through their door I'd be greeted by a unanimous cry of "Rook! Here come da Pancake Loll Kid! Har har har!"

One particular night, after dropping my girl home and ordering my pancake roll (with extra abuse), I was happily meandering up the road home when a maroon Ford Cortina swerved abruptly in front of me. Suddenly two uniformed cops jumped out, grabbed me by the scruff of the neck and pushed me into a shop doorway. When I asked them what the hell was going on, they told me that I was under arrest. I don't know why I did it, but I took one look at the plain-clothed maroon Cortina and then at them and said "Well, how do I know you're real cops?" This turned out to be the equivalent of waving a red flag to a bull and any measure of niceness that they were going to afford me went right out the window there and then and they started pushing me around.. "If you like, we'll take you down to the station right now and prove it to you!" I took their word for it and over time would become accustomed to spotting plain-clothed police cars, being that they were all maroon Ford Cortinas with uniformed cops in them...

I was told the reason for my arrest was because I fitted the description of someone who'd just abused the staff of the local Chinese restaurant and smashed his head through the plate glass window when refused service. I pointed out that as I had no blood or broken glass on me and had instead just finished off a particularly tasty pancake roll from said establishment that there was a chance that they could actually be mistaken in this case (wave, wave). With that they grunted (effortlessly), bundled me into the back of the car and took me to the scene of the crime for identification. As we arrived, the scene was still one of chaos and confusion (Confucius?), there was broken glass everywhere (and puddles of blood) and the staff were all running about wailing and freaking out. As we stepped out of the car the police presented them with their recently captured fugitive from the law. They took one look at me, then a very slanty look at the cops and said "No you bruddy iriots! That not him.. that "Pancake Loll Kid!" I was hastily bundled back into the car, driven home where they then apologised to my parents for keeping me out so long.... bruddy iriots.

THE PORTOBELLO ROAD SHUFFLE

I'd started frequenting the Portobello Road market every Saturday and was very pleased to discover that a lot of the bands I was into were either based around that part of London or appeared frequently thereabouts. The scene there felt really comfortable for me, I no longer felt like a square peg surrounded by round holes! It was like I'd found my tribe. I dug the music, the weird shops and market stalls, the underground comix, the wafts of aromatic incense emanating from the Hindukush Tibetan clothing store and the Head shops, the freaks, the bikers struttin' proudly around their shiny chopper motorcycles outside the pubs and of course, the sexy bohemian chicks in their bra-less kaftan blouses, nipples swinging freely in the breeze.. I first went there around 1975 with my school friend Chris and was just blown away by it all, it was like that earlier scene at the holiday camp that I'd witnessed but this was a lifestyle rather than an excursion! By the next Xmas we'd been regular visitors and to make a bit of much needed cash we'd hassled Chris's Dad into helping us make little 'Acrobatic Archies', little wooden jointed figures that would do somersaults on a piece of string between two wooden sticks. They were easy enough to knock up, they weren't plastic toys and they turned out pretty good so when we set up on a street corner there (you could get away with that sort of thing then!) the passing punters snapped 'em all up. We made enough money that day to buy all our Xmas presents and still had some spending money left over!

By that time the area had gone from being a relatively affluent part of London to a playground of bohemians, beatniks, jazz musicians, poets and writers, it had taken a stroll thorough marshmallow clouds and down and then downer to become a slum for the recently immigrated Irish, West Indians, Asians, winos, whores, junkies and burnouts from the Acid daze. It was a time of OZ, International Times, BIT, incense and Mick Farren. Under the Westway flyover there was a 'free' shop, yep, that's right, everything there was free to take. It was mostly shitty, donated stuff but, hey, if you were permanently off ya tits and living in a shop doorway then a change of clothing would have been most desirable, regardless of the style. There were a lot of Head shops and I'd eagerly started an Underground Comix collection (jeez, you could get away with this stuff?) which I still have today, stuff like the Fabulous Furry Freak Brothers, Wonder Warthog and anything by my favourite artist Mr Robert Crumb. Being a budding artist myself, I was amazed and truly inspired by all of these highly talented artists and the oh-so-risque topics that they tackled.. There were these huge, grand, Edwardian town houses (now worth millions) being squatted by legions of freaks, weirdos and drunks with huge padlocks on the doors and windows to stop the landlords from evicting them and also other freeloaders moving in on their space.

I'd met a guy down there called Cliff, he was quite a bit older than me, more like an elder brother and he happily showed me around all the hippest dives in the area. He looked a bit like Donald Sutherland, tall, skinny with a mop of long, blonde hair and a Dennis Hopper moustache. He was the archetypal Notting Hill dude and could often be seen strolling about in either a 'mock' Victorian style getup, black velvet cloak, top hat and cane or dressed in his tatty cowboy hat, boots and tasselled suede jacket a la Easy Rider. He introduced me to a lot of crazy characters and his squat was the first one that I'd ever visited, right on the Portobello Road overlooking the Electric Cinema. He was also the first to show me how to over-ride an electricity meter and get the juice for free! A necessity for the squatters during those cold, English winters..

The first time I stayed overnight there, he'd just met a French chick called Claudine, she was very much the hippy chick and I thought they made the perfect pair. We toked and smoked all night long and I had my first hit of Cocaine, which inspired me to listen to most of his substantial record collection throughout the night, checking out the bands I hadn't heard of yet. I remember especially he'd just bought Bob Dylan's 'Blood on the Tracks' and, probably helped by chemical state of mind at the time, suddenly ol' Bob began to make sense, I got him! They also took me one time to the Electric Cinema to see 'Janis' a documentary about her life (and death). Unfortunately death reared its ugly head a bit closer to home for me when, not long after, both Cliff and Claudine in a fit of smack-induced depression made a suicide pact and gave each other o.d's. That experience in itself was a reality check for me and it helped keep me on the straight and narrow as far as needles were concerned, their untimely death served as an extreme warning for me and prevented me from ever going down THAT dark road... I met a lot of people around then, most of them older than me but who kind of took my friends and I under their patchouli-soaked wings. S'funny when I think back now, but there were a lot of dealers about, as you can imagine, and due to their (understandable) wish to remain anonymous we only ever got to know them by the geographical location of their birth and their first names. Hence we got to meet an awful lot of Irish Micks, Geordie Daves and a plethora of Scottish Johns.

A TYPICAL 1970'S VISIT DOWN THE PORTOBELLO ROAD

Steve and I would catch a bus on the Saturday morning (ish) or maybe jump the fence at North Acton train station and sneak onto a train or sometimes we even just walked there (we only lived a coupla miles away and we had a lot of energy to burn!) and upon arrival we would kick into the ol' regular routine...

*Arrive at Notting Hill train station on the Bayswater Road, if a train had been caught, work out cunning plan to get past the guard without tickets (usually involving subtle manoeuvres like barging through the crowd or jumping over a secluded fence/barrier.

*Due to Steve's unpredictable bladder, I'd have to wait outside the public toilets at the station as he 'syphoned the python', trying hard not to look like some kinda gay pickup as I waited patiently for him to finish. It was really dodgy in those toilets and very difficult to piss with an audience.

*First stop, the huge 'Record & Tape Exchange' store just outside the station. That one had a rare-record collector's section upstairs with lots of albums we wanted but couldn't afford, stuff like the 'Glastonbury Fayre' triple album with its previously unreleased tracks by the Pink Fairies, Hawkwind, Gong and the Grateful Dead among many others (I did eventually get myself a mint copy of this and I have it sealed in a lead-lined container at an undisclosed location). They were mean bastards at that shop if you were hard up and had to sell some of your records to them, you hardly got anything for 'em, but they did sell their records a lot cheaper than new, plus, if you timed it right you could get 'preview' copies of new albums that the music journalists had reviewed (or not) and promptly taken down to the Record & Tape Exchange for much needed beer money, often before they'd even seen general release!

*On to the infamous Virgin record store, as in THE only Virgin record store, pre-global domination, you've got Mike Oldfield to thank for that! It was most kool in there, they had a line of listening booths with headphones but you had to queue up to have a go.. the place was always packed with freaks listening to 'Tubular Bells' shouting "..And Adolf Hitler on vibes!" at the appropriate moment. I've always loved that original Virgin Records logo though, the one with the naked twins, my Dad reckoned at the time that if they truly were 'virgin' records then you should have to punch your own holes through them (thanks for the input Father!).

*'Round the corner and over the road to the other 'lesser' Record & Tape Exchange searching for old MC5, Deviants and Stooges albums. I also had a really bad habit then of buying really obscure albums if they had interesting covers. New album cover art had started to become rather bland, you know the sort, boring photo of the band on the front, track listing on the back.. we liked the big, fuck-off fold out jobbies with the psychedelic art and booklets and suchlike, stuff like Hawkwind's 'Space Ritual'. Unfortunately, most of the albums I bought purely on the strength of the cover art turned out to be in that shop for a very good reason, they were shit. They were either bad 'pseudo' psychedelic bands made up to cash in on the scene (maaan) or they were dodgy disco bands which just happened to have a sci-fi theme.

*Onwards to the top entrance of Portobello Road, sniggering and smirking in deep, manly voices and punching each other in the arm as we passed the window of the Gay Boutique with its leatherette underpants and Freddie Mercury leather biker caps and onwards into the merry throng. There always seemed to be more people coming up the road towards us as opposed to tackling it from our end so if there was anybody we knew down the 'road we'd eventually bump bullet belts with them.

*Down past the 'don't even bother looking' expensive antique shops and stalls with their garishly painted rocking horses in the windows and brass gramophones frequented by curious American tourists who would snap up anything if they were told that the Queen herself had brushed but a few feet from or had farted upon said curio. I knew a woman who worked in one of those antique shops who had a real, plummy, posh accent but was originally a prostitute in her native Liverpool.. now the pearl necklaces were real ones! She once confided in me that in order to get her 'clients' over with as soon as possible, she'd run her hands under the cold tap until he was ready to do the business, once those icy hands were encased around his throbbing manhood, it was soon all over red rover...

*Arrive at Heinekey's pub, stare in awe at the Hells' Angels profiling by their kool choppers, with us wishing we could be that kool and that we had those kind of bikes (and babes!). Both Steve and I had to make a choice at an early age whether we would get into music or motorbikes, we couldn't afford to do both! We chose to focus on the music and decent guitars and amps didn't come cheap! We've both managed to make up for it since then of course! My sister Paula's boyfriend at the time was a Rocker in the true sense, y'know, the studded leather jacket, turned up drainpipe jeans, quiff etc. and he rode a BSA Gold Star. He'd let me ride it shakily around the block and occasionally I'd go bitch and we'd shoot up the A40 onto the North Circular road and awaaay. So, we'd go into Heinekey's, survey the scene and look for familiar faces, pull up a coupla chairs and enjoy a few bevvies, catching up with all the latest bullshit.

*Eventually exit pub and stagger drunkenly onwards down the road, taking time out to praise/abuse any buskers that we passed. One of the regulars was this old guy who had a parrot and a music box, he'd be constantly swamped by tourists fighting for a chance to be photographed with this rough-ass old parrot as if it was the last one on the planet. Enter nearby army surplus shop and admire collection of Nazi regalia (shock value only folks!) and muskets. Exit shop sniggering and snickering at this bald guy who resembled Adolf Hitler in a t-shirt with a large swastika on it that could always be found goose-stepping up and down the road all day, much to the disgust of passers-by (and the many Jewish antique dealers).

*Swaggering ever onwards until reaching Finch's pub, catching up with more fellow deviants and playing 'spot the undercover cop' (there was a lot of it about at the time). We'd often see Lemmy at Finch's, occasionally his guitarist 'Fast' Eddie and Philthy the drummer. Mick Farren seemed to ALWAYS be in there, often completely rat-assed and it was no surprise to see many other 'celebrities' in there too. I remember seeing Roger Taylor the drummer from Queen in there, hanging out an' profiling, dressed completely in white desperately hoping for someone to recognise him so that he could ignore them. Maybe Freddie was up at the Gay Boutique getting a 'fitting', eh?

*Out of that pub eventually, shouting "hi" to Blind Bob the busking accordion player and singer who always played outside. I don't know why we shouted, he was blind not deaf! He seemed to always be there, come rain or shine, he was amazing, I'm sure unscrupulous people would put things like bottle tops into his hat but we never did it, just in case the whole blind thing was an act, he was a big fella! Onwards and upwards to the first of many Head shops to add to my collection of comix while Steve checked out the bongs and eventually arriving at the legendary 'Mountain Grill' restaurant (chippie!) for greasy cholesterol input and a large cup of stewed tea.

*Under the Westway flyover to the undercover market, stopping off to see Rory the infamous electric guitar busker still playing the lead guitar solo that he'd started at 9:00 that morning. He had a little practise amp that he would have cranked up to 11 and be twiddly diddly lead guitarin' from dusk 'til dawn.. he must have had fingers like leather ol' Rory! I remember he eventually found a band that could keep up with him, they were called 'The Invisible Band'. I'd like to say that I never saw them for humour purposes, but I did!

*Get pulled to one side by a group of cops usually containing at least one young 'trainee cadet', we were convinced that this was an integral part of their training (unwilling volunteers that we were), with the same ol' repertoire… "Where ya been?" "Where ya goin'" "What ya got?". On one occasion we'd bought some punk singles to check out the scene and there was a single in my bag by a new band called The Police. We remarked as they pulled it out that ok, it was a fair cop, seeing as we had a police record.. gee.. no sense of humour those guys.

*Swiftly out and away from the boys in blue, under the flyover and over the road to the music store on the corner where we'd check out the guitars, amps and effects pedals (but we never played 'Stairway to Heaven.. ok, maybe we did!) the staff in the shop would try real hard to be cool and let us play as long as we liked (through gritted teeth) maybe it was because we liked a bit of excessive volume?

*Give our regards to little (another) Bob who was always hanging around the same spot, who turned out to be a mate of my Uncle Eddie. He was this wee fella, but he had the coolest black leather jacket we'd ever seen and he'd spend most of the day profilin', ya know, hanging' out with his leathery tassles swingin' and studs gleaming in the hazy, winter sunshine. His kool added a couple of feet to his stature, kinda like the Fonz, he was a short ass too.. we'd hang out with Bob a while, chewing the fat, secretly plotting how we could relieve him of said awesome piece of apparel.. I wonder where it (or he) is now??

*Past the rastas and their heavy dub sound systems pumping out over the street and the heady smell of sensimeeeelia wafting over you.. as dey would biddy deng deng all de day.. rite? There'd be a queue of 'em, dressed in their finest army surplus and red, gold and green bobble hats patiently waiting for a chance to grab the mic' and biddy deng deng themselves. I never minded a bit of deep, heavy dub and roots reggae myself, Steve hated it. Not far from them was the infamous old 'Frendz' shop. It was a leftover from the old Underground Press days and seemed somehow frozen in time, a relic of those rose-tinted, innocent (and depraved) times. There were dusty old books like 'The Politics of Ecstasy' by Timothy Leary and 'The I-Ching', all manner of exotic oils and scents and best of all a huge pile of old, yellowing, leftover and unloved copies of Underground papers and magazines such as, Frendz, International Times, OZ etc. I think I eventually musta bought them all as no-one else seemed that interested!

*Sometimes we would venture onwards past the convent with its high, stark grey walls (some of the things they would have heard over those walls would have beggared belief!) and past the stalls which had the junky, old crap on them that nobody wanted before reaching the end of the road, turning about and doing it all again on the way back.. only uphill this time!

HIGH FRIENDS IN PLACES (LEST WE FORGET)

There was another Steve kickin' around at the time, he'd been a friend of the other Steve for longer than I'd known him, they grew up not far from each other. He was part of our posse from the beginning, he looked like a cross between a straggly Steve Marriot and some sort of dodgy, hippy used car salesman with his long, stringy hair, a tatty old velvet jacket and a spivvy pencil moustache. He loved to be chemically induced and loved to share that love! We'd often arrive at the West End of London some nights not even knowing how we got there.. we'd just start talking and walking.. from North Acton!

Another guy on the scene was called Colin who sort of vaguely resembled Robert Plant, but with a beer gut. He had the long, blonde cork-screwy hair thang going on, appropriately tatty leather jacket and skin tight loons but that ol' beergut would hang precariously over his bullet belt. He was a bit of a dick at times but knew a lot of people on the scene. Then there was dear ol' Scruff (Scruffus Bruttanicus). We met at a Motorhead gig (playing as Iron Fist and the Hordes from Hell – Came out as the 'What's Words Worth?' live album) at the Roundhouse, where he was doing the occasional bit of roadie work for them and we became inseparable for a while, like The Three Amigos. We all shared the same ridiculous sense of humour and laughs would be many and often. He suffered from asthma which gave him a kinda wheezy snigger much akin to that of Muttley the cartoon dog from Wacky Races. Often that snigger would evolve into a breathy chuckle before exploding into a howling guffaw.. by that time, all present would be just laughing at his laugh having completely forgotten what the original joke (if any) was about. We also had someone else to hang out with who lived relatively close to us and when you're walking home from the West End to North Acton at some godforsaken hour of the morning (as we often did) an extra dude for company never went amiss. Especially when he resembled Neanderthal Man in a leather jacket! He had one of those faces that would relax into a miserable expression, so he never looked the 'cuddly' type...

One night, a whole posse of us were crashed out on the floor after a particularly good party and we'd all slept really badly, mostly due to a) our age b) speed and c) Scruff's incessant laughter, but by the time we'd woken the next morning, Scruff was nowhere to be seen, or so we thought. All that remained was his smelly old boots (his pongy feet were the stuff of legend!).. we were pondering the reasons for his possible abduction when Steve shouted out "Maybe his 'Odour Eaters' ate him!" which produced a mighty roar of laughter that far surpassed any attempt made by Scruff overnight. He also played a mean bass guitar and he liked a bit of dub reggae as well as his Hawkwind and Motorhead and eventually became bass player for my first incarnation of the Magic Mushroom Band (by then Steve was off doing other things!). The last I'd heard of Scruff he'd done really well for himself as a dub reggae bassist and engineer working for Youth (from Killing Joke) who was fast becoming a dance music 'guru'. He also had a reggae band called 'The Herb' (Speed Machine? The Magic Mushroom Band? The Herb? Anyone sense a bit of a theme running through this?).

OUR FIRST BUST (MAAAN)

Through those formative years and beyond we had our fair share of run-ins with the law. It's not that we went out of way to get pulled so often, but I guess we just looked so guilty! I've lost count of the times we'd get pulled by the cops down the Portobello Road for a quick search, we were almost on first name terms (but not quite!). I guess we were a safer bet then trying to foil IRA terrorists...

There we were tho', still wet behind the ears but livin' life to the max, but on one particular occasion we found ourselves with a problem, big time. We were due to go to a Motorhead gig but horror of horrors, we had no dope! Nothing! We searched and searched for someone with a bit to spare but nix, nada. So in sheer desperation we committed the ultimate sin, we did something that we swore we'd never do which was to buy a bag of 'mystery' grass from a rasta under the flyover down the Portobello Road. He could tell that we were desperate and charged us accordingly. Desperate times call for desperate measures though, we didn't want to turn up at the gig without anything to smoke! So we did the deal and off we went to the gig that night. We met up with loadsa people and had our usual riotous and righteous Saturday night shenanigans... we drank, we toked, we snorted, we rolled up, they rolled up and eventually me and Steve decided to make our way home, bleary-eyed, totally wasted but happy.
We were only a couple of miles from our respective homes when suddenly a (yep, you guessed it!) plain-clothed police car screeches to a halt beside us just as we were crossing over the Uxbridge Road in Shepherds Bush. Out jumped two police officers, one male and one female. I'd never witnessed this dynamic combination before and Steve and I looked at each other with confident smirks as the male cop politely asked us where we'd been, where we were going and why we were smirking. He wasn't getting much sense out of us and suddenly the female cop launched into us with a barrage of threats (must have been that time of the month) and in no time had us spread-eagled across the bonnet, searching through our

pockets. We'd split the remaining weed between us and had our bags well stashed 'pon our persons but seeing as we didn't want to further aggravate the situation and knowing they'd eventually find them anyway, we handed over our bags of grass. We figured they'd probably just confiscate our weed, slap us on the wrist for being young and stoopid and send us on our way under a cloud of shame. Wrong! They instead wanted to make a meal of it and were intent on making an example of us so we were arrested on the spot, bundled into the cop car and taken immediately to Acton Police Station.

They threw us in a cell and we were individually searched again.. this time a bit more thoroughly. Earlier that night the last thing we imagined would that we would later be in a police cell, trousers around our ankles with policemen looking up our bums.. s'funny how things turn out, eh? We weren't allowed to call home, but they did inform us that they'd sent officers 'round to our parents' homes to let them know that we'd been arrested, they wouldn't tell them what for though... so you can imagine the nice, warm reception waiting for us when we eventually got home! The police eventually let us out of the cell early the next morning and told us to report back there a week later when the cannabis would be back from the forensic lab and they'd have the results and charge us for our crime.

The week that followed was a long and painful one, we'd had our asses whooped by our respective parents and we dreaded the outcome.. major bummer all 'round. When the next Saturday finally arrived we walked down to the police station ('dead man walking' style) and approached the desk sergeant. He got us to sit down and looked up from his paperwork with a sullen expression on his face (our sphincters were going nine to the dozen). "Well... do you want the good news or the bad news?". We looked at each other in a bemused fashion and decided to go for the happy bit first. "The good news, I regret to say, is that we won't be charging you for this offence". We couldn't believe our ears.. we were free.. whoo hoo!! Somehow we'd managed to beat the system (maaan).. take that ya fascist pigs! But of course, we hadn't got to the bad news bit.. "The bad news is that you didn't actually purchase marijuana, you bought a bag of mixed herbs.." Well, upon hearing that we both burst into uncontrollable snorts of laughter and patted each other on the back. We couldn't work out whether he was pissed off because he had nothing to charge us for, or if we'd been the highlight of their week and they'd had many a joke at our expense. He even asked us if we wanted it back, we graciously declined and hightailed it out of there while the going was good. It turned out that because we were all smoking each others dope at the gig, nobody noticed they were puffing on mixed herbs, we didn't know at the time how badly we'd been ripped off by that shonky ol' rasta but in this instance... we were really glad that we were!

CRANKIN' THE SPEED MACHINE

It all really started coming together for me musically when I got my Fender Stratocaster. A 1969 maple neck, sunburst guitar that is still my main instrument today and I tell ya, as soon as I picked it up I could instantly play twice as well (or at least it felt like it!). Hendrix played a Stratocaster, so 'nuff said. I'd like to say at this point that Jimi Hendrix was, and still is ma main man, he was such an inspiration to me, watching him gyrating, fucking his guitar as it screamed through those cranked up Marshall amplifiers. It was he who taught me how to use the guitar as an extension of your soul (and dick). Even now if I hear his music, I just have to pick up that guitar and play, just like yesterday, then I'd get on my knees and pray...

Around the same time, Steve switched to bass guitar and bought a rather bitchin' Rickenbacker bass.. black as night and twice as.. er.. dark. I remember us going into the army surplus store in Portobello Road and buying some WW2 Nazi stickers and sticking them all over our guitars (they were a bastard to get off when I later had my guitar custom painted – bloody Germans!). We were baaad muthafuckers I tell ya, hanging around with our guitars and amps on the street waiting for our

Dads to come and pick us up! We'd jam at each other's houses but the complaints were getting louder than the music so for the sake of decent home cooking, freshly washed socks and undies (and an easy life) we booked some rehearsal time at a studio in Churchfield Road behind Acton High Street. It was deep in the bowels of the building under a music shop and we could make as much noise as we liked.. so we did. We would try to get those Marshalls as cranked up as we were (if ya get my drift), so that the mains hum was as loud as the music (they weren't our amps). We'd written a couple of tunes already and we had some favourite songs that we wanted to play.. but we needed a name... what were we? A Speed Machine!

The first of our troubles was that we couldn't find a single drummer who would play the sort of stuff that we liked. We asked so many people, we were desperate. At the time, bands like Motorhead were in this sort of 'netherworld', they couldn't be classed as Heavy Rock or Progressive and they were too old and even uglier than most of the punk bands. We were fully into getting our hair to grow as long as possible, still loving that "Mummy, I want you to meet my new boyfriend" look and we wanted a freaked-out drummer that shared our vision. We were almost down to asking people in the street, in fact we'd go up to any long hair at a gig and ask "Oy mate, do you play drums? No? Do ya know anyone that does?" But to no avail, any prospective drummers would flick their hair back in an important manner and inform us that Motorhead/'Fairies/MC5 were "Way too heavy, man" and they were in much too much of a progressive state of mind for all that and anyway, they were all waiting for Phil Collins to drop dead so they could get HIS gig. Over the years I've seen a lot of HIS albums in the charity shops so I guess he did alright for himself..

Salvation eventually came in the lanky, gangly freaked out metal-fork-in-the-toaster hair explosion that was the amazing Deso. He was perfect, he had the huge fuck-off Hendrix afro going on, dressed in black velvet, with bells and rings hanging off him and best of all, and most importantly, he bashed those drums like a freaky demon possessed! His hair would be thrashing about, narrowly missing getting caught up in his drumsticks as he thumped the bejaysus out of his ratty old kit. He was the first drummer I ever saw that had a pair of bongos strapped next to his tom toms, a sort of shoestring budget precursor to the roto-toms.

He also had a weird, spaced-out hippy girlfriend called Sam, as hippy chicks went she was an olympian, by that I mean that if ever there was an Olympic event for the hippiest hippy chick she would have won it. She lived with her parents in Surrey in a huge Victorian mansion and her attic bedroom was bigger than the whole top storey of my house. It was all decked out with droopy nets, old candles melted over bottles, pungent incense, ethnic velvet cushions, ultra-violet lighting, the whole freaky enchilada. It made me want to do up my own bedroom a little more, I just had a large Budgie poster (liberated from a gig at the Roundhouse), a 'Land that Time Forgot' Raquel Welch poster, a stack of records and comix and my neighbour's son's Easy Rider magazines which he never got back. There was a mural on my ceiling that I'd done of the Hawkwind 'Space Ritual' cover, the product of a stoned/tripped out, sleepless teenager with nothing better to do at four o' clock in the morning and, oh yeah, a very stiff black leather jacket standing by itself in the corner.. But then, I wasn't coming home very often at that time..

I still have the recording of Speed Machine's first 'session' (and I mean that in all respects), we were chomping at the bit to get in there and set up, this had been a long time coming! We were that excited that we decided to go 'hell for leather' ('scuse the pun) and popped and smoked everything we had. It turned out to be a good job that we'd set up quickly because in no time at all we were transformed into gibbering, electrified epileptics. UP went the volume and tempo as we launched into an epic jam, faster than the speed of complaint. You can hear me starting the thing by suddenly launching into a demented guitar solo, I was just getting used to the power of the Fender by then and it was hitting that sweet note that Strats and Marshalls make when they come together. Even the feedback was in tune as up, up and away I went, twiddly-diddlying away like there was no tomorrow.. in my head I was atop some fiery mountain, the wind blowing in my hair (probably coming from the force of the speakers!), lightning shooting from my guitar at dragons as they chased sweet, young, virginal maidens up my leather studded thigh… ahem. When it eventually dawned on me that I may have been doing this for quite some time, I looked over at Steve and Deso who proceeded to thunder in with an earthquake of an intro and we were cooking on gas baby, for the rest of the session. Even in our accelerated mindstates it seemed to last forever. But it was probably only about an hour.

We had some great sessions like that, in squats and at parties but unfortunately, due to our excessive nature and our penchant for ligging and parties we never actually got to play at a regular gig venue. We were possibly one of the first bands to ever get by on reputation alone, kinda the 'Paris Hiltons' of our day!

OL' SMOKEY

Ah yes.. the good ol' Smokey Bear's' Picnics! Sorta nice idea if not a little naïve, the idea of skinning up in broad daylight at such a high profile location as London's Hyde Park seemed like a good 'un at the time, but of course, our good ol' boys in blue didn't see it that way and put a cunning plan into action. They'd dress their boys up in afghan coats, sandals and granny specs and be eyed very suspiciously by the rest of us in our tatty leathers, beer-stained/hash-burned t-shirts and bullet belts wondering what the hell they were thinking, it became quite a sport picking them out among the crowd!

The whole point of the thing of course was to make a 'statement', we all wanted to be free to enjoy a herbal supplement without recrimination. So the plan of attack would be a very simple one, turn up en masse, sit in a huge circle and skin up. . Suffice to say that the gathered 'freedom fighters' would get totally blasted and the MAN would be powerless to do anything about it. That was it and thousands turned up to take part. Of course there possibly could have been even more people make it on the day if not for the fact that they probably got the wrong day, forgot about it completely while watching Dr Who on TV or saw a TV detector van down the road and hid in a cupboard under the stairs, missed or took the wrong bus/train, saw a rainbow and decided to find its end, or were standing around confused by the severe lack of amenities, cops and fellow protestors as they gathered at the completely wrong end of Hyde Park.

LIGGIN' IN THE RIGGIN'

Apart from attending every Motorhead show possible, we went to as many other gigs and venues too. We had an abundance of energy, both pubescent and chemical and the idea of sitting at home watching Coronation Street and drinking cups of tea with the family was not an option at the time, we had people to go and places to meet, baby!

We'd swagger off to venues like The Music Machine in Camden and Chalk Farm's Roundhouse to check out bands like The Pink Fairies, Stray or another of our favourites the Welsh rockers Budgie. Anyone who saw Budgie live in the '70's has to agree that as a live band they really kicked ass. We loved 'em, good ol' Bludgeon Riffola, criminally underrated as a band. Most of those sort of venues put pretty good support bands on too, although we were too busy yappin' to all and sundry to take them all in. We'd be yakkin' and a clakkin' from the moment we joined the queue outside, we'd yak yak at the bar, in the toilets (carefully stepping over the 'mandie' freaks lying comatose on the floor), out into the auditorium and eventually yak yak our way to the front of the stage. After the show of course, we'd do it all in reverse.

I remember we went to the Music Machine on one particular night to see a band called 'Kittyhawks'. It was basically a band made up from all the people that weren't in Hawkwind anymore, we're talking Lemmy, Nik Turner, Dik Mik and others, it was a real one-off and we were really looking forward to it. We did our usual early arrival and hung about outside the venue socialising and we waited and we waited. Eventually someone came out of the venue and announced that the show had been cancelled.. major bummer! The only consolation was that while waiting for all that time, being the social types we were, we pretty much met everybody else in the queue and by the time we all had to disperse, we all headed off en masse to the nearest boozer, some of us ending up at a bizarre party somewhere that was hosted by a druid, or was it a wizard? I forget which (witch?).

With Acton being relatively close (read walkable) to Hammersmith, we got to frequent the Hammersmith Odeon on a fairly regular basis. They had all the big league bands there like Black Sabbath. We didn't have much luck as far as seeing a good live Sabbath show was concerned though.. all that black magic maybe. One time we went to see them and at one point popped outside through the fire exit for a sneaky spliff, only to hear someone slam the doors behind us, we were locked out! Another time, although we managed to stay in the building for the entire performance, Ozzy had got really bad flu and kept going off stage so we were treated to numerous guitar, drum and even bass (?) solos. Regardless of that though, they were true pioneers and very inspirational. Blue Oyster Cult, Humble Pie, The Tubes, Hawkwind, Rush we saw them all and many more... We were really chuffed for Lemmy and Motorhead when they finally broke the big time and headlined there, it was a real triumph and a huge "up yours" to the doubters and naysayers.

The best thing was that it was so great to be out there among so many likeminded freaks, fellow black sheep into (and often on) the same things as us. We'd all hang out after the shows at a chippie around the corner in Fulham Palace Road, steam billowing from our sweaty, hairy heads and clothes into the night. The Fulham Palace Road was also home to the Greyhound pub, one of a few really good venues at the time which featured lower league bands, I guess you could file it under 'pub rock', but that doesn't really do the place justice.

Best of all was the legendary Marquee club in Wardour Street in seedy Soho. We went there A LOT. Punk had well and truly reared its ugly (but necessary) head and we'd often go and check out that scene too. There were odd, quirky bands too, like Alberto y los trios Paranoias doing punk spoofs with lines like "Gonna cut ya liver out and nail it on the door!" and they also did a reggae version of 'Where Have all the Flowers Gone?' with the singer bobbing around on stage with an oversized rasta hat with curly telephone leads hanging from it (I wonder if he knew the same school friend?).

We'd get so cranked the whole evening would often turn into some kind of weird, circus freak show in which we were the major players. Sometimes we'd go down there and our lil' posse would expand at a rate of knots and we'd end up trogging off somewhere else after the show, maybe a pub, or a party, or a party at a pub, or just go and sit in a park somewhere... Xmas Eve, New Year's Eve we did them all at the Marquee. In no time at all the place would be buzzing, especially us, big time, and we'd be out there in orbit.

One night we decided to go and check out local new 'hot' punk band The Ruts at a pub in Acton High Street, Steve knew a lot of the punks there as a lot of them had been in or hung around his old band Firebird. In a moment of madness before leaving for the gig, in a desperate moment to try and do something 'punk' so I wouldn't stand out so much, I asked my Mum to put my hair into lots of plaits while it was wet. As it turned out I couldn't have stood out more if I'd tried, I thought it looked real stoopid so I undid all the plats and of course, as soon as my hair dried it all went 'Pooffttt!' into a big, spirally, curly, girly mass and no matter what I tried I couldn't get it to straighten out again so I just though "fuck it" and left for the gig. Once all the giggling and chortling had died down we got to the pub and had a great time.. well, at least I WAS an (unwilling) individual at that gig and how 'punk' was that?

By day we'd hang out at the grooviest markets, the aforementioned Portobello Road, Kensington Market, Petticoat Lane, Tottenham Court Road, Carnaby Street et al. Our local High Streets in Acton were just so plain and normal and boring and didn't cater at all for 'Space Warriors on the Edge of Reality' like us. Kensington Market was great in those days, a twisty, multi-level cornucopia of weird and wonderful stuff and people. At that time 'Biba' the iconic swingin' sixties fashion store for foxy chicks was still up and running and the quality of the talent was unequalled. Real hotties, from their bra-less blouses to their skimpy miniskirts or hot pants (otherwise known as 'mumble pants' because you saw the lips move but you couldn't hear what the cunt was sayin'). The best place to be there was in the café where the freaks would gather, topping up their caffeine quota and discreetly passing around the Jamaican Woodbines in preparation for another stoned-out wander around the place. It was still at that time a hippy market I guess, lots of bongs, pipes, bells, beads etc. but I do remember when punk came to town there appeared t-shirts and trousers for sale that had been purposely ripped with a blade and then pinned back together again with safety pins. We'd spent most of our lives trying to avoid having to do that! Our flared jeans did have to eventually go the way of the dodo, which in the end was no bad thing as at least with the straight-legged pants we weren't getting our legs so drenched on those many long, wet meanders around London.

AND JESUS WAS HIS NAME...

At this point in my tale, I'd like to give an honourable mention to a certain character who never really got any credit or kudos for being such a familiar face at so many freaky/happenings/gigs/festivals etc. We only knew him as

Jesus. Now THERE was a real hippy, he always wore a sort of kaftan-esque type over-shirt and robes, with beads, shoulder bag and sandals and a weird kinda monk-ish hair style that was very long at the back. He always reminded me of one of those space hippies from the Star Trek TV episode 'The Way to Eden', also a little like what Brian Eno would have looked like had he ingested too much of the brown acid in the 'sixties. He'd often have a small entourage with him mostly comprising of pretty, stoned young chicks and strange, sweaty fat dudes in Demis Roussos mu-mu's.

I swear he was at EVERY gig or festival we ever went to, be it heavy rock, R&B, metal, even punk.. there he'd always be, right up the front swaying and gyrating, bashing his little tambourine and blowing his little flute, all to no avail of course because he'd be drowned out by the bands and constantly pelted with glasses and bottles by who people who wanted him to sit down and let them see the show. Fair play to him though, he just stood his ground and did his own thing. Some gigs would feel a bit strange if he wasn't there, that's how much of a regular feature he was. When the Magic Mushroom Band eventually got to play at the Marquee many years later, I was very pleased to see him in attendance, so much so I impulsively did what I thought I should do as a reward for his dogged determination and invited him up on stage with us. His eyes became as big as saucers and he was up there in a flash before you could say "Be careful with that tambourine Eugene!". Of course, I soon came to realise why so few bands had offered him the opportunity.. it was really hard to get him back off again!

LIVING FOR A LIVING

As a pacifier to my family I'd gone to the local 'Careers' office in search of a job. I told them that I'd done well in Art at school and wanted to do something that related to that. Their first attempt at finding me something suitable resulted in the discovery of a vacancy for a person to put up advertising posters on the billboards at train stations.. what th'? I can't remember my actual reply but I'm sure it went along the lines of "Fuck off!".

They did eventually find me an excellent job working for a company called 'Pictures' that provided 'props' for the film & TV industry. The owner was James Hill, by then a famous director in his own right, he directed the movie 'Born Free' among others as well as TV shows like The Avengers and Worzel Gummidge. In fact, it was while having dinner with Kate Bush discussing a possible role for her in Worzel Gummidge that he mentioned to her that she had a huge fan who worked for him (me!). The next thing I know, I receive in the mail a large, signed photo of Kate and a card with "Dear Garry, I hope you're happy, love Kate B" written on it. I've often wondered what she meant, did she mean was I happy in life? Or did she mean was I glad that I'd managed to make her sign another bloody photo and card? Only kidding, she's a sweetie.. and wow, amazing.

James was also a World War 2 hero in the RAF, he'd been shot down over German territory and shared living quarters in the POW camp with Clive Dunn (from Dad's Army!). He'd escaped twice and they broke a different leg each time they recaptured him to try and deter him from doing it again. He was played by Donald Pleasance in the movie 'The Great Escape' (He'd never show you the palms of his hands, they were badly burned when his plane went down).

When I say that his company provided film and TV props, I'm not talking about made-up things, I mean they were the real deal. Not only was the warehouse full to the brim with pictures, ornaments, rugs, drapes, sculptures, statues and objet d'art from all over the world, but they had stuff going back a coupla centuries too. The building itself was an old, converted dairy (in Shepherds Bush!) and it was painted a chocolate brown on the outside and salmon pink on the inside, kinda like working inside a large strawberry choc ice.

We provided many props for the movie 'Raiders of the Lost Ark', one time a truck driver from the set arrived to pick up more props and he called me out to his van. As he opened up the back, loads of rotting corpses spilled out! They'd just been made for the scenes in the tomb. He even had one strapped into the passenger seat in the front of the van, elbow resting out of the window. He turned up a few days later with his van full of weapons, machine guns, bazookas, the lot. For the movie 'Alien' I remember the props buyer rifling through a hospital supplies catalogue, sitting on the phone ordering copious amounts of silver foil duct-tubing for the insides of the Mothership. For 'Star Wars' an airforce jet-fighter 'scrapyard' was used to supply lots of bits and pieces for the Jedi fighters etc. We did all the Pink Panther movies too and I remember them all freaking out because if Peter Sellers took a shine to a particular prop he would just take it home with him, regardless of its value!

I loved that job and stayed there for the rest of my 'formative' years, it was nice having a bit of money for once, I was always going to need more records, comix, guitars and effects pedals! Best of all the bosses there didn't care about how I looked and really looked after me. It was my manager Judy's husband David who lent me the two hundred pounds to get my Stratocaster, he'd only met me twice but he opened up his wallet and said "Here you go, pay me back a fiver a week, that'll guarantee that you'll have to work here for a while." I'll always be grateful to him for that generous gesture, I never knew that people could be so generous..

A lot of famous actors, directors and various crazies walked through those doors too. I remember the doors literally 'swishing' open one day as Jon Pertwee sashayed in dressed from head to toe in black leather, a shock of snowy-white bouffant hair, medallion swinging through his equally snowy chest hair with a foxy babe on each arm. He'd come to discuss 'Worzel' business, what a dude! I'd grown up watching him battle with the Daleks from behind the safety of a cushion, or behind the sofa, or preferably from another room (but still seeing it all through a crack in the door). Even ex-Pink Fairy Larry Wallis turned up one day, it turned out that one of the girls I worked with had known him since the 'sixties. I must admit I didn't recognise him at first, he'd just cut off his trademark mattress of frizzy hair and he'd porked out a bit too (as we all do eventually!). We chewed the fat for a while and he later sent me a copy of his new solo single 'Leather Forever' (maybe it was written about my old jacket!). Julie Christie strolled in one day and she was as beautiful as she looked onscreen, I tried not to drool in her presence.

The atmosphere was really laid back at Pictures, there was free coffee, tea, wine, cookies and smokes on tap and if we stayed in the building during our lunch break we could order whatever we liked from the Italian restaurant next door. I was more than happy to volunteer to collect the food that we'd ordered over the phone, but on one particular day I really wished I hadn't put my hand up. I'd gone next door to collect our meals but was left waiting for an unusually long time, suddenly there was a loud 'craaasshh!!' that came from the kitchen followed by lots of wailing and crying from the waiters. Eventually the older guy came out and said "I'm a vary sorry innit, but da chef he jus' died..". I was speechless.. would he have lived if I'd eaten somewhere else that day? I went back next door empty handed and explained the situation. I was promptly sent back out to a nearby fish n' chip shop.. Hell hath no fury like women with empty stomachs.

Sometimes we'd all just stay back after work and carry on chatting, drinking and smoking.. I should add at this point that I was the only male (and a very sexually charged one at that) among three or occasionally four very bohemian women. I've never minded being in the company of just women, apart from when they vented their frustration with the male species on me because some guy had just stood them up. It was an absolute pleasure to be around those ladies in my formative years.. a real learning curve when it came to women in general I can tell ya! As my hair got longer and longer I think at times they would just forget I was a guy and I saw a glimpse of the harsh, scary world that was '70's woman! None of them wore bras, having burnt them all in the '60's and yes, to get ahead in the film business in those days it helped if you looked like you were prepared to 'put out' at the drop of a hat.

There was a girl who would come in part-time to do some cleaning, Anoushka was her name, she was Swedish and had shacked up with a drug-dealing taxi driver who lived down the road. I'd go to their place for many a snort and a toot and I guess they must have thought I was wide-eyed and drooling due to the potency of the drugs, well not completely! Anoushka was a stunning blonde, to die for.. I could have quite happily murdered the boyfriend, buried his body and spent the rest of my life between her thighs. She thought I was 'funny' which is something I suppose. One day she was running late and had to come in to do some cleaning. It was a stinkin' hot summer's day and as she rushed into my despatch room she threw off her coat and there she was, standing there in just black fishnet stockings, suspenders and a g-string, talking to me about what a mad day she was having! Swedes, eh? So yeah, being the only guy in the building they did seem to enjoy practising their flirting on me and I didn't put up much resistance! I'd often get an eyeful of bare breast or cotton panty gusset as they sat and chatted, often they'd just strip off and try on clothes that they'd just bought. The place often resembled a Carry On movie with me as Sid James chasing them around the building as they yelped and screamed (or vice versa), all in the 'best possible taste' of course...

It did get all a bit too carried away one time though, I'd only been there a coupla months and June, one of my favourite girls there decided to creep up on me and put some ice cubes down the back of my shirt. When I eventually peeled myself off the ceiling intent on instant revenge, I grabbed a fistful of fresh ice cubes, chased her back up the stairs and threatened to stick them down the back of her jeans. "You wouldn't dare" she taunted.. well, no one taunts me and gets away with it so I lunged at the waistband of her jeans and as we fell to the ground she kinda twisted 'round to foil my plan and I instead ended up shoving the ice cubes down the front of her jeans. Not my original plan at all but Dr Fate likes a good laugh every now and then and suddenly there I was, lying on top of her on the floor with my hand down the front of her jeans with a fistful of ice and pubic hair. We all laughed a very embarrassed laugh, I climbed off her and we decided to cool it a bit ('scuse the pun), but as I turned to sit down at the big desk she grabbed a (by now thankfully) cold cup of coffee and threw it at me. Now, if there's one thing that growing up at a tough school does for a lad, it teaches you the art of evasion at an early age. I ducked easily and the coffee went flying way over my head straight into the face, hair and all over the dress of our manager Judy. The silence was painful.. you could have heard a pubey cube drop! There was the boss, sitting there at the desk dripping from head to toe in cold, wet coffee. I gingerly reached for a towel and offered it to her at which point she turned to me, frowned with the mother of all frowns and then promptly burst into uncontrollable laughter. We all soon joined in, mixing the guffaws with tears of relief and I made a vow there and then to be a bit more selective about where I deposited ice cubes in the future. Poor Judy had to do business for the rest of the day sitting at her desk with just a blouse on while under the desk she was in just her knickers with a tea towel over her lap.

Another one of the girls, Miranda (the one who knew Larry Wallis) had been around the Ladbroke Grove scene since the '60's, she'd helped out with the lightshow for Hawkwind's infamous 'free' performance outside the gates of the equally infamous Isle of Wight festival and had also appeared naked on the front cover of an issue of Oz magazine. When she told me that I rushed home, rummaged through my collection whooped with joy when I found I had that copy. This was all very exciting stuff for a young teenager who'd often felt like he was born ten years too late (happy for that NOW tho'!). I remember staying over at her apartment in Kensington one night with a girlfriend, we'd babysat her daughter in exchange for endless spliffs and a double bed for the use of in the spare room, although me and the girl got so wasted we never left the sofa.

When Miranda eventually came home, obviously in a very similar state to us, she disappeared into the bathroom and then came back out into the lounge stark bollock naked and asked us if we wanted to jump into bed with her! I was totally 'up' for it but my girl freaked out and we had to go home by taxi immediately. This became a bit of a common theme with the girlfriend in question. I once took her to see a Russ Meyer movie called 'Beneath the Valley of the Ultra-Vixens', I thought it would be some kind of fantasy epic, well it was, but of a different sort. When the lights came on for the intermission she observed that she was the only girl in the audience and that a lot of the guys there were fumbling around in their raincoats, she again freaked out and we had to go home by taxi immediately. Sometimes, if it was real sunny, we'd forgo lunch at work and go over the road to the local park where the girls would whip off their tops.. gee it was a tough job but someone had to do it, Miranda had huge, dark nipples like chocolate buttons... yum.

Then there was Marge, she had a great pedigree too, a real good time, rock n' roll chick if ever there was one. I've never seen anyone quite fit a pair of Levi's like she did. She had a son by the guitarist Micky Moody who later went on to play with Whitesnake, he'd also been in a band called Juicy Lucy, their album cover had a picture of the underground cartoon character 'The Chequered Demon' on the front and was called 'Get a Whiff of This'. Jeez.. how I lusted after her.. I used to follow her around at work like a dog on heat. I don't think she even had a clue or cared about that, but then I was a very horny young buck. On the same night every year, Pictures would have an anniversary dinner and my first one of those got way, way out of hand. Always a posh affair, a Chinese restaurant in Chelsea had been booked and there were about twenty of us, four staff, the boss and his missus and various hangers on. The champagne started flowing immediately and we were well on our way to getting severely lashed. We'd all vowed at work that day not to eat any lunch so that we could consume as much as we could at the restaurant (we weren't paying!). Being poor white trash, I'd never tasted champagne

before and although I could take or leave the taste it was
having the desired effect on me and the girls, the waiters got
abused, one of the girls chased the chef around the kitchen
trying to grab a kiss, it was chaotic. I'd ordered a curry and the
spices kicked in so I grabbed one of the conveniently placed
water bowls and took a huge gulp, the place instantly fell into
silence followed by loud guffaws from all present.. yep, I'd
drunk out of the water bowl that everyone had just rinsed their
fingers in. Well... I didn't know! I was more concerned about
picking up the right fork! Our boss James had a film projector
and screen set up for a showing of some of his movies but by
then we were so far gone we just laughed, farted and giggled
all the way through them. Eventually we said our goodbyes and
Marge and I got a taxi to Hammersmith Broadway. I was in no
state to try and make it home so I walked Marge back to her
place in nearby Barnes, just a stagger away over the
Hammersmith bridge. We were laughing so hard that we had
to stop and sit down for a while, I eventually got her back up on
her feet but no way could she walk so I gave her a very
precarious piggyback home. We eventually got back to her
place and it was another very groovy pad, lots of ethnic
hangings and candles, she was slurring by now and said while
undressing in front of me that I could crash on the sofa as she
flumped unconsciously onto her bed. I spent most of that night
just a wall's thickness away from this groovy chick totally off
her tits very probably lying naked on her bed. I entertained all
sorts of unsavoury thoughts and wished with all my heart that
she'd come to and drag me protesting into her den of iniquity.
Of course, she was out cold and I didn't see her 'til breakfast.

Yep, many good, good times working there at Pictures and it
sort of came along at just the right time. I think now, looking
back, things were getting out of control for me and it wasn't a
situation that my folks could handle or understand so I sort of
gained an extended family who could give me sound,
experienced advice and who genuinely cared for me and the
type of guy I was (am). Those years were a lot of fun and it was
eventually very hard for me to leave that job. So a big thumbs
up to Acton Careers Office for that one!

SURREY SEEMS TO BE THE HARDEST WORD

Through circumstances which elude me now, me and my mates had heard about a 'rock disco' that was held above a pub called The Bull in East Sheen every Sunday night. It was a fair-sized room with a decent sound system and we met a lot of new boys and girls there. The deejay was pretty good and he'd slowly build the tempo up over the night always ending up with 'Freebird' by Lynrd Skynrd so that us guys could grab a girlie and have a bit of a bum squeeze during the slow, meaningful bit and then go freakish mental in the faster bit. Me and the boys were a little bit in the minority mixing it with the kids from the affluent Upper/Middle Class suburbs of Richmond, Putney and Barnes, being poor, working class boys, but no-one gave us a hard time about it and anyway, that scene was pretty classless anyway. Most of them still lived with their parents in these huge mansion houses and the parties there were awesome, with no shortage of stimulating additives.

I eventually hooked up with a sweet young thing called Jacqui, at the time she resembled a startled deer, but I later found out that she always looked like that when she was speeding. Fortunately for me, she loved sex too and no sooner had we done the Freebird she dragged me outside where we promptly went at it hammer and tongs in a nearby alleyway. We did it everywhere, at gigs, in parks, by the river, at parties.. It had been a while for me so I appreciated the exercise! We became an inseparable team for a while, three couples, myself and Jacqui, Steve and his new girl Indrani, Deso and Sam... and Scruff.

It was about that time that we began to frequent Richmond Park, a beautiful, spacious place owned by the Queen, with wild deer roaming around and in the right places at the right time of year an abundance of magic mushrooms. Ahhh.. magic mushrooms.. thank you your Majesty! They were to kick in the next phase of my evolution. The infamous writer Terence McKenna had a theory of evolution that involved monkeys coming down from the trees to eat magic mushrooms (unwittingly I'm guessing as they were probably after the dinosaur dung that they grew in) and through constantly tripping their little tits off, developing thought and communication skills. That was how I felt too! We'd played around with acid and other hallucinogenics but we were always righteously stoned and speeding and drunk at the same time, so we didn't know what was doing what.. or why and we didn't care. For me, it changed my perspective on the world for sure, my music, my artwork, my outlook on things, I wasn't so strung out anymore.. and the Grateful Dead finally made sense! Fortunately we always had an expert along with us when were picking them, I'd just grab all types and hope for the best, but of course, once identified we'd see them waving their little pointy caps at us. During the 'season' those paddocks could get quite busy with lots of dishevelled figures hunched over in the early morning mist shouting out to their mates "Oy! Is this one?" There'd always be some fool going around eating them as he picked them, something I'd often been warned against doing, and you'd see them wobble off, trying to find their bicycle.

Richmond also had a very cool hippy market and my girlfriend worked on one of the stalls and brought me home lots of (liberated) assorted paraphernalia. There was also a great pub opposite the train station called 'The Orange Tree' that had live traditional Irish music. We'd all get tanked up and be tiddly diddly jiggin' with the best of 'em.. to be shure. There was a guy that we met called Andy who was a tall, stocky, public school, rugby playing 'what ho' type who'd somehow crossed over into our nightmare world of drugs and debauchery. His Dad was the groundsman for the local golf club in Barnes (not far in fact from where Marc Bolan tied his yellow Mini 'round the old oak tree – sorry) and they lived in a huge house on the grounds of the golf course. Having no neighbours around to freak out, we immediately saw it as the ideal venue for a Speed Machine jam and after-party, so we organised it on behalf of the hapless Andy. It was a great party, but something happened to me on that night... normally, if I'd had a line or two I could play like a demon and twice as fast (or so it seemed) but on that night I couldn't get it together at all.. I just found myself with this annoying plank of wood around my neck and my fingers just weren't co-ordinated with those bits of wire stretched across it at all.. that kinda freaked me out a bit and I began to wonder whether I should cut back on the pharmaceuticals and mellow it all out for a while.

NOT LONG-GONE GONG BUT HERE AND NOW

Perfectly synched with our mushrooming 'awakening' was the news that we received on the grapevine about a band called Planet Gong who were touring and playing for free (!?) travelling around the country in a big orange bus. Although the band was led by Daevid Allen and his partner Gilli Smyth, his backing group was really a band in its own right called Here and Now. Daevid entered the music scene initially via 'beat' poetry, then the fledgling Soft Machine in the '60's and onwards and Gongwards into the '70's with his quirky space jazz/rock band Gong. At this time however, Daevid had already left Gong (we'd seen the Daevid and Gilli – less Gong and found it a bit too much jazz and not enough space), he'd brought out some great solo albums, as had Gilli, and they were now embracing the punk ethic with their hippified message of 'Floating Anarchy'!! Me and my friends had been suffering serious space-rock withdrawals what with Hawkwind taking a sabbatical and re-emerging with the more 'new wave' sounding 'Hawklords', so when we first heard Planet Gong we were blown away.. it had spacey, cosmic moments, but with a real, driving punky attack to a lot of it, like a cross between Hawkwind and the Sex Pistols and judging by the huge crowds that the band attracted, we weren't the only ones stuck between these two netherworlds! It suited us down to the ground because the music was just like us, spaced out but with a lot of energy to burn... There was Keith the bassist who resembled a cross between a Dickensian Oliver Reed and Lurch, Steffy the guitarist who had even longer hair than me, wore an emerald green all-in-one body suit (I'm namin' and shamin' Steff!) and had lips that could out-Jagger Jagger once he'd launched into one of his many (and highly influential to me) guitar solos. There was Kif-Kif the drummer, a skeletal, highly under-nourished looking individual who played the drums with the power of someone extremely nourished (!), squeezing free-form rhythms from a very battered old drum kit and Gavin the synthi player who burbled and gurgled and 'whoooo'd' with his EMS VCS3 synthesiser in all the right places. There were also two girl singers, both pretty and extreeemely sexy, who would have us all fighting over who it was that they were looking at with their 'come to bed' eyes.. The sound engineer was a chap called Grant Showbiz who later went on to perform in an excellent project called 'Moodswings'. I think we only got to see a couple of Planet Gong shows with Daevid and Gilli before they departed for further solo projects, but Daevid had left Here and Now with the bus and p.a so that they called continue with the free shows. There was a live Planet Gong album and single released on Charly records and further releases from Here and Now in their own right were soon to follow (even a John Peel session on Radio One!). Because the tours were free we could afford to follow them to as many gigs as possible.. often helping with the equipment (or pushing the bus – you don't remember THAT do you guys?).. all good people tho'.

After my first experience of Daevid, Gilli and Planet Gong, I began searching through the record racks of the Record & Tape Exchanges for Gong and related albums, not too difficult a task in those Punky/New Wave times and there were many to be found, sitting there collecting dust. I also found myself buying a few non-black t-shirts and my now familiar goatee beard started to sprout forth from my chin.... The main reason for choosing to grow the beard was that, without it, with my long, brown centre-parted hair, people (especially my Mum and Dad) would often liken me to Francis Rossi of Status Quo which would drive me to distraction, so I grew a goatee beard and I've spent the rest of my life being told that I resemble Billy Connolly.. It's funny, I read his life story a while back and Jeez, how could I possibly be compared to him, I mean, he was a huge Pink Fairies fan, married an Australian woman and could play a mean didgeridoo.. actually, hang on.. er...

The most common venue for us to see Planet Gong/Here and Now was at a place called Meanwhile Gardens in Westbourne Grove, not far from Portobello Road. It was a small piece of wasteland that had a circular embankment and the band would play in the 'dip' in the middle, thus forming a natural amphitheatre and we, the audience would sit around the sloping edges that surrounded them. For what was basically a piece of urban wasteland, it was actually a really cool place to see a band, everybody had a really good unobstructed view and best of all, it was outdoors so we could smoke and toke our tits off...

On one particular night, we'd been to see the band at one of their regular haunts the Kingston Tabernacle and hadn't thought about how we'd get home after. The guys in the band very generously offered us a lift back to Shepherds Bush and after dropping us off there, we headed to the centre of the Green for a little herbal supplement. Not long after we got there, we noticed one particular police car was circling the Green, slowing down on occasion to stare through the darkness at this little gaggle of hippies huddled in a circle in the early hours of the morning (in the winter!). We knew what was about to happen so as they launched into their offensive 'Sweeney' style and drove across the grass to apprehend us, someone threw the communal tin of dope onto the ground and squished it into the mud. We were asked the usual questions and they searched us when we said that we were clean of any illicit substances 'pon our persons. Frustrated at finding nothing on us, they left us with a warning and told us to disperse immediately, ironically, the one issuing those commands was actually standing on the dope tin at the time! We waited 'til they left, skinned up and then ambled over to the all-night Kentucky Fried Chicken place and ate chips and drank coke with all the resident drunks and assorted fellow undesirables....

ASKEW ROAD ADVENTURES

As previously mentioned, our assorted drug related busts and associated adventures had finally sent our parents off the deep end and while Steve got evicted from his home, I just chose to stay away and avoid the lectures. As luck would have it (or so we thought) Steve and Scruff had heard about a big, old house in Askew Road that had been recently squatted. That was a great location for us, being pretty much on the border of Shepherds Bush, Chiswick, Hammersmith and Acton. Property there now is worth extremely silly money, but at the time it was really squalid, a regular haunt for winos and weirdos and very much gangster central. There were pubs in that road that you just didn't go into, period. But, like I say, the location was excellent and I was still working at Pictures at the time, which was actually right around the corner.

The house had three floors and the rooms were huge, so we all got one each. I remember one of the rooms at ground level had this old rasta living in it, he'd roll these huge spliffs of just grass in sheets of newspaper rather than cigarette papers.. kafff! Cha Mon!!.Ya got well wrecked but bejaysus.. the stench!! Steve and Scruff had excitedly moved all their stuff in, but I left mine at home. I'm so glad I did that because a lot of good (and expensive to replace) stuff got stolen from there.. golden rule number one – never leave a squat empty.. ever (it might get squatted!). We did have some great jams and parties there though, after a particularly good one Jacqui and I collapsed into our bed and after a while we both felt in the darkness that a cat had somehow got in and had made a nest between our legs. It was wriggling about trying to get comfortable and we could both feel the vibration of its purring through the blankets. We eventually lit a candle to check it out… and.. there was nothing there! We could still feel it on our legs too! We immediately jumped out of bed, went back downstairs with the die-hards and when we eventually returned the ghost cat had gone.. or had it??

THE PIN AND THE SILLY PRICK

One occasion I recall that nearly had me shuffling off my mortal coil prematurely through nearly laughing myself to death was a time when I was invited back to a guy called Andy's house in White City. I'd met him via work and at that punky point in time, us freaks kinda bonded if we met as there weren't that many of us left by then. We'd chatted about music, drugs etc. and having reached those important common denominators, I accepted his offer of a 'session' at his place. He was sharing a large rented house with a bunch of straights but they'd all be away that evening....

Andy was a short, skinny straggly kinda guy from 'Oop North' with long, greasy black hair held from his face by two large, jug-handle shaped ears. He was a fellow Frank Zappa fan and the album 'Zoot Allures' had just been released, so we eagerly started skinning up and cranked the hi-fi to maximum. I don't know what he was putting in his spliffs, but in no time we were absolutely wasted and by the time we got to 'The Torture Never Stops' on the album, I was tripping, smiling, thinking, worrying, laughing, panicking and trying to relearn how to breathe (you know... THAT stoned!). We agreed that we should maybe follow that with a mellower album to calm our nerves a bit, so he lit some incense and plopped some Tangerine Dream onto the record deck. ZZSSCCHHOOOMM! Now I was out in space, among the cosmic stars, but in no time I was worrying about my breathing again, where was I getting my air from out there in the cosmos?? I eventually calmed down and got into it and was soon ready for another hit.

This time though, Andy asked me if I'd ever tried the pint glass, paperback and pin trick? I'd never heard of it. So I listened in awe as he explained that if you fancied a pipe or a bong but there weren't any around, or indeed had run out of rolling papers but was too stoned and paranoid to go out and get some, all you needed was a small lump of hashish, a paperback book, a pin and a pint glass.. you put the pin in through the front cover of the paperback book pointing outward, placed the hash on the pin's tip light it, blowing out any flame so that it would slowly start to smoke and hastily place the upturned pint glass over it. In no time at all the glass would be full of smoke, with none of it wasted into the atmosphere (maaan). You then gingerly pushed the glass to the edge of the book cover, tipped it back ever so slightly and sucked out all the contents (apart from the burning hot hash and the pin of course..).

"Bloody clever idea that!" I thought, as I sat back on the bean bag and gazed in awe as Andy produced a small lump of hashish, expertly positioned it onto the tip of the needle that was protruding from the paperback book and proceeded to light it. Now, at this point I would like to remind you once again that we were both really, really ripped.. we're talking Cheech and Chong proportions here. We'd already raided the larder and eaten all the food and drank all the tea and due to our unquenchable thirst we were reduced to drinking pints of good ol' London tap water.. mmmm. Pleased with how his demonstration was going thus far, eyes fixated on the the the hashish glowin' and smokin' nicely, Andy reached behind for the pint glass and with a superior expression upturned it to place it over the burning orb of hash. With an uncanny synchronicity, the music stopped, in fact all sound everywhere ceased, just in time to hear a very faint 'ppssstttt' as he instead poured the pint of good ol' London tap water all over the dope, the pin and the paperback book.. it was a Michael Moorcock novel too.. most uncool.

Well, that silence decided to hang around for a bit longer to get maximum effect out of the situation and to see what would transpire. For a brief moment there I felt deep pity for the man, I imagined how deflated I would have felt in his place and how humiliated he must feel.. but then, looking down at the soggy, blackened knob of hash and the soggy book, I felt a rush of laughter rumbling up from my guts and I let out an uncontrollably hysterical, raucous roar.. he was not too chuffed about this which only made it worse for me and the more I tried to suppress it the worse I got and I once again found

My first Magic Mushroom Band circa
1978 featuring Scruff on bass, Deso on
drums and Jacqui on backing vocals.

myself having real difficulty breathing, only this time because I'd laughed all the air out.

If I ever need to go to a 'happy place', that's one of the memories I'll recall.. it's bringing a smile to my face even now as I type this.. I never saw Andy again....

DAWN OF THE MUSHROOM MAN

It was while staying at the Askew Road squat that Steve and I finally came to realise that we were both at a crossroads musically and different musical paths beckoned. I still loved my Motorhead and Pink Fairies and rockin' out, but I was beginning to get into the spacier stuff too, it was quite nice not playing at 200mph all the time! We both still wanted to do our music more than anything, but them was crazy times at the squat and I wanted to mellow it all out a bit and I wanted to do the same musically. Steve however still wanted to have the harder edge, by then he was really getting into all the heavier punk bands but as he was getting darker, I was getting lighter so we decided there and then to lay the Speed Machine to rest.. the end of an era and the dawn of a new one. It was then that I hung up my bullet belt and invested in a woolly hat.

Due to a (by now) mushroom consuming frenzy and my discovery of the delights of Space Rock and the free Stonehenge Festival, I decided to put a band together that best summed up where I was at that point in my life, hence the name The Magic Mushroom Band, too easy really! Of course over time, this name would prove to be a curse and a blessing at the same time. My girlfriend Jacqui, Scruff and Deso were up for joining in too so we got together and jammed out a few ideas or ten..

By then I'd bought a Watkins 'Copycat' echo unit and my Floyd was becoming very Pink..... Jacqui was into doing 'spacey chants' (a la Gilli Smyth) which surprised me somewhat as she was a very timid girl and not accustomed to the limelight (or any light – startled deer, remember?). I'd also mastered the art of 'glissando' a technique involving the rubbing of a metal rod or bar (I've always found a scalpel handle to be best) over the guitar strings through an echo unit, something that had been pioneered by both Syd Barret and Daevid Allen to great effect. It produced a sound somewhat like a huge wash of stringed instruments, sort of a poor man's Mellotron. The one thing that we were seriously lacking though was a good 'bubbly' synthi player.. it wasn't fair.. Hawkwind, Gong, Here and Now AND Pink Floyd all had excellent synth players but we couldn't find one. The best synths for all the requisite swooshing, space-helicopter sounds were made by a company called EMS. They produced both the 'VCS3' which was a real Dr Who affair with a multitude of knobs, switches and cables kinda like some sort of spaceship console and the venerable 'Synthi A' which when closed up just looked like your average businessman's briefcase but when opened revealed a synthesiser with a 'dummy' printed keyboard at the bottom and above it there were 'patch pins' that you placed into little holes, kinda like a weird version of the 'Battleship'game that we all played as kids.

We asked around everywhere, but nobody was interested, until we eventually heard from a guy who we'll call Paul the Chef. He'd replied to an ad we'd placed in the Melody Maker, he was a chef by day and lived in a very nice squat in Kingston (not far from the Tabernacle in fact). He was one bizarre dude, he looked relatively straight (because of his job I guess) but he had a Korg analogue synthesiser and although not a patch(pin) on the EMS synths it nonetheless still produced the required bleeping and swooshing that we'd been searching for. His girlfriend was a snotty bitch though, I remember that much! She didn't seem to like us taking her man way to do something that didn't involve her, a common problem for all musicians since early man picked up a stick and a skull and started pounding out a beat.... Paul was also the local dealer and I remember one day me and Scruff popping 'round to his place and unbeknown to us he was having a meeting with other local dealers to 'check out' the latest batch of merchandise that had recently been smuggled into the country. We were invited in anyway, on the condition that we be cool at all times as they were serious types and this was serious stuff, seriously guys... Things almost immediately took a bizarre twist though when Paul suddenly emerged from his kitchen with a large carrot. We all proceeded to sit in a circle, Navaho style and we stared in awe as Paul took a small carving knife and began whittling away at this carrot. I looked at Scruff and he looked at me and together we conversed with our eyebrows "Say nothing.. be cool" "Yes, I agree.."

This was our first experience of seeing a carrot used as a chillum and although clever in the extreme in a sort of 'survivalist' way, me and Scruff started to get the dreaded snickers as it was passed around, pulled on and commented about in a serious 'dealery' way and by the time it approached our end of the circle (how do you get an end to a circle?) we were starting to lose it big time. I was the first to receive it and managed to get it into my mouth without incident. I was just about to take a huge pull when suddenly Scruff leaned over to me and whispered into my ear "Hey, what's up Doc?". In doing that he instantly brought home to me the fact that there we were, sat in a circle of high-fallutin' dealers, smoking a large carrot. That was it.. suddenly with a huge "Snooorrrfff!!!" and a "Snnnuucckk!!" I guffawed up into the chillum causing its contents to billow like an erupting volcano up and out, over the assembled throng, showering them all with hot ashes and burning embers. People were frantically patting their hair and clothes saying things like "Uncool man, way uncool..." while me and Scruff in the meantime were rolling around the floor in uncontrollable fits of laughter. We were escorted out of the place toute suite and literally tossed into the street weeping and sniggering.. most uncool.

It wasn't long before it was all cool again with Paul though and we became regulars at his place. It had a nice vibe to it and as the visits to Richmond Park increased so did our sessions at Paul's pad. I remember Jacqui and I leaving his place once and we got onto a train to head back to my house, the mushrooms we had taken were kicking in big time and we collapsed into our seats in fits of laughter. It was only after a while that we noticed the train was very full at one end with people but there was a lot of space around where we were. I remember trying to work out why that was and then I noticed that although we seemed to be sitting quite still in our seats, the open doorway of the stationary train was (to us) actually swinging from side to side like a huge pendulum and to try to compensate for that in our psilocybin-induced state we'd unwittingly both been swinging from side to side ourselves, in unison. The rest is a blur, but I guess we got home ok!

With our newly formed Magic Mushroom Band we eventually got around to organising a jam at a rehearsal studio near Westbourne Grove, I forget its name now but it was right smack bang next to an area known as 'The People's Independent Republic of Frestonia', a series of streets and houses that'd all been squatted by freaks and the like and they'd declared it an independent republic. They even had border guards and their own council! The studio itself seemed to be an old converted warehouse and it had a huge plush rehearsal space for the 'upper league' bands and a cheaper basement affair for us 'would-be's'. On the night of our first jam there was a newly formed band called 'Asia' who were practising there for their first world tour. In that band was Steve Howe (formerly of Yes and Tomorrow) and Carl Palmer of ELP and while they were out we sneaked upstairs to check out their gear.. wow!! Steve Howe must have had about eight guitars lined up there in front of a huge stack of amplifiers and Carl Palmer's drum kit was massive, topped off by a huge gong at the back. We eventually pushed our jaws back together and headed back downstairs before we were discovered... We set up our own equipment (in a lot shorter time than Asia would've!), checked the mics, set the echo units on stun and away we went. We played pretty nonstop for what seemed like eternity, Paul blended in pretty good and made all the right noises on his synthesiser. I'd written a couple of tunes by then and we jammed through those too (in fact they went on to be included in the original live set of the far more successful Magic Mushroom Band Mark 2). We'd recorded the session and upon listening back to it later were very pleased with how it all went and the hunt for gigs began in earnest.

We'd met some freaky types who were part of an organisation called 'Free Tibet' and they were looking for bands to play at a benefit gig (the first of many in my life!) where all the proceeds would go into a fund that would enable them to go to Tibet and.. er... free it. Of course, they were all so out of it they never got as far as leaving London, but their hearts were in the right place. They were squatting an old, derelict greengrocers shop in (pre-yuppified and very squalid) Covent Garden. We happily agreed to do a show for them and just as we confirmed a date, Paul hit us with a bombshell, he couldn't play with us any more due to work commitments.. damn and blast! We reckoned the girlfriend had put him off the idea, that seemed a more plausible explanation as he'd really enjoyed himself at the jams.. so there we were.. debut gig all sorted and no synth player.. what to do?

Hastily we placed another ad in the Melody Maker and this time we had instant success. Enter 'Thamby', of Ceylonese (Sri Lankan) descent who'd spent his teens growing up in Tottenham. He was as dark as night with a huge mop of black curls framing his face, in fact he reminded me of an Aborigine when I first met him. He always wore a silver bomber jacket as worn by his hero Tim Blake the synthesiser player with Gong. We went to visit him at his house in Southall and had a bit of a jam, he had an EMS Synthi A and a Mini Moog (excellent!) and he also had a van (also excellent!) and he was very keen to be a part of it all.

On the day of that first gig we arrived at the venue way too early, we were that excited! We'd squeezed most of our equipment into Thamby's Ford Escort van and caught the train to the venue, guitars in hand. We went down some rickety stairs to check out the 'performance' area to discover a dark, dank cellar that had no ceiling to speak of, just joists and old cables. The organisers had kindly constructed a 'stage' for us out of a combination of large sheets of chipboard and milk crates which meant that once we were set up on stage everything would bounce up and down with the slightest of movements.. including us! The amps and speaker cabs were teetering precariously, the mic stand kept bouncing back and hitting me in the mouth making me more than a little reluctant to smile at the audience and little, skinny Jacqui looked like she was going to be catapulted across the room at any time. It was absolute chaos, but.. at the end of our 'set' we were greeted with much applause by a then, fair-sized audience (for a first gig) and Tibet was temporarily rescued from the dark clutches of its Chinese oppressors....

Through a mutual friend, we'd also discovered a whole string of squatted houses on the A3 near the 'Robin Hood' roundabout on the way to Kingston. The 'Convoy' (the original bus-dwelling gypsy hippy types) were all camped up there with one bus parked out front of each individual property and one of the houses had been made into a rehearsal studio. We had a great jam there but at the end of the session both Scruff and Deso hit me with another bombshell, they didn't want to do it anymore. Scruff really didn't get on with Thamby's enthusiasm, he used to call him 'Gungadin', they both instead wanted to get into the Ska and R&B stuff that was becoming popular again at the time... The Specials, The Selector etc. Fair enough, things were forever changing and evolving at that time so I just had to 'go with the flow'. About a year or so later they invited me to do a live show with their R&B band at an outdoor festival in East London.. it was fun and good to play with them again.

Poor old Deso died not very long after that and it was very weird how that came about. Apparently he'd gone to visit some family in Ireland with his new girlfriend and on their way back he'd become separated from his girlfriend at the train station. The girlfriend eventually made it home but he never did and his body was eventually found by the train tracks somewhere and no-one ever discovered what had happened... did he jump?

Was he pushed? He always seemed a pretty happy go-lucky guy to us, it was a real loss and it hit us all hard, especially Scruff who'd been the closest to him....

KNICKERS TO 'TWICKERS

Jacqui and I had been together long enough by then to want to get a proper place to live. We'd left the craziness of the Askew Road squat and we couldn't handle living at our family homes anymore and as luck would have it, my Uncle Brian's girlfriend Sandra had a rather tempting offer for me. She was living at the time in a two-storey, four-bedroom flat in Twickenham, right on the High Street above a shop. The view out of the windows at the front were of the bustling main street and directly opposite was the Twickenham Odeon cinema and the view out at the back was of Eel Pie island, where Pete Townshend of The Who had a recording studio and the River Thames rolling by.. choice location or what? To buy a place like that, even way back then would have been way out of most peoples' budgets, but my Auntie Sandra was a canny lass in the '60's and had taken advantage of a loophole in the law that allowed you to take your landlord/lady to court if you felt that your rent was unfairly high, wherein the judge would put a 'freeze' on the rent from that point on, so it often never went up at all. So, flash forward to the late 'seventies and she was still paying just twelve pounds a week! The flat actually belonged to a woman who owned the shop beneath and she was forever trying to find an excuse to evict her.

My Uncle Brian was going to America for two years and desperately wanted Sandra to go with him, she really wanted to go too but was concerned about the flat being left empty for so long and the landlady doing something sneaky in her absence. When they both discovered that Jacqui and I were desperately looking for somewhere to live it seemed like the perfect solution, she could go to the 'States with Brian and we'd have a posh flat in Twickenham to live in for two years at twelve pounds a week.. AS LONG AS WE DIDN'T DO ANYTHING TO ATTRACT ATTENTION TO OURSELVES.

We couldn't believe our luck! We packed everything we owned, not a single sock was left in my room (which had been hastily decorated in pink and my sister moved in before I changed my mind) and after calling loads of favours we got it all into our new abode. Of course, I was only nineteen by then and compared to all the shit that I have NOW, it wasn't really that much stuff.. certainly not enough to fill a two-storey four-bedroom flat, but that was nice in itself in a kinda spartan, open plan kinda way.. best of all though was that I allocated myself a music room! I could finally go into that designated space, switch on my amp, grab my guitar and share my riffs and licks with the passers-by in the street below.. whether they liked it or not.. are you beginning to spot the fundamental flaw with this arrangement yet?

Sometimes we'd wake up in the morning, look out at the back view and see yet another car floating upside down in the river, we got quite used to the sight after a while. There was a slip-road from the High Street which took you down straight to the river where you suddenly had to turn a sharp right or left at the last minute to avoid driving straight into the water. At night this was obviously more of a problem, especially if you'd had a few too many shandies, people would often become a (very damp) cropper... even drunken walkers were known to stagger unwittingly into the murky, unforgiving waters of the River Thames. Walking along the river one day, I discovered a secret walled-garden at the back of an old, abandoned convent, I saw a big old wooden door ajar and couldn't resist peering in.. there was no-one around so I ventured in. It was absolutely beautiful in there, so tranquil, it had obviously been well looked after at some point but was now completely overgrown.. and unoccupied. We'd often go there, either for a little toke or a little lovin' (or both) and we thought we were the only ones that knew of its existence... I guess no-one else cared..

Unfortunately, and unsurprisingly upon reflection, after only a month and a half of living there, somehow(!) word of our loud parties, large groups of giggling freaks hanging out the windows and the constant waft of aromatic fumes reached the landlady who got her solicitor to put a very stern letter through our door while we were out..

"Dear current occupier,
It has come to our attention that you are living at this property and you are not the listed tenant. You are not permitted to stay at this address and I shall be contacting the tenant proper to enquire as to whether they have indeed vacated this address."

Bollocks, damn and blast! Poor Auntie Sandra had to hightail it back to Twickenham from the 'States just to make sure that she wouldn't lose her flat (she did eventually have to give it up but she kept it for a few years longer). We had to clear out our stuff immediately.. nowhere to live again, this was getting ridiculous! Homeless again! By now, there was no going back to the family home, my old room had already been commandeered and anyway was now a particularly girly shade of pink and covered in horse posters courtesy of my sister Paula who at that point, to be fair, had been sharing a bedroom with our younger sister Sonya. It was while 'round at Thamby's house in Southall that he suggested a meeting with the rest of the guys in the house and it was agreed that we could have the 'box' room that at the time was just used for storage, if we contributed to the rent thus making it cheaper for them.. excellent! Saved by the bell!

SOUTHALL – LAND OF THE MUSTARD COLOURED DATSUNS

The 'Southall' years were a very strange and illuminating time for me.. like a lot of my friends I'd always fancied going to India to 'find myself (maaan)'.. but I could never imagine getting myself that sort of money together for the trip or indeed surviving outside of the tiny world that I inhabited.. I was not a worldly man. So, fate gave me the next best thing. Suddenly, here I was in a town swamped with Asian culture, every shop seemed to have sitar and tabla music emanating from it, the clothes they wore were almost painfully bright and plenty of full-on markets that resembled what I had imagined Eastern Bazaars to be like. The cinemas showed only Asian movies, Bollywood style and the music shops played only Asian music and the heady smells of the different herbs and spices wafting from the supermarkets were very aromatic. Apart from (obviously) the weather and the London buses it felt to me just like being out there in deepest, darkest Indiah! But I never contracted Malaria or Dysentery (or Delhi Belly!) AND I could still hop on a bus to go and see my Mum and Dad or go to work. It was also my first real experience of living in proper 'shared' accommodation, something which definitely had its share of ups and downs I can tell ya...

Thamby (meaning 'little one' in Ceylonese) was a real character and like the other guys in the house was about five or six years older than me. Born in Sri Lanka (then Ceylon), his family were servants of a rich, white family and it was them who gave him his 'English' name, which was Richard. He just so happened to share this house in Southall with two other Richards which got very confusing for me (and many others) as time went by. Thamby was a bugger for getting things on 'H.P' (credit) and not paying off the instalments. He always had to be the first on the block to get the latest technological marvel but he was always broke! He would brazenly stroll into a music shop, go straight to say, a new flashy synthesiser setup and after a bit of a chat with the salesman and some hasty form-signing, he'd be out of the door with the stuff in boxes under his arm. Whenever the debtors would (inevitably) call 'round at the house asking for Richard, he'd be standing at the door, black as the ace of spades with Ravi Shankar playing in the background telling them... "Nah mate, nobody of that name lives here innit..". Poor Thamby was to die relatively young in his early forties after numerous heart attacks and losing a leg, but as is often the case with those kind of characters, he squeezed a lot more living into those few short years than some people do in a whole lifetime...

Upon moving in we immediately became the young ones (literally) in the household. The other guys had been through their 'wild days' and 'crazy music' and were busy trying to settle down to a gentler, more adult way of life, which meant abstaining from such distractions as drugs (!) alcohol(!!) and meat(!!!). Luckily for me, living in Southall/Asia meant the vegetarian options were countless and could be bought almost twenty four hours a day, so the 'no meat' option was a pretty easy transition for me (if not a little whiffy at first!) and something I quite happily embraced. I obligingly smoked my reefers in the garden as far away from the house as possible and seemed to be backing off naturally from other more damaging stimulants and it seemed the perfect environment to do it in, no peer pressure at all.

The music the guys in the house were listening to was a lot different to what I was used to and it became a very important education for me as a 'hungry for knowledge' musician, they had all at one time or other been heavily into Gong, but they were also fans of the broader 'Canterbury Sound' (commonly summed up musically by a fuzzed-out organ and bass guitar and extremely English vocals). The main protagonists and inspiration behind the scene was the band 'The Soft Machine', named after a William Burroughs novel of the same name who in the 'sixties rivalled the Pink Floyd as the top UK psychedelic band of the time. As I mentioned earlier, Gong's Daevid Allen started with them as did Robert Wyatt the drummer who became wheelchair bound after falling out of a window after a particularly 'happening' party. He later appeared on 'Top of the Pops' in his wheelchair singing a version of 'I'm a Believer' by the Monkees. He's blessed (luckily) with a beautiful, haunting, sweet voice and he went on to do such projects as Matching Mole and numerous solo singles and albums for Virgin and then Rough Trade records in the 'seventies and 'eighties.

Also part of that scene were such bands as Caravan and Hatfield & the North and National Health who often shared/stole band members, it was a very incestuous scene out there in Canterbury! It was clever 'Art School' music kinda flirting with jazz and rock but not in a squiddly diddly oobeedobee way that the American counterparts such as Mahavishnu Orchestra, Return to Forever and the like were doing, wanking all over their fretboards. S'funny, around that time Daevid Allen had his punk single 'Much too Old' reviewed in a music paper where they applauded him for rhyming Chick Corea with diarrohea! Both Caravan and Hatfield & The North shared the same lead vocalist and bassist, a lovely guy called funnily enough... Richard! He, like Robert Wyatt, had a voice that could melt the hardest of hearts. I was in fact honoured in later years to have a recently reformed Caravan (of Dreams) share the bill with the Magic Mushroom Band at a gig that we'd put on.

There was this whole vast array of music, all styles that I'd never heard before and I was hungry to assimilate it all.. it was great stuff! Arthur Brown's Kingdom Come, Ivor Cutler, Can, Pat Metheny, Todd Rundgren, it just kept on coming... I still enjoyed what I had listened to before, this stuff just expanded my mental 'reference library' – the part of my brain that makes the songs up. I also benefitted from my housemates' reluctance to relive the past by inheriting lots of their records, books, pipes and stuff either dirt cheap or free, because they needed the 'space'. My record collection grew substantially during that period! I constantly craved input – more music! Give me more! Feed me!

I'd also just discovered a Sci-fi 'kid's' comic called '2000ad' which was fast becoming something of a cult item.. Judge Dredd, Sam Slade Robohunter, Strontium Dog etc. The quality of the artwork and stories blew me away and I was very proud (as a twenty-something 'kid') to get a cartoon of Judge Dredd that I'd sent to the comic printed in Thaarg's editorial page on the inside cover. It really inspired me to experiment more with my drawings which was and will always be a great form of therapy for me.. BORAGG THUUNG EARTHLETS!! But the eventual Judge Dredd movie? Sylvester Stallone? Come On!!!

S'funny... like the soon to follow 'Hitchhiker's Guide to the Galaxy' phenomenon, it's amazing how so much of that dialogue has found its way into the modern English language, eh? So long and thanks for all the fish then...

TO THE MANOR 'GAWN

With Scruff and Deso both now gone, Thamby and I decided to to try some stuff as a spacey, 'ambient' duo, lots of echo guitar and cosmic synthesiser sounds (I guess we were an ambient act before the term really existed) we did a really far out version of 'Within You Without You' (which the Magic Mushroom Band would later expand on) but which Thamby insisted on singing..... now, he was a wizard on the ol' synths there's no denying that, but as a singer he left a lot to be desired.. I eventually got my way and we did it instrumentally..

We were invited one day by a nice chap called Phil from Newbury to play at a Lord's Manor near Bath. It turned out that this young guy had inherited the whole estate from his Lordly father complete with huge mansion house, various outbuildings and courtyards and rolling acres as far as the eye could see. Unfortunately he also inherited the associated debts, he was so poor that he couldn't keep the place together and it was falling down around him. We arrived just as dusk was settling in and as we approached the huge wrought iron gates with stone eagles atop them we saw a large, creaking sign that announced that we'd arrived at Avebury Manor. We drove on through, along a seemingly endless drive and eventually arrived at the huge, gothic mansion. We parked up and began to unload our equipment and were helped by a couple of 'chaps' who offered to carry stuff for us, the birthday party for the Lord was to be held in the belltower!

We entered through an enormous, creaking oak door and wound our way up the cold stone staircase in what turned out to be the 'West Wing' (we'd never been in a house that had 'wings' before!). Past ageing rams' skulls and weapons mounted on rough, cracked wooden shields that littered the walls and out into a corridor that had tatty, faded velvet curtains hanging limply on broken poles and once-proud suits of armour rusting on decaying mannequins in the musty, dusty dampness and finally arriving at the door that led to the belltower. As we wound our way up yet another twisty (but final) spiral staircase we entered the main bell-tower room and were greeted by the sight of a huge crowd of upper-class party people all completely off their tits who clapped at our arrival and eagerly awaited our performance.

We were introduced to his Lordship the birthday boy who was dressed in Eton schoolboy type clothes but wore a brightly coloured bandana around his head, 'Deer Hunter' style. He had a certain 'eccentricity' about him probably caused by his bloodline staying as close to the 'gene-pool' as was legally allowed.. he was a pretty 'far out' character who spent our entire performance in an upside-down lotus position (yes, on his head!). Everyone seemed to enjoy our set and they offered us some vegetarian stew after, but we noticed some dead flies floating around in the pot so politely declined. We were thanked for the performance and we bade our farewells to the Lord of the Flies and his entourage and decided to get the hell out of there as soon as we could.. too weird!!

We eventually found our way back to Thamby's van and drove on down the driveway, looking back when we reached the gates to see the creepy silhouette of the old mansion house being backlit by a full, blood moon as his hounds howled in the courtyard. Thamby put the pedal to the metal and we were off quicksmart.. but, as was often the plot in any decent Hammer Horror movie, no matter what direction we took we always ended up back at those gates to the Manor. I kid you not! We tried going in totally opposite directions to previous attempts and there we'd be, right back where we started from. We tried in vain to find someone who could give us directions but there was nobody about, all the villagers were asleep (or dead!). We were seriously just about to lose the plot when, somehow, we found a lane that took us up and out to the good ol' M4 and back to the safety of the West London smog.

WITHIN YOU, WITHOUT YOU

The lease had run out at our house in Southall and couldn't be renewed, but luckily our Sikh landlord had another house to rent to us that was next door to his home on the other (nicer) side of the Uxbridge Road. It was closer to the railway station for me and, more importantly, closer to the best Indian takeaway in town (or anywhere!). It was just a 'greasy spoon' but for Indians, so it was dirt cheap, but very tasty, the proper stuff as opposed to the posh overpriced slop that was usually dished up to us whiteys in the 'proper' flock-walled restaurants that we'd frequent after a night on the hops. We were virtually living on Indian takeaway food by that point as we'd got tired of coming to blows over who's turn it was to cook or do the dishes.. instead, to keep the peace, we just ate takeaways out of the foil dishes. We were such regulars there and we'd always order the same thing (Mater Panir) that in no time, we'd just walk in and say "105!" wherein all the Indian staff would crack up with laughter for the duration. This stemmed from the first time that we went in there and asked how much the meal would cost. The guy serving said nothing and instead smirked and pointed out of the window instead.. I saw nothing of any consequence out there and returned my gaze to him as he widened his eyes in a more deliberate fashion and pointed.. er.. more pointedly at a passing bus. I looked at the bus, then at him and then back at the bus and in sheer desperation for me to 'get' the joke he suddenly blurted "105!!"... "You see?"... "105 bus!!" I continued to stare at him blankly as he continued, rather deflated and resigned to the fact that we'd missed out on the funniest joke ever "That's how much it costs...". One pound and five pence, see how cheap it was??

The new house was bigger than the previous one but had less rooms, so Jacqui and I got what was originally the front lounge as our bedroom. There was still a communal dining/TV room next to the kitchen which was conveniently closer to the kettle anyway. Jacqui had been working at a bank for quite a while by then, I knew the money was good but I couldn't understand what got her into doing that in the first place, she was such a space cadet. As time went on we seemed to be edging further and further away from each other, having less and less in common. She'd go out on her own to socialise with her fellow bank workers and I'd often be out and about doing my own thing. She'd also started having really intense nightmares about being held up at the bank, but still wouldn't give it up. It finally reached a point when I had to suggest that she leave, for her own sake and find someone else more suitable for her new lifestyle, I was in no rush to change mine. It was very hard to do, we'd been an item for quite a while by then and experienced a lot in our time together. She didn't take it very well (not helped by the other guys in the house who hadn't had a woman since Arthur Brown sang 'Fire' on Top of the Pops and they took her side, making me feel like a complete bastard) and after moving back with her Mum would phone me constantly, sobbing down the phone.. I felt so bad.. but I knew it had to be done.. time to move on.

So, now it was down to me, Richard, Richard and Richard (Thamby). Luckily for me (and anyone else who phoned asking to speak to Richard) one of the Richards eventually moved out to be replaced by a Derek. Derek and I got on really well, he was a left-handed guitarist from the Isle of Sheppey and was still partial to the occasional Jamaican Woodbine. The guys would always advertise any rooms available for rent in 'Time Out' magazine, so we were always guaranteed to attract characters of some extreme at least, from ardent dungaree-wearing feminists to devil-worshipping masters of the Black Arts (but more about him later..). Through all this time, I was still spending my Saturdays hanging out down the Portobello Road and would often bump into Steve the Speed Machine somewhere along the road. We went through some crazy scenes together in our formative years so I know he'll understand when I say that I was getting a little concerned about him. He was still the crazy trouble-magnet that I knew and loved but I sensed a real danger around him. He was immersing himself into a deadly dangerous smack-induced world while I was eating vegetarian curry and listening to Steve Hillage's 'Rainbow Dome Musick'.

JUST MY 'MAGINATION

We never, ever attracted any sexy chicks back to our place though and my sex life during the Southall years was not one to shout out about. The only females around seemed to be either large, negro women or butch Socialist Worker's Party women who were just plain ugly and had given up on trying to get laid (by men at least) and decided instead to put all their efforts into bringing 'Power to the People'. There was one girl who used to come 'round on a semi-regular basis who liked me to fondle her large, floppy tits but that was as far as I was allowed to go.. that to me was kinda like being allowed to smell the food but not eat it! The Indian chicks were as invisible to me as I was to them and most of them had moustaches anyway. Let's not forget that by then my hair was down to my waist and my beard was reaching 'biblical' proportions. It wasn't so much that I'd let myself go, more like I'd let myself grow (and grow) and in what was by now the beginning of the 'eighties I wasn't in a cast of thousands anymore.. I was alone.. a 'Neil' surrounded by 'Rick's' and 'Vivians' and truck drivers would honk their horns suggestively at me from behind before promptly speeding off as I turned to wave at them.

I was coming out of 'Pictures' once and walked by a nearby bus stop where there was a little old lady reading a copy of the Sun newspaper. She looked up at me in horror, looked back at the paper, looked up again at me in sheer terror and scuttled off. Needless to say I was a bit freaked out by this and decided to go and get a copy of the paper myself. Once I'd got past the topless models and katchy, kooky, kocknee headlines, I got to the page in question to find a photo of a guy leaving a courthouse who looked JUST LIKE ME! He had been to an all-night party somewhere with his girlfriend and apparently she'd overdosed during the night and he freaked out when he woke up next to her lifeless corpse and to avoid any hassle with the law he'd burned her body on a bonfire in the garden. Obviously his cunning plan had flaws.. hence the court appearance!

I was also at the time getting stopped a lot in the street by people asking me if I WAS Billy Connolly. The chicks at the time saw me as an amusing timepiece and if it wasn't for those sexy girls where I worked, I think I would have gone crazy.

There was a girl, Joanna who I met on the train to work, I noticed her getting into my carriage one morning. She had a mass of brown, corkscrewy hair and a big fur coat (if she'd worn a top hat she would have been a ringer for Marc Bolan, not that I would've.. er.. he WAS a pretty guy, come on!). As is the commuters' way, you would always try to sit on the same seat or part of the carriage at least (if possible, one time I gave up my seat for a blind man and he told me to "Fuck off!"). There was a smoking carriage then so it was an obvious choice for me and the fellow puffers. She was standing right at the opposite end to me but she'd noticed me and I'd noticed her, we kept giving each other furtive glances and subtle smiles throughout the journey. This went on for quite a few mornings, but with her getting onto the carriage further and further along, all the time getting closer to where I sat. Eventually she got on and sat down right next to me and straight away we started chatting. She was from the Midlands and I instantly fell in love with her accent and we had a lot in common with mutual interests in music and art and eventually the conversation got around to the ol' Mary Jane. She said she had plenty back at her place and would I like to go 'round there the next evening for dinner etc.? (etc.? what was included in the etc.?). Well, does a bear shit in the woods? You betcha! We made the date.

I arranged to meet her at her place in Hayes at 7:00 in the evening. I couldn't believe my luck, at last! Some action! I couldn't stop thinking about it (and her) all that night and the next day. I bought a nice bottle of red wine (so the man said) and some flowers, I was firing on all four love-cylinders I can tell ya.. I got to her door and eagerly rang the bell, flowers and wine in hand (and clean underwear on) to be greeted by Joanna wearing just a loose-fitting dressing gown.. what the?.. we exchanged greetings as I tried to peel my eyes away from her glistening cleavage and she invited me in. This seemed to be turning into one of those stories that they have in the porno mags, ya know the type.. 'Suddenly her gown fell open to reveal two ripe mammaries and a luscious pubic mound..' kinda t'ing. She made her excuses for not being ready and as she turned toward her bedroom door said "Why don't you go on in and make yourself comfortable (excellent!) while I finish dressing (damn!), dinner's almost ready, my BOYFRIEND is cooking it... ????????!!!!!!!!!! Piddleshitfuckdamnandblastit! Boy, did I ever get the wrong end of the stick or what? As you can imagine, he wasn't too chuffed about me turning up with wine, flowers and a slight erection in clean underwear and I swear I saw his face turn decidedly evil as he turned to add 'flavouring' to the meal he was preparing. As you can imagine, the meal itself was rather awkward with me joking about how I always take flowers, wine and an erection with me wherever I go, yup, that's me, good ol' flowers, wine and erection man.. yep.. sheeit! Their pot WAS good tho' a little too good in fact and added to the queasiness I was beginning to experience after the meal. I made my excuses and left as the pain began to worsen and by the time I got home I sprayed the bowl at thirty paces, narrowly missing my clean underwear..

OY, YOU!!

After our dabble as a duet, Thamby and I decided that it'd be nice to get back to having bass and drums again. He'd had a band previous to meeting me which he'd called the 'You' band (named after a Gong album) and set about contacting the original members to see if they were up for getting together for a jam. Gary, his original bassist was in another band by then called 'Karma Kanix' (always thought that was a really clever name) but, yes, he was up for a jam.. and the drummer Alan Hitt (yes, Hitt) was too. For the drummer, 'Hitt' was such an appropriate name as he would always turn up at rehearsals or gigs with either black eyes, broken bones, or bruises administered by jealous boyfriends, or from getting run over by a car or falling off the back of a bus, whatever.. it's no coincidence that the word 'drummer' sounds so very much like the word 'drama' eh, fellow musicians?? His younger sister was a gorgeous sweet thing and had a crush on me, but she turned out (fortunately discovered in time) to be a lot younger than she looked and as desperate as I was.. jail bait was not an option!

Gary knew of a street of squats in Maida Vale called Bristol (but changed graffitily to 'Crystal') Gardens and one of the houses was a rehearsal studio (as you can tell by now this was often the case back then, the only way to get away with having bands playing in your house was to put a practise studio where the neighbours were either pissed off with you already or just plain didn't care!). The guy who lived there was a drummer himself and was appearing at the time in a stage version of 'The Hitchhiker's Guide to the Galaxy' as the percussionist in the band. It was believed that he was the heir to the Winchester rifle empire, but that might just have been stoner bullshit. It was an archetypal old, damp, smelly London squat.. there was an old man upstairs that no-one ever saw. Looking out of the rear window I remarked on the little white bags that were swinging like Xmas decorations on the tree in the garden. "Oh, that's just his shit! He craps in the carrier bags then tosses them out of the window.. if we're lucky it'll get caught in the tree.." I guessed right away that not too much sunbathing would be going on in THAT garden in the Summer... We carried our gear down the wobbly stairs to the basement, set up and proceeded to have one of the best jams ever, we were on fire, baby! Gary was (and probably still is!) an amazing bass player, he was nicknamed 'Bap Bap' because he'd mastered that 'bappity bappity' rhythymic style of bass playing

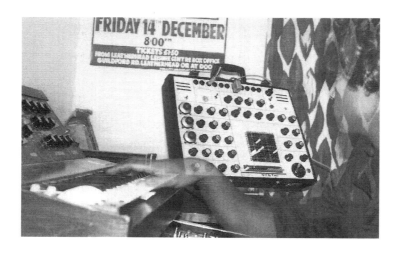

An eerie photo of the long deceased and much missed
Thamby with his beloved EMS Synthi A and Mini Moog.

that was popular at the time. Because they'd all played together before I found myself jamming with one of the tightest rhythm units that I'd ever experienced as we peaked and we troughed at all the right moments. Unfortunately Gary had too many other commitments to be able to join us, plus he'd just become one of the 'Orange People' (Rajneesh) and don't get me started on all that malarkey!! There was a glimmer of hope in the oddball that was Colin, he too was a very competent bassist although really a drummer (!) and had played in the You band before, so he knew the material inside and out. He resembled Clark Kent, as he wore these huge, framed glasses with the lenses as thick as the bottom of a bottle but he was tall, stocky and as strong as an ox. I remember during one rehearsal, in a fit of boredom, he proceed to lie on his back and tilt a Ford Transit van almost onto its side, using just his feet! He wasn't able to commit either though, I think he got a job out of town, maybe on the Planet Krypton or something...

So, there we were again, without a bassist once more so we placed yet another ad in the Melody Maker and waited patiently for a bite, like fishermen on the bank of a river but without the smell. It wasn't too long before we received a huge, hand-written letter in the post, full of CAPITAL LETTERS and EXCLAMATION MARKS!!! with hastily scrawled stars and moons and smiley faces throughout. It was from a very keen young chap called Wayne who lived in a town called Bracknell in Berkshire. I'd been there once with a girlfriend called Joyce whose Uncle let us stay at his house so that we could go to the Jazz Festival there and shag on his sofa after. Wayne was very much into the same stuff as us, just a year younger and had been playing bass for some time jamming with his guitarist, identical-twin brother Craig. We contacted Wayne and arranged a date and time for him to come down and have a talk and a play.

We were sitting in our house, equipment all set up when we thought we heard something... it was a very faint noise, but there nonetheless. As we cautiously approached the front door we realised that there was actually somebody or something there scratching on it. As we opened the door to shoo away whatever it was, we were greeted by the sight of Wayne, tall, blonde, wispy, with John Lennon specs, afghan coat and obligatory bobble hat (it was Winter tho'), looking not a little like the character that John Hurt portrayed in the movie Midnight Express. He had just enough meat stretched over his bones to give him a temperature and looked like he was having trouble holding up his bass guitar case. He opened his mouth to speak, but instead we got a barely audible squeak, it was then that we discovered Wayne's intense shyness (something that did diminish in time thankfully!). Of course, once the bass guitar was strapped around his neck he could play like a demon possessed, he wasn't a drinker but puffed like a magic dragon and we were to become good buddies and fellow musicians for many years.

There we were at last, the You band was finally complete! We recorded a (very rough) 4-track demo at our house on a Teac reel to reel recorder (that, yes, Thamby had bought on H.P). We did it in the smallest room (no, not THAT smallest room) so we could only record one person at a time. No great problem for most of us, but the drummer had to put his rhythm track down first.. to nothing. He had to memorise each segment of the song, which would be an instrumental, all the rhythm changes, everything and get the length right.. so we'd all be conducting him through the doorway, waving our arms like, er.. demented arm wavers.

If gigs were on the agenda then we needed to get some decent transport. Thamby's black Escort van had long given up the ghost, so he went out window shopping one day and came back with a white Ford Transit van, bought (you guessed it) on H.P. We wracked our brains for a cool logo to paint on the side of the van and in a fit of inspiration Thamby came up with the idea of a fluorescent UFO travelling past a planet in space (I tell ya, for someone who never did drugs, ol' Thamby could be a real space-case!). We made up a huge stencil and sprayed it all up, it was quite a feature on the Southall landscape for a while there, the Indians couldn't for the life of them work out what the Ceylonese guy was selling from his van, spaceships? Planets? That ol' van saw us through many an adventure and eventually died from exhaustion. Problem was, what to do with a dead van outside your house Thamby? Easy, just tow it across London to a seedy Council estate in East London, park it up, let the tyres down, race back home to Southall and report it stolen.. easy innit?

Our first gig together as the You band came about as a result of a chance meeting with a fund-raising group called 'Cartwheel' at the Festival for Mind, Body & Spirit at Olympia. I was there to eat all the free veggie food samples, perv on the girls doing yoga and crash out in Steve Hillage's Rainbow Dome after a coupla doobies in the car park. They said that they were actually rolling a huge cartwheel around the UK collecting money for various causes and they offered us a chance to play at a (here it comes) 'benefit' gig at a disused church near the East India docks in London. Our 'set' was a bit rough in places but it had its moments and Wayne's posse who had come down from Bracknell for the show were very supportive.

It was such a cool scene in Bracknell at the time, I really couldn't believe it when Wayne invited us to play up there for a friend's birthday party (at the local crematorium!). It was a great party and we all had a good time, I'd brought 'Robert' with me, an inflatable remote-controlled robot that spent the whole night mingling, profiling with the guys and chicks as they fondled his controls. The radio control unit had a great range on it, I would often set him up outside the front of my house on the footpath and have him trundling up and down the road and turning 'round to come back once he'd reached the end.. it freaked the shit out of a lot of the Hindus and Sikhs and nearly caused a few car crashes! There I was living in Southall, wondering where all the freaks, bikers and hippies had gone and the answer that night was right in front of me.. they were all in Bracknell! It had a lot to do with the proximity of the town to Reading, home of the infamous yearly festival and the last bastion of Heavy Rockness. I eventually moved to

Bracknell myself and had many, many happy years there.. but anyway, I digress!

So, the Cartwheel benefit gig went well and it was suggested that we should play at the equally infamous Stonehenge Festival that year. We had a good couple of months to work out a decent set of tunes and a very good reason to do so.. most of the numbers would be instrumental (to stop Thamby singing). He had a penchant for odd song titles ol' Thambers, he sometimes had a weird grasp on the English language and would be fascinated by certain phrases or signs. 'Freshly Cut Sandwiches' was one that springs to mind and another was 'Caution, Sudden Air-Brakes' which he renamed 'Caution, Sudden Tea-Breaks'. He was a truck driver at the time and was once told by his boss that the truck he was driving had faulty air-brakes. They would work ok, but didn't make the legally required 'hiss' when stopping at lights or intersections, so for legal purposes could he wind down the window and audibly 'hiss' with his mouth whenever he had to stop. The silly bugger did it for a while before the penny finally dropped...

Thamby was, to me, one of the real pioneers of the east meets west fusion of synthi styles, way before bands like the Orb and suchlike brought it to the mainstream (he would have loved that scene tho' but sadly died before it happened) and all of the You band instrumentals had that Eastern flavour. It was a lot of fun for me and a real learning curve with all the 'pentatonic' scales and notations. I wrote my first ever 'Eastern' flavoured instrumental number during that period and called it (T)urban Paranoia which became a popular live track for the Magic Mushroom Band in later years.

LEY LINES, CRAZY TIMES

The Stonehenge Festival loomed on the horizon and we were as ready as we were ever likely to be. We'd also discovered that Michael Eavis of Worthy Farm in Pilton, near Glastonbury (home of the festival) was into renting out his barn for bands to rehearse in. It could be booked for the whole weekend and we could sleep there too, so we decided to book it for the weekend before the Summer Solstice and head on to the Stonehenge Festival after. We had a great time at Worthy Farm, Michael was a really nice chap and very affable as were his family and co-workers (this was before it became the home of the huge uber-festival of today!). One of the guys who was living and working there was Andrew, he used to do the 'Acidica' lightshow and also knew Miranda from 'Pictures' where I worked. We had fresh milk every morning and the rural vibe was most good.

Onwards to the (in)famous Stonehenge Festival then.. growing every year from its initial weekend-long mid-summer jaunt to almost a fortnight of non-stop Rock n' Roll, Wheelers, Dealers, Mystic Healers and Convoy Craziness. As we arrived at the scene we saw the usual array of colourful tents and buses and teepees as far as the eye could see, but something was amiss… no main stage!! The familiar 'Pyramid' stage (owned by Nik Turner) had not been set up yet. We met up with Sid Rawle (who looked like Willie Rushton on acid) and he very kindly led us to a relatively large marquee and said that we were very welcome to set up and play there if we could blag a generator. Apparently we were one of the first bands to arrive on site! As we opened the back of the van up, people started to gather 'round as a crowd and there were excited murmurings coming from within "Are you a band then?" "Are you gonna play for us tonight then?" "Do ya wanna hand setting up then?". Boy, these people were seriously starved of some entertainment! No sooner had we explained our generator dilemma people were scurrying about shouting "They needs a generator!" "Somebody lend them a generator!" a guy in a small tent was spotted running a light bulb from what looked suspiciously like a hastily disguised generator and they somehow managed to persuade him that it would be a really good idea for him to part with it and we were in business.

It was dark by the time we'd set it all up and to save fuel the

only lighting was from candles and with a nod and a wink, off
we went and launched into our set. The rehearsing had paid off
and we were playing really well, but something was awry..
things were sounding a bit bizarre. By then both Thamby and I
were using 'Echoplex' echo units which relied on magnetic tape
to provide the much needed echoes. Trouble was, that poor
little generator was having trouble keeping up with the
demands on it and the power output was seriously wavering,
thus making the echo tapes seem to speed up and slow down
and it was also doing all kinds of weird things to Thamby's
Mini Moog, making it bleep and fart and drift out of tune.. but,
for all that, it was our first festival appearance, the people were
loving it and the marquee was fit to burst with the amount of
people who'd come to check it all out. We finished our set to
humungous applause and they wouldn't let us off the stage...
there was clapping and chanting and whooping and hollering
and we didn't want to stop.

As we'd worked our way through our set we'd noticed a
growing number of kids had started to gather at the front of
the 'stage' (as was often the case at festivals). These were the
convoy kids, scruffy little urchins, angels with dirty faces and I
could tell that they were desperate to have a little turn of their
own. Once we'd exhausted our 'repertoire', Sid came up onto
the stage and made an announcement that some rotten bastard
had stolen his son's acoustic guitar and would they be so kind
as to give it back, this was soon followed by chants of "Give it
back! Give it back!" I handed a microphone to a kid at the front
of the pack and he suddenly shouted "We don't need no
education!!" so I started playing that riff and the band
eventually picked up on it. By the second verse all the kids had
gathered around the mic and they (and most of the audience)
were singing along. The response we got from the crowd when
we finished THAT was phenomenal.. people were laughing,
screaming and crying with joy, it was a very special moment
indeed. I have it on cassette and if I ever play it, I get tingles up
my spine, especially when I think about that poor little
generator glowing bright, molten red in the night.

ATTACK OF THE WASPS

Of course, after such a high as that Stonehenge performance, the only way to go was back down. This was confirmed not long after when Thamby announced out of the blue that he didn't want to do it anymore. He was developing that fashionable early 'eighties cynicism to all things hippy (and he gave me all his paraphernalia to prove it!) and went in search of a solo career. He did eventually bring out a single under his own name called 'Acquaintances' backed by a cover of Robert Wyatt's 'O Caroline' on his own 'Freshly Cut' records.

So, there I was, still in Southall, a hippy outcast. There was still a great scene in Wayne's Bracknell, but I didn't have any transport and was still working in London. I'd been 'given' my first credit card by my bank that had two hundred pounds on it that needed spending so to cheer myself up I waltzed 'round to the nearest music shop and bought a 'WASP' synthesiser. They'd just come out and were the duck's guts for the price.. they featured two 'oscillators', lotsa knobs and had a printed keyboard like the EMS Synthi A. It came in a black, moulded plastic case with yellow controls (like a wasp) and could do a lot of the whoopy sounds that I needed.. and all for just two hundred pounds! The only problem was that I needed two extra arms grafted on if I was to play that AND my guitar at the same time, so I advertised for another synth player. Bear in mind that this was the 'eighties now and New Wave, New Romantics and Weird Hair bands ruled the (air)waves. So not many cosmic synth pixies about then.. until I got a reply from Adrian. Adrian was a veeerryy complex character, he turned up at my house on an old MZ 250cc motorcycle (with very little exhaust) and his own WASP in a rucksack on his back. He was a pretty nervy, hyper kinda guy, very excitable and emotional but once he'd hooked both synths together he made those little boxes burble and scream. He was a very quirky and inventive player and I liked his energy and enthusiasm (especially in the wake of Thamby's constant cynicism), he looked a lot like Rik Mayall but with long, golden locks. He was, I guessed straight away pretty camp as well and it was no shock to me when he confessed that he was gay. I was working in the movie business don't forget! It wasn't a problem for me at all, I didn't want to shag him, I just wanted to make beautiful music with him! The main problem for him though was that he confessed that he really felt like a woman trapped inside a man's body, this was something I had no experience in and I could see he was really tortured by this, but the plot eventually became even more bizarre when he eventually met a butch lesbian, fell in love with her and apparently after he left my band he had a sex change and changed his name to 'Adrienne'!?

Anyway, as a player I couldn't fault him and we enjoyed many a crazy, spaced-out jam. He was deemed too weird by Thamby and the others in the house who all spoke in VERY DEEP MANLY VOICES when he was around. We made a couple of really good jam tapes together and at one point had a little ambient thing of our own going on which we called 'Who Needs the Egg?' (named after a Deviants song).

DARK ANGEL

A room became available at our house and as usual it was advertised in 'Time Out' magazine. As mentioned before we'd seen our fair share of weirdos apply for a room but nothing prepared us for the dark, satanic lord that was Neil.

Neil was from Worthing in Sussex, he would wear nothing but the darkest black, wore a silver pentagon around his neck and talked incessantly. He couldn't look you in the eye when talking, instead he'd kinda look around you, or past you with his deep, icy blue eyes fixated on anything but yours. But for some reason (maybe because he said he really enjoyed housework!) we let him move in. It wasn't until he'd paid his deposit, unpacked his solitary rucksack and settled in for the 'getting to know you' chat that we fully realised what we'd done. When I say he talked, I mean MAN he talked! He probably spoke more words to me in the short time I knew him than me and Steve the Speed Machine ever did, even at the peak of our speed-snortin' days (and that's saying something!). He worshipped Alistair Crowley and Jim Morrison and never to our knowledge slept. He'd wake us all up in the night vacuuming the stairs or washing the dishes, but none of us would complain outright as we didn't want to do those things ourselves the next day. He wasn't working at the time so he'd be on his own all day tidying up and driving himself crazy with his own company and as soon as we'd walk through the door he'd be on us, rambling on about something or other.

The only time I ever saw Neil shut completely up was, ironically, when I got him some speed to see what would happen.. Once it kicked in he just sat upright in his chair and didn't mutter a single word, but his eyes were spinning like the fruit on a one-armed bandit! He's also the only guy I've ever seen spin out on nutmeg too! Sometimes when we had people 'round for a social, for no reason whatsoever he'd run frantically down the stairs from his room, dance through into the lounge stark, bollock naked wiggling his wiener at all and sundry, grab a beer from the fridge and dance back through and up the stairs again. He eventually got a job as a postman (and was probably the only one to turn up early!) and moved out of our house into a converted water tower.

TROUBLE INNA KINGSTON TOWN

I was lucky enough to still have Wayne and Mr Hitt available to me on bass and drums respectively as well as the (pre-sex change) Adrian on synthesisers so I decided to form a new band 'Ali Katt & His Baghdad Boogie Band' and we played (as you can imagine) Eastern/Egyptian flavoured Space Rock. We wrote songs with exotic titles like 'I Want my Mummy' (geddit?), 'Me and my Camel' and of course, we did a spunkier version of '(T)urban Paranoia'. After a couple of decent rehearsals we felt we were ready to perform live and set about organising a debut gig somewhere. It proved to be a lot harder than I thought.. our stuff was not exactly 'flavour of the day' I can tell ya! Eventually I managed to wear down the landlord of the Three Tuns pub in Kingston after convincing him that we were going to be the next Pink Floyd and could fill the place with ease…

I excitedly contacted all of the music papers, informing them of our up and coming showcase and invited them all along to the show. We fly posted most of Kingston and Wayne had organised a posse of friends from Bracknell to come down and give us a bit of well needed support. We had to provide our own p.a so we hired a large one (with engineer) and some coloured spotlights. After the luxury of a soundcheck, we all got comfy and waited for the crowd to start forming outside.. and we waited… and we waited. Wayne's posse had shrunk dramatically from the original estimation, it was midweek after all, but thank the gods they did turn up as they were the only ones there! No-one else came, not even a punter from the next bar to check us out on the way to the toilets.. nix… nada. We just decided "What the fuck? The show must go on.." and we actually played a really good set, although every time I glanced over at the landlord his eyes seemed to be getting slittier by the minute.. he was fuming. By the time we got to our last number of the night he looked like he was just about to burst a blood vessel. As soon as we finished he stormed over and laid into me about the lack of punters and the expense of it all and don't even think of him helping to pay towards the p.a and lights as the door money would hardly cover anything.. blah blah blah.. We did eventually manage to pacify the p.a man with a whip 'round of cash and a bit o' smokeable and after that we packed and loaded the equipment and got the fuck out of there as fast as we could with the landlord still going off in the car park shaking his (tight) fist at us as we drove off.. asshole.

Oh well, them's the breaks. Maybe Ali Katt & his Baghdad Boogie Band were before (or after) their time and after that disaster both Wayne and Alan decided to quit.. I didn't blame them. Hmmm.. so no band again then!

POLICE & THIEVES (IN THE STREET)

The 'eighties were well and truly upon us now and Punk/New Wave had brought politics back into music for the first time since the radical 'sixties. Bands like the Clash and Crass were spouting radical ideas and being very vocal about challenging 'the kids' to question authority and the unfairness of 'it all'. This was to bring benefit gigs back into vogue, where 'name' bands would perform for a minimum fee or indeed for free (something which almost broke The Magic Mushroom Band on more than one occasion) in the name of their preferred 'just cause'. Thus we were all invited to Rock against Racism/Famine/Nuclear Power/Animal Cruelty/Homophobia etc. Basically anything that challenged the 'norm' (which drastically need challenging!).

Unfortunately for every action there is a reaction and this was very much the case with the race issue. Bands like Sham 69 and Skrewdriver (no matter how unwittingly) through displaying a skinhead image managed to attract hordes of National Front and British Movement aficionados who would 'Sieg Heil' their way through most of the performances. This in turn incurred the wrath of the militant factions of the SWP (Socialist Workers' Party) and other anti-racist collectives. If truth be told, as much as they'd condemn the racists for their violent anti-social behaviour many of them weren't that much better themselves. It was just a case of which badge you wore on your lapel. Sure, Steve the Speed Machine and I wore Nazi regalia during our rocking days s'true, but that was always just for the outrage of it all as it was for the original 1%er outlaw bikers of the 'sixties. We also wore t-shirts with 'fuck' written on them and I don't remember Hitler sporting one of those. I would have made a terrible racist anyway, I idolised Jimi Hendrix and was extremely partial to the odd curry or ten…

The inevitable eventually happened and Southall with its large Indian/Pakistani West Indian population was chosen as the venue for the predicted war of ideologies. It had all started with a rumour (no mobile phones then!).. on the streets, in the shops, down the pub..

The (before their time) Ali Katt & His Baghdad Boogie
Band Mark 1

(Above) Myself, Adrian, Nigel and Ormond

"Busloads of skinheads are coming up from the East End to smash the place up" and before you knew it, shop owners were boarding up their windows and barricading the doors.. it was quite surreal... On the first (and worst) night of the riots, I had decided to take a stroll down the High Street, but I didn't get that far. As I turned the corner at the bottom of my street I was greeted by the sight of hundreds of angry militant protesters and the SWP were rallying people together with megaphones as they drove around in jeeps pointing out to the angry hordes which shops to loot first (it wasn't ALL about race methinks..). I must admit I didn't see many, if any, skinheads that night. I know that there were some that had turned up, but not quite the invading army that was anticipated. They must have taken one look at the sight of a huge mob of angry Asians and West Indians (and middle-class white people who were more than willing to be angry on their behalf) and hot-footed it out of town quick smart.

The police were (of course) unprepared for such an event and apart from letting everyone know that they had sirens and flashing lights and weren't afraid to use them, they were about as effective as the proverbial chocolate teapot. I chose to stay at home and wait for it all to blow over, I didn't fancy getting a brick in the face from either side and what with me looking like Catweazle on acid (therefore obviously a deviant!) the police in their infinite knowledge were sure to round me up as a ringleader. Most of the 'action' was in the High Street (where all the good electrical retailers were), but it wasn't until we switched on our TV for the evening news that we realised just how close the fighting and associated chaos had got to our home. We saw numerous shops and buildings blazing out of control and people kicking in shop windows and running off with televisions and other assorted luxury items and then the cameras panned 'round to show a newsagents burning down.. our local newsagents! We all rushed to the door and looked up the street to see poor Mr Patel's newsagents ablaze and there were people running past our house being chased by cops with the big riot sticks. We hastily closed our door, locked it and sat back in the lounge with some music on.

Southall was never the same after that, the innocence had gone and its charm with it. The people were really angry and you could taste it in the air. I noticed a lot more Asian drunks appearing on the benches around town and it got to feel really dodgy walking around there at night, something I'd never felt there before. I'd often walk home at all hours of the night on my way back from a gig that the other guys in the house didn't want to go to (make that most of them then!). More and more things were getting stolen from and off of cars in our street, muggings increased and there were more reports of rape (quite how all that related to urban frustration I never worked out..) it was getting, like I said.. dodgy and the harsh reality of living there came crashing down on me on one particular night..

I still had the converted front room as my bedroom and after a particularly good day, I eventually said my goodnights to the others and retired to my chambers. Due to the large Jamaican Woodbine (See? How could I be racist?) that I'd finished moments before, I was deeply asleep in no time at all. Having discovered the joys of having a double bed all to myself, I adopted the traditional 'starfish' position and went to the land of nod where I dreamed of beautiful hippy chicks tapping on my window wanting to come in and share my bed with me. The tapping and scraping sound they made on my window seemed so real, maybe I wasn't dreaming? For whatever reason (a deluded desperate mind?) I hazily, lazily crawled out of bed, had a bit of a stretch and ripped open the curtains. Unfortunately, I wasn't greeted by the sight of hippy chicks lusting after my body, I instead found myself staring at a large, black dude, all dressed in black too, with a knife in his teeth trying to break in through my window.. who was now staring right back at me.. I knew he was staring because all I could see in the inky blackness were these huge, white orbs that displayed a look of terror, surprise and shock. I instinctively started shaking my fists and ranting and raving and made a dash for the front door. I angrily swung it open and lurched into the front yard and as I reached the front gate I saw him jumping over a fence at the bottom of my road. It was only after he'd gone that I realised what at least one of the expressions on his face was for.. I was naked. I cupped my manhood and hastily beat a path back to the safety of my room where I collected lots of wire and string and tied all the windows closed permanently.

LAKE FLACCID

As for my rather unsuccessful sex life in Southall, salvation eventually came (literally) in the shape of a sultry siren, hippy chick who for the purposes of this tale I shall call Lulu. She lived in Bracknell and was very tall, bright, beautiful and extremely bohemian. I'd already met her a few times as she was a memorable character among the Bracknell posse. We always got on very well and would chat and flirt, something which although fun at the time, became an extreme source of frustration for me because she was in a relationship with someone else at the time.. and I knew that 'someone else'. Apparently it was 'cool' as they had an 'open' relationship.. I never knew one of those to ever work out before, but what the hey? I was hot to trot (almost overheating by that time) and the signals were most definitely there, so we arranged for her to come down and visit me in Southall. After the 'girl on the train' debacle, I was really hoping I'd got the signals right this time...

The night before the visit, I cleaned my room thoroughly and put all my records into alphabetical order. At last! If all goes well, I'd soon be back where I belonged.. between the thighs of a fine woman and she sure was a sight for these sore eyes. After a Southall diet of Indian women with moustaches, leftist-marxist-lesbian activists and mad Irish women I thought all my birthdays had come at once. Just as planned, Lulu was waiting outside the train station when I pulled up in my recently acquired (for free) primer-grey Mini (car not skirt). I'd suggested we go down the Portobello Road and hang out there for a bit, she hadn't been there that much and I was more than happy to be her guide…. So off we headed. We had a good time there, we were pretty relaxed in each other's company but there was definitely an underlying sexual tension there too. So, feeling cocky (in more ways than one) I suggested "Hey Lulu! I'm from London and I know these city streets like the back of my hand.. I've walked most of them with Steve! Let's go to Camden Lock Market now!". So we jumped into Hell's Mini and off we drove towards Camden.

A couple of smokes in the car later and I'm beginning to wonder where the hell we actually were. Sure, some of the streets and landmarks looked familiar, or so I thought, but I would have been too out of it to pay any attention back then anyway. Sometimes I could see the streets that I actually needed to be on but they all seemed to be at the wrong end of one-way streets. At one point I even ended up going around and around Trafalgar Square on a boiling hot Saturday afternoon in thick, choking traffic with no air conditioning and a rapidly overheating mini engine coming to the boil, trying to cover my tracks by explaining to Lulu that I wanted to surprise her with a really good view of Nelson's Column.. by this time my own column was rapidly diminishing in the heat. Eventually by some lucky twist of fate (or the fact that I'd attempted every other route) I found my way onto the M4 and home to Southall.

The guys back at the house had got wind of her visit and had been winding me up the night before with "Whoo-Hoo"'s and "Wha-Hey"'s. I just smiled back at them, secretly hoping that they'd be right. Thoughtfully, they'd made themselves absent from the house by the time we (eventually) got back (or pretended to be). We were both hot and flustered for lots of reasons, but also relieved to be back and we saw the humour in what had just happened, this was a great relief to me, I should never, ever, try to be cool, that's just about the uncoolest thing to do! We were still laughing as we fell into my room and collapsed on the bed. Lulu rolled a spliff as I chose a suitable record to put on, fluffed up some cushions and lay beside her. My lower brain was feeling better by then and most of my blood was eagerly coursing its way down there. We had a little fruity play fight and after a while she made her excuses and went upstairs to the bathroom with her bag over her arm. I was feeling great, after such a long drought of intimate contact with a female, there was this freaky, gorgeous, hot chick in my bathroom and she was here for me!

In no time at all, my door swung open and in she sashayed. This time wearing just a short halter-neck top, no bra obviously as her ample breasts were swinging freely and her nipples were raised beneath the flimsy material like Braille. She was also sporting a very short denim mini (skirt not car). We fell back together on the bed again and we tickled and giggled for a while, somehow (!) I found myself tickling her upper thigh and she suddenly laid back and lifted her skirt to show me that she wasn't wearing any panties. I had to put my hand there just to check that it wasn't an illusion, it all seemed too good to be true!

Yeah baby, rock n'roll! Freaky music, stoned and sexy on the bed, I felt like Keith Richards with the sexiest groupie in town. I fondled and groped and rubbed and sucked like a thirsty man getting his first drink of water after being lost in the desert. She seemed to be enjoying it although I couldn't help but get the feeling that it was really all for me... oh well.. fuckit.. no.. this feeling was beginning to nag and gnaw at me.. no!... of all times.. not now.. pleeeeze! Here I was, in a perfect situation, able to do what any red-blooded male would give his right nut for.. this, my gift from the Church of Fate, a reward for patience in my times of drought. Of course, by now, I had this little voice in my head saying " You're not good enough, she thinks you're crap. You're not pleasing her at all and she's just doing it for your sake.. annnd.. what about the 'other guy'? Will she tell him you couldn't get it up?" and it's getting louder and louder as she starts to unbutton my flies. By the time 'the beast' is finally released, its heard those voices too and its flagging fast like a wilting rose.. nooo!!! Fair play to Lulu she tried everything in the book (and some from the movie) but to no avail. I was truly flaccid, but not placid, it was like trying to stick a sponge into a letterbox. I guess the shock of actually being able to do it, having it all laid out on a plate for me after such a long time was just too much and with a loud, pitiful, anguished moan I had to admit defeat, apologise profusely to Lulu, change the record and make a cup of tea.

You know those religious fanatics, the ones who flog themselves with branches as penance for their sins? I did a very good impersonation of one of them after Lulu had gone home. Fortunately that nightmare scenario hasn't reared its ugly head (so to speak) too much since.. maybe all that speed caught up with me? After that occasion we managed to make up for it a few times, but it was never a relationship, the other guy was still in the picture and I felt really bad about that (after). It had no future and so we had fun while we could. Fate had a more positive outlook in store for me, when I met my true love at one of Lulu's infamous parties. Of course, jealousy wasn't a card that could be played!

MAKING PLANS FOR NIGEL

Things seemed to be going from bad to worse at the house and I felt I had to move on. The chance came when I met a drummer called Nigel, also from Southall, who had a spare room going in his council house and was also looking to join a band. Oh merciful fate how I adore thee! We had a jam (in his lounge!) and got on very well.. he was a wild and crazy drummer, excellent to jam with and he had a similar style to original Hawkwind drummer Terry Ollis who he knew. When the lease came up for renewal at the other house I made my excuses and left. Nigel was sharing the house with an old school friend called Terry and let's say that hygiene was not at the top of anybody's list (including mine!). The place seemed like it hadn't been vacuumed or dusted for years and there were old, green-with-age terrapin tanks festering behind the sofa and the garden was full of dog shit courtesy of Sam, a huge German Shepherd that lived in the garden by day and shat in the kitchen by night. The electricity was on a coin-operated meter, only seeming to take ones that we didn't have at the time and it was always freezing cold there, so baths were few and far between. But it was a home nonetheless and I was very grateful to Nigel for freeing up a room for me.

There was a bit of a 'peeping tom' situation there a bit later though.. Not long after I'd moved in it transpired that the house actually belonged to Nigel's Mum and her elderly boyfriend Bert and they'd decided to move back into the house and reclaim the master bedroom. Like a lot of my own older relatives, Nigel's Mum looked the archetypal hard-nosed Londoner with the tight, purple-rinsed curly perm and drawn-on eyebrows, she looked scary but had a good heart. The boyfriend Bert seemed very old and very frail, to the point where you wondered that if you shouted too loud he would suddenly clutch his poor little heartsie and kark it right there and then. He resembled a cross between Mr Magoo and the old fellah from the Benny Hill show, the one always getting his head slapped. Not only did their arrival curtail most pot smoking activities, it was very difficult not to keep bumping into each other all around the house but I also discovered that ol' Bert was getting a good old eyeful of my sexual activities. I hadn't noticed anything straight away being too busy catching the 'love train' as much as I could after the aforementioned drought period.

So, there I was in bed in the throes of passion when suddenly an eye appears through the keyhole of my bedroom door. I thought I was seeing things at first, but no, there it was again, blinking and staring.. the eye of an old codger who obviously hadn't seen firm, young flesh in a long time. It kinda put a dampener on things, but I put it down to experience and didn't make a fuss about it to anyone. The next time I attempted a lust-fest, there it was again, the pupil widening with every exploratory sexual position that I attempted. I got out of bed and very noisily went over to the door, by which time the eye was long gone, having scuttled off with the rest of Bert back to the master bedroom. The only thing I had to hand at the time that could block his view was a packet of rolling papers, so I pulled one out and stuck it over the keyhole and resumed the grunty stuff. Occasionally I'd glance over at the door, but all seemed well, the eye was gone... or was it? I suddenly began to notice that every now and then the paper would puff upwards, revealing the open keyhole and a recently-returned eye! The cheeky bugger was blowing through the keyhole and grabbing a quick eyeful before the paper settled back down again.. at that point I leapt out of bed and shouted "Fuck off Bert!!".. the eye never appeared again.

The other housemate Terry really should have been in MASH, what a crazy dude. He always wore army surplus clothing and collected old army field equipment, radios and the like. I remember him making his own fireworks one year, his 'jumping-jacks were made from crow scarers and his rockets nearly took out a plane.. he was a nutter.. but also a real clever electronics whiz.. even that far back he designed his own Star Trek game on his Sinclair ZX-81.

Once again I was without a bassist, but luckily Nigel had a cousin called Ormond who was a kinda dread-less rasta (so wasn't averse to a little sensi) and played guitar with local reggae band 'Misty in Roots'. They were having some time off so he agreed to play some bass with us in his downtime. The jams with him were very bizarre, all he'd ever played was reggae so his bass playing style leant towards that, regardless of what we were playing at the time. We did have some good, fun, righteously stoned sessions but they never came of anything. We decided to change the name of the band to 'Psychic Attack' and heavy up the sound a bit. Ormond promptly disappeared in a puff of logic (well.. ganga) but luckily for us Steve the Speed Machine was around at the time, living just down the road in Ealing and he was up for jumping in on bass. It was good of him to stand in for us, but no matter how we tried we couldn't secure any gigs, we even hired a van and went to that year's Stonehenge Festival but we couldn't blag a generator this time (maybe they recognised me!).

This Space Warrior was fast becoming a Space Worrier and when Steve finally acknowledged that our musical tastes were just too incompatible by then and left (along with Adrian), I almost contemplated blowing it all out.. almost. Nigel and I tried to keep it all together, even finding Clive a new bassist and recording some great sessions, but by then the writing was well and truly on the wall.

I couldn't change how I was, what I did or what I liked, it was all or nothing.. so would it have to be nothing?

LOVE, KINSHIP & MUSHROOMS

My old Dad has always said to me in times of despair "Don't worry son, when you hit rock bottom the only way is back up again.. you can't go any further down" and he was right.. just when I thought of jacking it all in, two very important life-changing events occurred almost simultaneously.

I got a call from bassist Wayne in Bracknell inviting me up there for a jam with some of the local musicians who were into the same sort of stuff, a very rare thing at the time (apart from in Bracknell! Hence why I eventually moved there for nigh on twenty years). There was Jimbo on drums and percussion (previously in 'Zounds') and although slight and wiry in appearance an amazing powerhouse of a drummer (and a huge Zappa fan to boot), Wayne on bass and twin brother Craig on guitar, plus assorted joint-rollers.. sorry roadies etc. We had a really good jam at a pub in Crowthorne (near Broadmoor). We all hit it off so well we decided that although most of us were already in bands, we'd drop everything else and make a go of it, it felt that good. As for a name for the new venture? Why not resurrect The Magic Mushroom Band? We reworked some of my old tunes and a wealth of Acid Rock cover versions to throw in for good measure.

Another rehearsal was swiftly booked at Windsor Arts Centre and at the end of the session a chap called Graham who organised things there offered us a gig in the December (1982). We worked out a full set of tunes and word started to get around.. the next thing we knew we had a full psychedelic light-show courtesy of Jon and Porij (Dancing Shiva – ex Acidica lights) which was to become a very important feature of our shows throughout the years. At the same time I'd met a young Australian chick fresh on the scene called Kim who was in the UK on a working visa and was looking to do some singing with a band. She'd already recorded a 'demo' with a local synthesiser player and wanted to do more. She came along for a session with us and I loved her energy, her voice and her. From the moment we met that was it, no more searching, I'd found THE ONE. We've been inseparable from that moment on, we came from such different worlds but nearly thirty years down the track I'm still chasing her around the house.

So, from the ashes of despair I rose phoenix-like with a new love and a new band and both would prove to be very successful undertakings! The dawn of a new era for me....

Mushrooms & Moonboots

An Autobiography

by

Garry "Moonboot" Masters

Foreword...

Garry 'Moonboot' Masters and his Magic Mushroom Band were to become major players in the Acid Rock/Psychedelic Festival resurgence of the 'eighties and early 'nineties, bringing some much needed colour to an otherwise grey and dull era...The band also became the launch pad for the 'Ethno-Ambient Space Beat' pioneers Astralasia and the all-acoustic, then electric Moonboot Oz. They released numerous albums and singles and gigged extensively over the fifteen years that were to follow....

Episode 2:

Mushrooms & Moonboots
(1982 – 2002)

December 1982.... the music scene was getting pretty dull, already 'post punk' the trendmeisters were tripping over themselves trying to create a new music 'scene', something unique without realising that by then, pretty much everything had been done before and in fact if you look at the first half of the 'eighties music scene in general, you'll soon come to realise that most of it was generally some kind of re-hash of styles that had gone before.. be it blue-eyed soul.. or sci-fi androgynists a la Bowie or smack flavoured Velvet Underground riffers or rockabilly rebels, skinheads.. basically anything went... as long as it wasn't anything to do with hippy music. This was a punk attitude that had stuck (particularly with the UK music press - most of whom were old hippies), but as I have described earlier in the book, the punk reaction was against the frilly shirted, fluffy, spandex, girlie-haired soft rock stadium bands, not the likes of the 'earthier' Hawkwind, Pink Fairies, early Gong etc. but anyway, that was how it was and to profess even a knowledge of said bands would render you so uncool as to not be allowed to play with the other children.....

WINDSOR BLOWING

As you can probably imagine, during the height of the 'New Romantic' era, the sudden appearance of flyers and posters advertising the debut gig of a group called the Magic Mushroom Band at an Arts Centre in Windsor (right across the road from the castle!) complete with full psychedelic lightshow and all its bells and whistles came as somewhat of a shock/surprise/welcome sight/curiosity to many that Xmas (Kim's birthday in fact..). Of course, we've never professed to being ground-breakingly original, all we were doing was playing the type of music that we wanted to hear ourselves, but at the time, those type of bands just weren't around or were scared to be too freaky for fear of ridicule. But as the size of the crowd waiting outside the venue on that night proved, other people were starved of that kind of scene too... and we were just young and stoned and carefree enough not to give a stuff what other people thought (quite a 'punk' attitude, eh?).

Now, sure we'd all gigged before with our other bands but somehow, this began to feel like a much bigger deal and we were all pretty excited in the days leading up to the show, personally I've never suffered from stage fright, but I remember some of the guys (and gals) getting a little jittery. But of course, nothing a little Dutch (Amsterdam to be precise) courage couldn't sort out.. The music press rather predictably chose to ignore the huge newsletter that I'd knocked up to inform them of the event and instead chose to relegate it to a microscopic line in their 'gig guides', no worries, because apart from the flyers and posters (hastily stuck up at prime locations around the area under cover of darkness) which caught the punters' imaginations, word of mouth seemed to be the main instigator for the large turnout.

We had no set plan stage-image wise (although my dear mum suggested that maybe we should all wear nice, matching shirts with mushrooms on them) to be honest the sight of that amount of hair, beards, beads and kaftans meant that just wearing our everyday stuff was enough to make us stand out in

The Magic Mushroom Band Mark 2, first gig December
1982 at Windsor Arts Centre

a crowd (as we did then anyway) and putting a swirly, twirly acid-laced lightshow into the equation took us from a cold Xmas evening in Berkshire to a 'summer of love' Haight-Ashbury style anyway..

Incredibly, someone managed to be together enough to record that first gig and on listening back to it now, you can tell that we were so fired up with energy, from each other and from the audience that it turned out to be one of the fastest gigs we'd ever done! During rehearsals we'd timed each song and added a couple more into the equation just in case we fell short of a full set but after doing an hour's worth of material in forty minutes, we decided to stretch out a few of the numbers and throw in a couple of jams too! The songs that I'd written for the first incarnation of the Magic Mushroom Band took on a new lease of life and energy and never sounded so good. Jim bashed the skins like there was no tomorrow, Wayne chugged along on the bass, while Craig and I traded riffs and competed with the volumes of our battling guitars, Kim sang her heart out and gyrated pleasingly on stage joined and complimented on that night by Craig's then girlfriend Laura.

Not having enough original material for a full set, we all had a say in what cover versions we wanted to do, for example 'The Snake' by the Pink Fairies, 'Up in Smoke' by Cheech & Chong (complete with hastily scrawled lyric board for the audience to sing along!) and a full on psycho rendition of 'Duelling Banjos' with me and Craig's guitars thrashing it out at breakneck shitkicking speeds.. Luckily the crowd lapped it up and we were tripping on the feedback and how well it all went.

I don't think any of us slept for about a week after that! The lightshow looked fantastic in the photos that we saw, you know the trouble with being the performer is that you never get to see the lightshows, we're always facing the wrong way! (Double annoying when you later discover that someone had decided to project a porno movie above (and on) your heads as indeed happened at one gig, eh Porij??). Anyway, after just that one show, the offers of other gigs started rolling in as word got around that there was this good time band playing the sort of stuff that we did.. bringing the sounds of Stonehenge to the suburbs... Not long after that I quit my job in London, Kim and I moved up to Bracknell and together with the rest of the band we formulated our plans for world domination..

MUSHROOMS ON THE ROAD

The first part of 1983 had us playing at various venues in an ever increasing radius, some were just support slots with bigger bands which was ok because nine times out of ten we'd be invited back to the same venues to headline in our own right. It suited us to headline, not for ego reasons, but because there were often up to eight of us on stage plus the lightshow and the main bands didn't seem to take too kindly to the kind of reaction we got from the crowd and indeed the space we took up on stage... often our problem was that there were a lot of people who wanted to be in the band but we just plain couldn't fit them in!

Throughout the Magic Mushroom Band's career there were generally three types of gigs for us (something most bands of our 'ilk' can relate to I'm sure!)

1) The well-advertised 'paid' gigs, with ample drinks and food for the band and entourage:
Most rare, often the venues were squats put together by 'anarchist' collectives (a la Crass etc.) and there'd be a huge list of bands performing and often we'd be onstage if we were lucky at around 3:00am. The well paid and fed gigs were real luxury and we felt like kings (and queens), real 'rock star' stuff of legend... funnily enough, the college and university gigs were always good for that...

2) The 'Benefit' gig:
We were always keen to do these, obviously it had to be a cause that we were sympathetic with, but they gave us good

exposure and showed that our hearts were in the right place. Often the reality was though that these kind of gigs nearly led to our demise on a lot of occasions. We had a lot of mouths to feed and petrol money to lay out and most of us had packed in our jobs to concentrate on the music, so often we'd find ourselves out of pocket but the cause was almost always worth it.. Problem was there was rarely any money left in the mushroom kitty, in fact we released our first ever 'live' cassette not just as a way to quickly get some of our music out there (the record companies weren't very forthcoming in those days for some reason, could they not imagine us on 'Top of the Pops'???) but also as a way to generate funds as the expenses very rarely got covered by our fee alone... in fact if it wasn't for the cassettes, posters and badges that we sold at gigs I doubt if we would have been able to keep it together at all...

3) The 'Free' Festivals:
No complaints there, we loved to do those (pre 'Battle of the Beanfield' anyway, more about that later..). We were often given free reign to do what we liked (generators permitting) and could 'space out' and jam a lot more. Obviously there was no kind of payment but we kinda treated them like little holidays anyway, we didn't have to shoot home straight after our performance plus it gave us a good chance to check out other bands for a change... and of course plenty of 'networking'.. we met so many people at the festivals and many remain friends to this day.. the phrase 'tribe' is an often overused one but I really can't think of a better way to describe it...

DUDE, WHERE'S MY CAR? AND MY GUITAR??

At the time Kim and I were living way up high in a tower block in Bracknell's town centre, you know the sort, pissy smelling lifts and endless echoing corridors leading to your flat. We'd just got back from our first (of many) gig at Bracknell's own Arts Centre called South Hill Park which is an old, converted mansion house set in its own grounds on the outskirts of town (more about that place later too...). The show had been great, as usual it was late and although it was the middle of winter we were all sticky and sweaty from the show and just wanted to get indoors as fast as possible. I took one look at all the equipment I had in the boot of the car, my guitar, my amplifier and a large box of assorted pedals and leads that I'd have to drag over to the lifts in a succession of journeys and said 'Ah, stuff it... it'll be alright 'til the morning!'

I know... famous last words... Sure enough after a good and well-earned night's sleep we went down to the car and lo, it was nowhere to be seen!!! It should be noted at this point that the car park for the flats backed onto the local police station yard and although often a potentially precarious situation given my chosen state of mind at the time and my chosen vocation (even they'd heard of the band!), I did feel that at least it would provide us with some kind of security as far as car theft went..... WRONG!! "Shit, bollocks, fuck and piss!" and other assorted expletives poured from my mouth as I kicked myself around the car park, how could I have been so stupid?? It was bad enough that we'd had our only mode of transport stolen but, shit man, all my gear too!! And there were gigs coming up. Of course upon contacting said local constabulary we were told in no uncertain terms not to expect to ever see our car or my equipment ever again and how stupid was I to leave it all in there in the first place?? That helped...

Anyway, as luck would have it our next gig was a fortnight later at the Bridge House not far up the road from where we lived. At the time it was a pretty cool pub, oldy-worldy style with a decent jukebox and an ample sized stage. It was an 'open' party that we'd been invited to play at courtesy of the Bracknell Chopper Club, we thought they were righteous dudes (with equally righteous motorbikes). Porij, one of our illustrious illuminators had been with the club and was at the time in the process of building a rather tasty Triumph chopper. Bikers were an ever present part of our scene, digging it just like everyone else, always welcome, never any trouble, grievances and attitudes were always left at the door. We were all looking forward to the show, the local ones were always fun (and not so much travelling after the show.. yay!!). Luckily I had a spare electric guitar, but everything else was borrowed, amp, pedals, leads etc. We finished our soundcheck early so that we could check out the cool, custom bikes that had begun to pull up outside the pub. The show seemed to be going down pretty well and all was good.. we'd been allowed an extra long set so we took a break halfway through and I thought it might be a good idea to make an announcement regarding my missing car as the police had been no help at all in locating it. I explained to the audience that it'd been stolen two weeks prior and that if anyone saw a dark green 1966 mark 2 Cortina (who in their right mind would have stolen it anyway? It ran like a real pig...) could they please get in contact with us... Now, I don't think for one minute that anybody present at that gig was guilty of the car's theft , but would you believe it, we got a call from the police the very next morning saying that they'd had an anonymous call from someone telling them where the car was parked! We shot around to a shaded back street and there it was, no damage to the car at all and as I opened the boot with trepidation, having almost resigned myself to the fact that all my gear would be long gone, would you believe, there it all was still... just as I'd hurriedly packed it the night it got stolen.... obviously it had just been taken to get someone home and it was an old banger, I don't think they could've bothered looking in the boot, do you? it just goes to show that it really does pay to advertise, eh?

FARNHAM CLOSE - TOO CLOSE

Before Kim and I moved into our flat (courtesy of Wayne) we'd spent a couple of weeks staying at the infamous 'Farnham Close' house which was a rental property in a cul-de-sac close to the centre of town. It had started out as a simple rented town house to a couple of guys, but it slowly became more populated as it evolved into a drop-in centre and out and out

24 hour party central place for the 'alternative sect' to hang out at. By then most of Bracknell was a 'new town' (read small gardens, crammed houses and paper-thin walls) and the mostly middle-class occupants of the cul-de-sac (French for 'nowhere to run') must have thought that the neighbours from hell had moved in. Most of the band (and assorted girlfriends) lived there as well and we would often jam and rehearse there. There were normally at least a couple of stereos blasting out at most times of the day and night (if you stood outside the house it was rather like being stuck between radio stations). There'd be motorbikes revving, Porij was building his chopper in the garage underneath the house and Wayne and Craig both had bikes too, and then there'd be various experimental light show projections beaming from the windows out into the darkness. I remember on one occasion, Porij had set up a projector with just its white light and was shining it onto the neighbours bedroom window opposite and Sarah, Wayne's girlfriend at the time, chose to simulate oral sex with a dick-shaped candle suggestively in front of it causing a most stimulating silhouette to appear on the opposite neighbour's curtains...

Apart from the aforementioned band members, there were many other interesting characters living there or who never seemed to want to go home.. there was Dave the Rave, a huge man who looked a little like Ken Dodd on acid with a very surreal sense of humour (as you would have), there was Nik Rampant who was kinda like a bohemian Ben Elton who possessed a very unique chortle and Phil the Gnome/Dwarf, a diminutive 'Tolkein-esque' dude who rode a Norton Commando and dug classical music and Wishbone Ash (but we still spoke to him), he later got into body piercing, so much that no-one saw him for ages... we feared that maybe he was so weighed down by his jewellery that he couldn't get up off the floor and maybe was wasting away on his carpet.. There was also the inimitable charm of Royston(ed), just back from living on a commune in Israel, at the time he looked like Robert Powell (circa 'Jesus of Nazareth'), he loved all the Gong/Space Rock stuff and after being persuaded to invest in a Gnat (like a smaller version of the 'Wasp' synthesiser that I had) and a

1983 The face of Stonehenge!

Casio keyboard, he was invited to join the band as our first keyboard player.. something he'd never been before, but we showed him how to get the twirly whirly sounds so loved by bands of our ilk (it's an acid/mushroom thing methinks...) and how to string a few notes together and he was in...

WE NEED A VAN, MAAAAN..

After a succession of petrified white-knuckle journeys convoy-style to various gigs in our clapped-out old cars, never knowing whether we'd actually make it home again, we had no choice but to get our own van. As usual there were little funds in the mushroom kitty but Craig and Laura had heard of an old Ford Luton box-van that was going for a song (one hundred and fifty pounds if I remember rightly-where were those warning bells???) the catch being that it was in an old barn in Hereford and would have to be collected...

I kind of volunteered (read 'was coerced') to drive it back and so we headed off to Hereford in Laura's mum's car. If I thought it took a long time to get to Hereford in a semi decent car, it was nothing compared to the journey back in the van. We eventually arrived at our destination and when they said it had been stored in a barn, they weren't lying.. it was 'primer' grey and still covered in bits of straw and pigeon shit, but it was a van and just what we needed...

After a few fruitless attempts at starting it, the van eventually coughed and spluttered into life and after bidding our farewells I headed off down the road following the others in their car. Now, the luton vans aren't known for their speed at the best of times, but this baby wasn't ever going over 60 miles per hour, not no way, not no how and what with the missing (ahem) tax disc and general tattiness we opted to take the back roads all the way home. 'Painfully slow' doesn't describe it, but I was trundling along headed home, enjoying a slight bit of speed on every downhill section of road. As you can imagine, some of the back roads out there are a little windy and precarious and it was precisely along one of those roads that I was 'belting' along, the wind behind me for once, when a rather stupid pheasant decided that now would be a good time to cross said road without looking.. before I knew it... PPPAAFFF!!!!!! I hit it like a cannonball and saw it's startled expression as it splatted against the windscreen, as most of its feathers flew through my open window and turned the cab of the van into a temporary snow globe. I tell ya it freaked me right out and as it was a skinny country road there was nowhere for me to pull over, so I had to keep on driving.

The rest of the guys in front were oblivious to what had happened and were merrily speeding along unaware that I was now trying to find a place to pull over, drenched in sweat, guilt and with a lot of feathers in my hair and beard. I felt so bad, poor thing didn't stand a chance, what kind of vegetarian was I? Just as these thoughts ate away at my conscience, I suddenly saw this claw appear at the top of my windscreen.. "Eeekkk!!!"... don't tell me that bits of the mutilated bird were going to start sliding down the windscreen in bloody portions.. just what I needed! As luck would have it, I eventually found a place to pull over, fully expecting to have to pluck any body parts out from various parts of the front of the van, but incredibly as I slowed down to a halt and went to climb out of the van, suddenly this dazed, almost naked, but alive, pheasant flew out from the van and off into the distance in search of some kind of temporary clothing. It turned out that when I hit it, it must have been sucked up the windscreen and under the little 'overhang' part at the front that the box vans have...

However, thanks to the wonders of gaffa tape, improvisational mechanics and bungee cords, that ol' van saw us trundling along to gigs for longer than it would have seemed possible (often full to the roof with equipment and people), it even made it to two Stonehenge festivals! It eventually shuffled off its mortal coil though, but still served us as an excellent storage container for our equipment at a car park by some flats where some of the band members lived. The landlord was ok with it being there because of the large 'OM' that had been painted on the roller shutter at the back. He remembered seeing a very similar van during the war in India and it seemed to be a comforting memory to him for some reason... result!!

NO SMOKE WITHOUT FIRE.... NOT THIS TIME

Due to the success of our first gig at Windsor Arts Centre, we were invited back for a repeat performance a couple of months later. Once again the turnout was impressive with a huge line of people queueing outside eagerly clutching tickets and waving to the Queen as they patiently waited for us to finish our soundchecks. We enjoyed playing there for many reasons, it had a dressing room (luxury!) a decent p.a (ditto) and a good sized stage with a huge white screen that pulled across as a backdrop, hence ideal for lightshow projections. On this particular night, Porij joined us in the dressing room after the soundcheck and said to us that there would be a surprise for us that night on stage, but he wasn't going to tell us what or when, just to expect something... we thought no more of it and put it down to the rantings of an excited lightshow operator.

We had suffered various delays with the p.a arriving late and the other support bands doing their thing and were running a bit late when we eventually headed up on stage, but the crowd was great, all fired up and ready for a party.. and what a party it turned out to be! We only got as far as our third song when about halfway through there was a loud KABOOOOM!!!!! and I noticed that most of the audience seemed to be looking past me and as I turned around to see what was happening I saw a large plume of smoke appear from between Jim the drummer's legs. As he continued playing, the plume grew and grew, swiftly became a cloud and then a dense fog which soon filled the entire venue! We eventually stopped playing when Graeme the promoter clambered up on stage, grabbed the mike and said "Okay, everyone has to, like, evacuate the building. The fire brigade are on their way and the show can only, like, resume once we're given the all clear". When he finished talking I noticed for the first time that all the fire alarm bells were ringing and so we were all ushered out into the car park and we watched as a fleet of fire engines pulled up and out trotted an army of fire fighters complete with axes, hoses and various other fire-fighting tools. After about thirty minutes of running around shouting things like "Where's the fire?" they eventually left, seemingly rather disappointed at not having anything to fight... fire-wise. The ironic thing though was that the venue was in fact Windsor's old fire station!!

Of course, the culprit was seen skulking around in the shadows of the car park until they'd left. Yep, Porij decided that tonight he would surprise us all by secreting a pyrotechnic smoke bomb under Jim's drum stool. Trouble was, he hadn't read the instructions on the box at all well... you see, they were for outdoor use only... by the time we got back on stage and fired up, we had time for two more songs which made it probably one of the shortest sets we ever did! Even funnier was seeing many members of the audience stumbling about holding their heads back and pinching their noses, it seems that the smoke bomb had red oxide in it and when it went off a lot of people were inhaling the smoke and when they touched their hand to their noses they thought they had nosebleeds! Hey, no-one said that being a Magic Mushroom Band fan was going to be easy... I bet Spandau Ballet never had that problem, eh????

STONED 'HENGES AND MUSHROOM RINGS

And so it came to pass that the Magic Mushroom Band didst make its way to the 1983 Stonehenge free festival for the first time. We were all so excited, we couldn't wait to get there and hurriedly packed in all the equipment, band members and associates into the van. We had so much stuff in there it was literally bulging at the sides. If there wasn't a speaker or amp or drum box there was a person squeezed into the available gap.. and we stopped to pick up hitchhikers along the way too..

needless to say, it was a very long, slow trip there.

It was always a breathtaking sight when as you left the A303 to turn right onto the Stonehenge road, you were greeted by the endless rows of colourful tents, marquees, benders and buses stretching to the horizon opposite the stones and of course the constant stream of bombed out hippies and hippesses stumbling around the road side. We entered the site and found a suitable spot to park, set up and skin up (but not necessarily in that order). As luck would have it, we befriended a neighbouring camper who happened to have a decent sized generator and didn't mind sharing it so we made up an improvised stage and started setting up the equipment. Later that day we were joined by another new band fresh on the scene playing their first Stonehenge too. They introduced themselves as the Ozric Tentacles (named after an imaginary breakfast cereal I think they said) and together we played throughout the night and forged a friendship that saw us playing many gigs and festivals together in the future. I don't know what time it all ended but I remember seeing the sun rise at least once...

A recently (and happily) pregnant Kim and I had to go back to Bracknell for a couple of days, but as the festival by then was usually around 2-3 weeks long it wasn't a problem, although we couldn't wait to get back there. As we re-entered the site, Kim was driving our car and suddenly she shrieked and swerved, just missing a naked cyclist. I think it caught her by surprise, she said after that she actually screamed because as he was bombing along on the bike his dick was flapping in the wind and it was a bit of a shock for her... that's the thing about festivals, especially free ones, pretty much anything went (apart from smack.. a bit of self-policing courtesy of the Convoy and Hells Angels saw to that if I recall) and for some people their first reaction to such total freedom was to get their kit off as soon as possible, not a problem, but it did seem that most of the ones who did get naked really shouldn't have.. not a pretty sight! Except.. well, as we didn't have much money, Kim and I had previously gone around some jumble sales back in Bracknell to get a load of clothes and shoes (past experience had taught me that for some unexplicable reason when out of it at a free festival, the first thing you lose are your shoes..) and we'd set up a stall to sell 'em cheaply to the poor wretches who'd done exactly that, plus we had a few tapes and stuff to sell too. As I was chief networker and generator blagger I didn't get to spend much time on the stall, but there was one time when Kim had to go off and do something and left me in charge of it.

That year, as in fact it was most years, it was hot... real hot and Salisbury Plain wasn't exactly renowned for its shade. So of course most of us did what most mad englishmen (and women) did and bared various parts of our virgin skin to the scorching orb above and cooked accordingly. I was sat at our 'stall' under an umbrella reading an underground comic I'd just bought, when I looked up and saw this vision of voluptuousness sashaying towards me with nary a stitch on.. man, she was gorgeous and totally should have been naked... always. She was the sort of chick who should have carried a card from her doctor saying that under no circumstances should she ever be given clothes to wear... Anyway, being the cool, together dude I was, I tried to hide my arousal and buried my face into the comic as she swayed and shimmied towards the table, her pendulous tanned breasts swinging as she walked and soft rivulets of sweat trickling from her navel down towards her furry pubic mound.... (see? I told ya I wasn't looking???). I looked up at her trying to stare just at her face, I tried real hard, honest. I did pretty well with one eye, it was very good and did exactly what I told it to do.. while the other one must have thought 'fuck that' and scanned her entire nakedness.. I must have come across as some kind of Marty Feldman impersonator and I have to admit it was quite a relief (for one eye anyway) when she found and bought a rather fetching pair of shoes and then left.

As I mentioned before, part of the requirement of playing at free festivals if you were poor, lowly musicians was the task of finding and befriending any generator owners and where they were located dictated where your next gig would be. Not a problem as there were always many willing volunteers to help cart the equipment around. One such donor was the owner of an ice-cream van in the 'high street' (where the vendors would set up). Not the best location as it was the middle of the day and people wanted ice cream but it did show our powers of persuasion. So we got all the gear over there and started playing and in no time at all a sizeable crowd grew. As I mentioned earlier, it was hot.. very hot, and as we played I noticed this cool dude behind me leaning against his recently parked, sleek black, shiny new motorcycle. At the time we were doing an anti-nuclear 'ska'-type song that I'd written (sadly never recorded) called 'Big Bombs' all about a chap who'd gone for a walk in the sunshine only to be witness to a hail of nuclear missiles raining down on him (whatever happened to 'boy meets girl', eh?) climaxing in a chorus of 'Big Bombs, Big Bombs, Landing in my Garden....' this became a live favourite and the crowd were often invited to join in on the chorus. This time, however, as we all launched into the chorus we were joined by a humungous explosion, courtesy of one recently blown up, not so shiny anymore black motorcycle with it's not so cool owner frantically trying to put out the flames. That's how hot it was!! The only down side of that festival was when someone pinched my mic, stand and echo unit from one of the stages but hey, this was an alternative society, but a society just the same and there were still rip off merchants and entrepreneurs... human nature ya see... swings and roundabouts tho'....

All in all, a great festival and we gained a lot of fans, many of whom were to come to gigs that we did around the country throughout the band's career. Apparently there was a call from the main stage for us to go on and perform but we were so out of it, we didn't get to hear about it until it was too late.

'TIL DEATH DO US PART(Y)

Kim and I had by then decided to have a baby, we knew we'd

be together for a long time within a very short space of knowing each other, it just seemed instinctive, something that caused a little consternation among others (including my family.. and probably Kim's in Australia too) but it felt totally right to us and in order to make it easier for us all 'round we decided to get married that July. It was something that neither Kim or I had given any thought to before but as I say it just seemed right and good. So we agreed that after the Stonehenge festival we'd tie the knot, July 1st to be precise at Bracknell registry office. Due to a severely limited budget (read dead broke), we decided to invite just immediate family, my mum and dad, my two sisters Paula and Sonya and my two nans (Kim's mum even flew over from Australia) and close friends. I'd invited Steve 'Speed Machine' up to be my best man, but unfortunately he didn't live up to his name on that day and turned up just as we were having photos taken after the ceremony!! I know he was upset about it, but he tried and that meant a lot...

It'll probably go down as possibly the fastest wedding ceremony ever held there, the registrar took one look at me with my waist-length hair and beard, resplendent in a white kaftan, waistcoat and jeans (Kim looked gorgeous tho') and the motley crew who followed us in and raced through the ceremony in record time, he couldn't wait for us to sign and get the hell out of their establishment! Job done we all headed off to the reception... luckily Kim was working in a pub at the time and her bosses laid on all the food and stuff and all was good. The only casualty of the whole day was our poor ol' green Cortina again.. someone had tied loads of cans to the exhaust and it was so rotten with rust that the weight of the cans pulled the exhaust off as we were going down the road! Also someone sprayed 'just married' on the bonnet and the spray must have eaten into the paintwork because it was still there plain to see many months later...

A HOME IS LOST - A JOB IS GOT - A JOB IS LEFT – A BOSS IS KILLED

January 1984, Kim and I had just spent Xmas in a homeless persons bed & breakfast 'hostel' in Askew Road (of all places) back in London. We'd lost the Bracknell flat we were living in because our friend who let it to us wanted to move back in. We'd gone to the Bracknell Council to see if they'd help us but they said that because we hadn't been in the town for long enough we had to go to a hostel back in West London where I came from... Kim was heavily pregnant by then and the owners of the hostel had very kindly put us in a tiny room on one of the upper floors accessible only by twisty, winding stairs. The owners of the 'hostel' were on a right ol' meal ticket.. we paid the council about twenty-odd pounds a week to stay there, but the owners were charging them over a hundred a week per room. Now when you consider that this was one of the big London Georgian townhouses with about five floors with umpteen rooms and they'd managed to squeeze people into every available space (there were often whole families in one room) you can imagine they were doing pretty well out of the deal and quite happy to house the homeless. 'Breakfast' consisted of egg on toast and one cup of tea every morning, that is, if you'd made it back in time for the 11:00 'curfew' the previous night, if you didn't you were locked out for the night..

Due to our constant lack of funds, I'd reluctantly found work again (not because I was lazy, but because it's a real bitch to work and do gigs at the same time). Luckily, I'd told the girls at 'Pictures' (where I'd worked before) that I was looking for work and although they couldn't help me themselves (which was a shame because that was what I was hinting at...) there was a new film & TV prop hire company opening down the road and it was owned by a lady I knew called Tessa and her husband Rick. I'd known Tessa through my work at Pictures, she was a very successful set dresser and had won recent acclaim for her work on the movie 'The Killing Fields'. We got on well, she was a sweet lady, always smiling and she was pleased to have me on board. Her husband Rick however was a whole 'nother kettle of fish entirely.. although never truly nasty to my face, I'd never met such an arrogant, pig-headed git of a man in my life. He should have been someone I felt sympathy for, childhood disease had seen him grow up to be a hump-backed midget, barely reaching waist height on me but he obviously decided to tackle his disability by taking the world head on and forcing it to accept him, again, it sounds admirable but it's how he went about it.

He'd managed to acquire great wealth due to a very successful waste paper business and various nefarious underworld dealings, through a mixture of clever business tactics and sheer arrogance. He had all the trappings of wealth that only poor people who become rich can acquire.. you know the sort, onyx ashtrays, brass dolphin-shaped taps, statues in the garden... he wore white leather loafers and had a matching Mercedes. He'd often pull up outside the business in his huge car, he always had a large cigar hanging out of the side of his mouth (He must have thought it gave him importance, I thought he looked like the Penguin out of Batman) but as he opened the car door, you'd notice that he was sitting on a pile of cushions and had extended foot pedals.. I know it sounds like I'm being really cruel here taking the piss, but if you'd met the man you wouldn't have liked him. But, for her own reasons, Tessa loved and married him and I respected her enough not to cause any ripples of discontent. The work was pretty heavy going, this company hired out metal 'props' to the film & TV industry, by that I mean old cast iron radiators, fire places, metal trunks, door furnishings you name it.. but the work was constant and paid pretty well, plus I learned how to drive a forklift.. that was fun!!

I had some interesting co-workers there... all men this time 'round... well... there was Derek the manager who was a real doom and gloom type of guy who couldn't speak to you without tutting and sighing, he always wore black and had the worst dandruff I'd ever seen, we all stood back when he sneezed... then there was Hamish, he was a real character, a real sixties leftover, not a 'burnt out' hippy as such, more of a spent Austin Powers/Jason King typa dude....... he still had the 'boofy' hair and frilly shirt, undone almost to the navel with a king-size medallion nestling in his chest hair and still fancied himself as a bit of a ladies man. If any ladies had no sense of smell then he would have been in like Flint, because he loved the booze and reeked of it constantly, it was best not to put him too near any naked flames... He did a lot of photographic work with the Yardbirds (being there with Giorgio Gomelski when Jeff Beck was asked to join the band) and others and designed some psychedelic posters in the 60's and was very pleased that he had some eager new ears waiting to hear the tales of his derring do's, as the others had heard it all before... often. We got on great tho' and because of his equally artistic bent, we'd often spend down time doing outrageous cartoons of ourselves or the others.. Then there was dear ol' Scurly, camp as a row of tents. Now, I'd met my fair share of gays in the film industry, easy to spot by their feather boas and pink lurex strides, but Scurly was my first introduction to the 'butch' variety. When I first saw him, I thought "'ello? who's this big skinhead with his rolled up Levi's and Doc Martens and what's he doing here?" But when he opened his mouth and this very camp, thick cornish accent came out (and he had a bit of a lisp and spoke from the back of his throat to make it worse) I almost fell down laughing. He had a wicked sense of humour (fortunately) and when he laughed his whole body shook... There was also Stewbie, a public schoolboy who desperately wanted to be a cockney (a la Jamie Oliver) he went on to do pretty well in the film biz..

I lasted there for about a year but eventually found myself having to choose between working or playing music, easy choice to make really (although not financially!) and so I decided to jack it in. The boss had been getting a bit psycho and there were problems between him and Tessa. I found out not long after that the problems were Rick's mounting suspicions that his wife Tessa was having an affair (with Hamish's brother no less) and one day he finally snapped and run her through with a sword killing her instantly. I was so glad I got out of that job before that occurred, I was really saddened and angry about it all... nasty stuff.

BLOWING THRU THE JASMINE IN MY MIND..

January 12th, Kim and I had been moved by the council to a 'smaller' homeless hostel on Ealing Common, which we actually quite liked. It was a converted Georgian house again but with huge rooms and tall ceilings, big picture windows and a view of the common. If we'd had to pay full rent for it we wouldn't have been able to live there that's for sure... By this time, Kim had passed the magic 'due' date for our soon to be released baby and was getting a mite frustrated. She'd been pretty sick during the pregnancy, but continued gigging with us until it became too difficult for her, she'd enjoyed the distraction. After a couple of weeks of inaction tho' she was beginning to climb the walls and somehow her energy levels had begun to climb again the nearer she got to the birth. On this particular night, we'd been watching 'Top of the Pops' and she'd decided to do some dancing on the bed, bouncing around on the mattress, she suddenly gripped her stomach and said "Oh-oh.. I think the baby's coming!!!". This was the line I'd been waiting for and as soon as I heard that, I was out the door and running to the nearest phone box (which was quite a distance, especially in the winter and I was just in my socks...). I grabbed at the phone and managed to blurt out 'Ambulance.... now... baby coming.. need help!', gave them the address and legged it back to the hostel. When I got back Kim was sitting calmly on the bed with her suitcase packed and ready.

We were taken to Queen Charlotte's Hospital in Hammersmith (same place where I was born) and Kim was soon booked into a bed in the maternity ward. Now, I'd heard that some women could go into labour for quite some time, so I opted to stay by Kim's side and made myself comfortable at the end of the bed... little did I know that she wouldn't be giving birth for another nineteen hours!! But, at around nine o' clock on Friday the Thirteenth (and a full <u>moon</u> to <u>boot</u>) Kim gave birth to our daughter Jasmine and the world instantly became the better for it.. we were so proud.

Incidentally, the reason why I adopted the pseudonym 'Moonboot' was not just because of my preference for boot-like footwear (I hate wearing shoes... weak ankles or something.. gawd knows...) but it was also because while we were thinking of names for the baby, I said that if it was a boy we should call him Moonboot or Merlin. Kim and our families and friends were desperately hoping for a girl and the much saner, chosen name of Jasmine and Kim had said to me that if I liked the name Moonboot so much, I should call myself it and see how I like it.

A HOME OF OUR OWN

Back at the hostel with our new baby, it was only a matter of time before Ealing Council would give us a place of our own. Unfortunately we were lined up for a flat in one of South Acton's notorious tower blocks, the same sort that I'd grown up in! Full circle for me and not a happy result either.. they were even more run down and depressing by then, but for us beggars couldn't be choosers. But then, out of the blue, we got a letter from the 'Guinness Trust', a Housing Association in Bracknell who we'd applied to for a place but never heard back. They asked us to get in touch if we'd had our baby as they had a flat lined up for us at their 'Boyd Court' flats in Bracknell. Joy of joys! We couldn't believe our luck, we called straight away and three weeks later, on my birthday in fact, we were handed the keys to our own place. The estate was really nice, not huge tower blocks, only three storeys high and we were on the first floor and the flats formed a rectangle with the car park in the middle and a kid's playground. A great place for young families, we're still truly grateful for the help they gave us and even with my looking a little 'out of sorts' they were nothing but very helpful and friendly to us. Even the neighbours were good and we never got any complaints... which was quite surprising really...

If we thought that previous places that we'd lived in were like 'drop in' centres then this was to be the 'Haight Ashbury' of them all, for as the band grew in popularity, so did our social circle and it wasn't uncommon for us to have a constant flow of people drop by for a cup of tea and a herbal supplement. In fact, most of my memories of those days seem to revolve around popping to the local deli (who had me on a first name basis almost straight away) for milk and tea bags, rolling papers and toilet paper. Many, many parties and many stories to tell about those times..

THE NAG'S HEAD

As word got out about the Magic Mushroom Band and the good-sized audiences we were attracting, we started getting offers of regular gigs at particular venues and by far the most regular one was the Nag's Head in High(!) Wycombe. It was a smallish pub on the outskirts of town but with a larger function hall upstairs and that's where the bands played. The owners didn't like us and the people we attracted but they seemed to like the takings at the door... funny that. The promoter was a guy called Ron Watts who had himself played in a band called 'Brewer's Droop' which goes some way to describing the sort of state he'd end up in by the end of the night... Credit where due tho', he'd made a bit of a name for himself by putting on the first punk gigs at the 100 Club in London against much opposition..

The Nag's head was your typical grungy, black-walled, beer stained venue but by the time we'd set the lights up it was miraculously transformed into a swirling, whirling psychedelic playground. Apparently Jimi Hendrix had trod the boards there in the '60's as had many other notables due to it being a regular venue for bands on the touring circuit.

Our first ever performance there was as support to a popular local rock band called 'Travelling Shoes', we were keen to get our foot in the door and it seemed like a good idea at the time. As previously mentioned, we had our usual bit of trouble fitting all our equipment on stage (in front of the other band's stuff too!) and I don't think the other band was aware of all the lighting equipment either! By then Jon had other commitments and couldn't provide his 'Dancing Shiva' lightshow for us anymore, but Porij had started collecting various bits and pieces and had put together his own 'Electrick Gypsies' lightshow instead, soon ably aided and abetted by a guy called Simon and together they pumped out a pretty good show for us... the show went down well and we were offered regular gigs there which we eagerly accepted.

It wasn't too far from home, the crowd was always great and very supportive and we met some good, influential and inspiring people there.. among them was Richard Allen founder of 'Freakbeat' magazine (and later Delerium records), Kosmik Ken high priest of the Deadheads, Dan the Man (mushroom artist supreme and designer of our wonderful posters and badges) and many more, too many to mention....

We also gained another addition to the band in the shapely form of Janey (Jane Reaction) who joined Kim on vocals, they got on really well and it was nice for Kim to have a bit of female company. Janey was a skinny, gangly thing with big, brown eyes and still at school when she first joined the band and she'd hastily slip out of her school uniform into her stage clothes at the shows (but never let us watch) and she was banned from talking about her day at school while we were in the pub. She did however display at a very early age, the beginnings of a very (and suitably) warped sense of humour which she retains to this day... It gave the band good balance having two female singers, they complimented each other very well, having very different vocal styles and they always looked great together on stage, I thought they had real presence and were a darn site easier on the eyes than us hairy ol' bastards (they got all the fan mail!). They'd often be up all night designing and trying on stage-wear and practising harmonies...

As I said before, the owners of the Nag's Head saw us as a necessary evil, but really didn't give a shit about us.. they often wouldn't open up right until the last minute so we'd often have to soundcheck in front of the audience (something I always loathed to do because it was like telling the audience the plot..) and then they'd try to quickly usher us out of the building as soon as we'd played our last chord! I won't even go into the fun and games we had trying to get money out of old Ron and his brewer's droop... the words 'blood' and 'stone' spring to mind.... One night we got down to our van to start loading it up and someone had smashed the windscreen in... funny that, it was parked up the side of the pub with the landlord's car behind it... gee, that was a cold drive home that night I can tell ya...

On another occasion Simon from the lightshow had brought his girlfriend Julie and her young son to the gig, they'd just been evicted from their house and had bought a bus (they eventually joined the Convoy and were involved in the Battle of the Beanfield, getting the bus trashed in the process), they didn't have a babysitter on this night so they brought the kid with them. No problem for us, he was a good kid, although knowing the landlords and the licensing laws we kept him backstage in the dressing room. Of course they found out about him and kicked up a right old stink, so much so that they refused to have him in the pub and Julie had to take him back to the bus.. we were all so pissed off about that, but the show had to go on. On the way home we apologised to Simon for what had happened and he didn't seem too worried, especially when he mentioned that he'd like to see the look on the landlord's face when he tried to drive his car the next day with a recently inserted potato shoved hard up his exhaust pipe.

The audience was always great though and we'd get to do many encores (often ending up longer than the original set!) and they gave us the freedom to experiment... so at one point we were playing there every month. Unfortunately, as was often the case, the cops got to find out about our performances and would often lie in wait outside the pub for the punters to come spilling out after the show and pick 'em off like the easy targets that they were..

The more regular we got there, the more requests we got from local bands asking for a support slot, something I always liked to encourage because we were often in that situation and knew what it was like and some bands went on to do very well, often better than us! (Kula Shaker for one...). We often got sent cassettes and one particular tape blew me away.. it sounded like some West Coast band from the '60's, free form improvisations and I really wanted to give them a go. Ron was reluctant at first, but the drunker he got, the more I managed to persuade him that it'd be a good idea. I forget the name of the band now, but on reflection it's probably a good thing... because when they set up on stage and started playing it was the horriblest, most god awful racket I'd ever heard in my life! I couldn't believe it! We all looked at each other in amazement, the band we'd heard on the tape was definitely not the one thrashing it out on stage, we looked out at the audience and they were grimacing too and by the second 'number' Ron had leaped up on stage, grabbed the mic from the 'singer' and told them in no uncertain terms to fuck off. After that we decided that rather than have bands suggested by Ron, we'd do our own support slots.. sometimes we'd have a jamming band (often billed as the 'Last Surviving Dinosaurs') and sometimes we'd do acoustic 'unplugged' sessions. They were great fun and always got the crowd warmed up for the main event.

Yep, it was the scene of many a 'drama' during our years playing there, whether it was our (highly unstable) p.a packing up, Porij going up in a puff of smoke at his lighting console during his delicate operation of controlling the projectors with a metal fork, us not being allowed to take our gear into the venue until the 'High Wycombe Pigeon Fanciers Club' had finished their meeting, the heat, the condensation, booking us to play on the night of 'Live Aid' to an audience of about eight who were all facing the other way watching the TV on the back bar..... it was one hell of a rollercoaster ride, but we loved it and especially the people who came to those gigs, they came to see us so often, it almost felt like they were part of the band.... which in a way they were....

MAGICK EYE - THE EPIC

Any reasonable band (if it's lucky enough) has that one particular tune that defines them and is immediately identifiable to those that have heard it. Many major league bands have them, be it Deep Purple's 'Smoke on the Water' or Lynyrd Skynrd's 'Freebird' or indeed Hawkwind's 'Silver Machine'. For the Magic Mushroom Band it surely was 'Magick Eye'. The by-product of a warm-up jam at a band rehearsal, it was based around a chugging, almost Bo Diddley-esque riff that I'd come up with on the guitar. The format was purposely kept 'loose' thus open to many different interpretations depending on our mood, with simple lyrics that I just threw together:

"I got my Magick Eye on you, what is this feeling coming through? I give to you and you take from me, why can't you just let me be? It's gonna grab you by the ear... it's gonna grab you by the ear.."

Huuuhhh??? It wasn't intended to make any grand statement, the words just fit good with the riff.

Altogether we recorded four different versions of 'Magick Eye' over the years, but it was when we performed it live that it really shone. Sometimes we would open our set with it, but more often than not it would be the set 'closer' and if the vibe was good it'd be stretched into a mighty opus. We would always start with a mysterious 'eastern' type drone (as all space rock epics should) and I would chant the words 'Magick Eye' while holding my fingers in a pyramid shape directly above where my third eye would have been if I had one. The audience loved this visual and before long they would all be doing the same thing, I always loved getting the audience involved, that was great fun and with Magick Eye in particular, I would break it all down for a while so that just the drums would pound the beat and then I would do an answer back with the audience 'Magick Eye!', followed by 'What have we got?' 'Magick Eye!' then a bit of 'Whoa oh oh oh oh' 'Magick Eye!' etc. Sometimes that song would last almost as long as the rest of the set... I guess if I was asked what song I would like us to be remembered by it would be this one...

IMAGINATIVELY TITLED 'CASSETTE E.P'

Up until this point, we'd had no recorded material released, apart from the previously mentioned live tape that we'd hastily cobbled together. It was better than nothing, but the quality wasn't the best. By chance we got to hear about a chap called Marcus who was working at the in-house recording studio at South Hill Park Arts Centre, he'd expressed an interest in recording us and suggested we make a 'demo' there. All we had to do was raise the money to pay for the session, not an easy task at that time (we rarely had any money!) but we eventually got some cash together from gigs and worked out a deal (or two).

We were to go on to record most of our work at that same recording studio, it was a brick out-building and very well soundproofed. A band could fit very comfortably in the main recording area and the mixing 'booth' took up the whole rear end of the building separated by a large, thick glass viewing window. After a bit of thrashing around and mass-debating (?) we'd decided on the tracks for the recording session, we worked it out that we could afford to do three songs which were:

Magick Eye - A live favourite as previously mentioned, this version featuring a rather 'excited' tambourine courtesy of me,

I was really getting into it out there in the recording room all on my own with the cans on digging the beat, until I momentarily looked into the mixing room for approval and saw the rest of the band crying with laughter. Far from being the cool, hip rhythm king that I thought I was, they said I resembled the 'Duracell' bunny... bastards... sounded alright in playback tho'.... hah!!!

Redemption Time - One of a few reggae tunes that we knocked out over the years, a throwback to my old Portobello Road years I guess. Reggae was always good to do live, especially at festivals. Bit of a political message in this one, again, easy to do with reggae. This track never made it to vinyl, lost in time and space...

Astral Action - One of the few original Magic Mushroom Band Mark 1 tunes that made it over to the new incarnation. A classic space rock structure, chuggy eastern riff, heavy on the chorus then into a laid back spacey mode before taking it higher and faster to fade.. Also never to be recorded again......

So, the tracks were down and it was then that we discovered the wonders of mixing, and also how bloody long it takes to do, if you can all agree on the final version that is... Marcus was being very patient with us studio virgins, but then he was being paid to. Marcus took the finished master to a cassette duplicating company that he knew called 'Angel Talk' they only usually did religious music but somehow he persuaded them to take it on and before long we had multiple copies of our first studio recordings. I knocked up a xeroxed cover for the cassette and after much beard scratching we decided upon the highly imaginatively titled 'Cassette E.P'.. well... with a name like ours who needed a catchy title??

BABYLON IS BURNING

So there we were, in the thick of it all trying to balance the paying gigs with the festivals, benefits and other worthwhile causes and such a cause came to pass in our very own home town...

There was an adventure playground not far from where we lived which was due for demolition to make way for a 'safer' (read sanitised) play area for the local kids. It was a really cool place with huge rope swings and climbing frames etc. and right in the centre was a huge wooden 'pyramid' platform. When we heard about the pending demolition we offered our services to do a show there to bring attention to the kids' plight. To be truly honest, I'd often looked at that pyramid and thought how good it would be to play on it, with the right 'lighting' it could very easily resemble the great pyramid (stage) of Glastonbury (Fayre) legend. We were up for it and hastily arranged a date with the play park staff who were very grateful for our help. Bracknell had a very good grapevine as far as that sort of thing goes and we were pleased to see a good turnout for the show, even better was the fact that we knew most of the audience so it was more like a party and in the party mood we did get...

All was going well, Dave a friend of the band had managed to acquire a (most rare then) video camera, but he got so trashed, when we saw it back it was either footage of the ground, the dark, or occasionally we'd get a glimpse of my 'Orange' amplifier... oh well... but we were cooking on gas that night, the sound was good and the 'stage' looked fantastic all lit up (courtesy of Porij)... maybe 'lit up' isn't the best turn of phrase as, actually, that's what we did.. we were oblivious to it of course, but apparently one of the smoke machines was a bit too close to part of the wooden stage and it had indeed caught fire and was merrily smoking away while we were playing. We were made aware of the situation by a line of cops appearing at the front of the stage trying to coax us down and away from the flames. Of course, we tried to ignore the 'fascist thugs' but eventually they got us off and shut the whole thing down.. so I guess in a way, although our hearts were in the right place, we actually helped the demolition get underway.... go figure....

I often think we must have been the bane of the local constabularies life, we were always setting up for free somewhere around town, be it in an abandoned cinema, outside the gates of the Bracknell festival, or in a field on the outskirts of town, but to be fair they never got heavy handed with us personally and maybe they thought better of causing too much hassle because often we'd be entertaining people who may otherwise have been out causing trouble somewhere else... better the devil you know, eh???

A RIGHT ROYAL RAVE-UP

We began to do quite a few shows around the Surrey/Hampshire area and another regular gig for us for a while was at a pub in Guildford called The Royal. The audience was very loyal (at The Royal!) but the band 'stage' was just a corner of the pub and once we'd all squeezed ourselves in and set up the instruments and lights there wasn't much room for the audience so it was a tight squeeze... especially when we had Jethro, a second drummer for a while. It was totally impractical having two drummers but a lot of my favourite bands had done it and I loved the sound, especially when Jim and Jethro had such different styles. On the bigger stages it looked awesome but at the smaller venues I must admit it was a bit of a squeeze. Also, there were no tables around for the punters to put their drinks on, so often we'd finish some psychedelic rock opus with a huge crescendo to be greeted by silence... the sound of 'one hand clapping'..... because the other hand had a drink in it!

The promoter, whose name escapes me now, was pretty much as I'd expected for those kinda gigs. Not really into the music as such, but he liked the amount of punters who faithfully attended each show. So we were on a regular gig there too... sometimes a bit too regular though. One particular time, me and Kim were sitting at home on a Friday night, suitably relaxed and getting into some movie or other that we were watching on our newly acquired (rented) video recorder and suddenly the phone rang and the conversation went something like this:

"Hello? Whaddya want??"

"Garry? Garry! This is The Royal... where the friggin' hell are ya??"

"Whaddya mean where am I? I'm at home relaxing..."

"Relaxing? You're supposed to be here! There's a queue of people waiting outside to get in and you're over an hour late!!!"

"Geddafuck outtahere! We're not supposed to be playing tonight!"

"Yes you bloody well are.. I've advertised it and everything, I told you about it ages ago.. it's written in my diary... errrr... no it's not.... bugger"

"Sorry mate, no can do... there's no way I can find the rest of the band in time, even if they were in a fit enough state to play which I certainly am not."

In the end I managed to persuade him to let the punters in, explain the situation and apologise to them (I'm sure he would have blamed us tho', just to save face), the DJ was the star that night and apparently it turned out to be a pretty good night... wish I'd been there....

After one particular gig there, we were approached by some members of the 'Road Rats' motorcycle club who wanted us to go on to a party at their clubhouse. I was totally up for it but some of the guys and gals were a bit nervous about it, so a somewhat slimmed down version of the band went on to play for them, any fears were totally uncalled for and they were really appreciative, so much so I really wished that I hadn't been 'designated driver' that night.. I was off my tits, I don't remember getting home from that one at all.....

One very special friendship that arose from those times was with the lovely Jake. He was a regular punter at the Royal, but we got to know him better through his record and tape stall at the local market where he would sell many a rare psychedelic gem. He had some great stuff for sale and I often wished I'd met him when I had money while I was still working, by that time all I could do was browse and dribble on the merchandise, he did look after me tho'. He was also an aspiring musician and went on to form a space rock band called 'Paperhouse' and then an ambient-dub act called 'Optic Eye/Optica'. His sister was a famous 'Page Three' girl of some notoriety. Jake was a lovely chap, a real important player in the scene but sadly, is no longer with us as his (never mentioned) epilepsy finally got the better of him recently...

Through our appearances at the Royal we were invited to play at the 'Torpedo Town' festival near Portsmouth. It was organised as part of a protest against a missile complex that was due to be built there. It was a great festival actually, a good amount of people were there, it had a decent stage and p.a, the local cops were well behaved and the vibe was most good. It was there I first met the curious Eugene Purple who did a very bizarre one-man show using tape loops and crazy stuff, he gave me a cassette after and I played it often, he remains a good friend to this day. It was also the first time it dawned (literally) on us that there would be nothing worse than going onstage after the Ozric Tentacles. We were to play many shows together over the years but often we tried to arrange to perform before them, because (especially at festivals) they would play.. and play.. and play.. and if it was going down really well.. they'd play some more! Great news for the punters but for us poor bands who had to follow them, by then we'd either started falling asleep or were too out of it to give it our 'all'.. and sure enough, at the Torpedo Town festival they played their li'l hearts out and we finally went on at dawn...

1984 - Y'ALL CUM BACK FOR MORE.... NOT

Before we knew it, Summer Solstice was almost upon us again and we were all looking forward to the approaching (and unbeknownst to us, the last) Stonehenge Festival. The van had a fresh assortment of gaffa tape adorning the wing mirrors/bumpers etc. and was running pretty well (considering). Jasmine was a six month old baby by then and so Kim and I decided to do the sensible thing and buy a new tent and camping equipment, stove etc. and we followed the van (and its many occupants) in our little white Mini, as did Porij and his girlfriend Jackie on his recently finished Triumph chopper. If the sight upon approaching the site was impressive at previous festivals there then this one beggared belief! It was absolutely huge!! On reflection, you could almost understand the government at the time getting a bit worried about this scene. Here were most of the nation's youth, potential future prime ministers all, getting off their tits 24/7 meeting and making friends lolling about with huge grins on their faces in the sun listening to all the cool free music and not a penny going into the governments coffers... how could this many people have so much fun for so long, for so little money??? Of course the local shopkeepers weren't complaining.. they'd never had so much custom before..

As usual, all was good for us... we did some great performances, sold lots of copies of our cassette and met a lot of new people and bands, in fact this one was probably the festival that led to the creation of our 'scene' as many bands formed for the Stonehenge festival and when it was stopped it all just switched over to the proper venues... so in reality, the 'scene' was created by the oppressors, thanks Mrs Thatcher, ya did us proud!!

For me and Kim however, it ended all too soon. We had to beat a hasty retreat after our last performance there, as we'd gone back to our tent after the show to warm up some milk for baby Jasmine on our new 'safe' camping stove. It'd started raining so we set it up in the entrance to the tent, all of a sudden this 'safe' stove decided to collapse on itself, splashing Jasmine's face with hot scalding water and in a fit of panic I grabbed the hot pan and threw it out of the tent. Kim and Jas were screaming so we gathered up all our stuff, threw it into our car and headed off out of the site to look for a hospital. By then it was dark and as was often the case, most people had lit fires so there I was trying to get the mini through a labyrinth of camp sites, smoky fires and pitch darkness. We eventually found our way out and headed to nearby Amesbury. I didn't have a clue where I was going or how to find the hospital but when I saw a police car up ahead I decided to overtake them and slam my brakes in front of them to get their attention (if it wasn't for the situation that would've been quite cool). Of course, when they saw me behind the wheel they approached my car rubbing their hands with glee..

To be fair tho', once I explained the situation they put Kim and Jas in their car and told me to follow them to the nearest hospital in Salisbury. Seemed like a good plan, except they burned off at great speed, but my poor little mini couldn't, plus I was running on the fumes by then so I soon lost them... But somehow the gods of fate were looking down on me, for as I took a succession of wild guesses at which direction to head in, I somehow found myself outside Salisbury hospital. I dashed into the emergency ward and soon found Kim and Jas... Jasmine was having her face bandaged as she'd got badly burned by the scalding water and I was met by a barrage of abuse from the doctors, nurses and cops who wanted to know what the hell I was thinking by taking a new born baby to a drug crazy pop festival?? Once I explained about the new 'safe' camping stove they calmed down a bit, especially when they looked at my hands which were badly blistered and burned, I hadn't really noticed as I was too worried about Jasmine to care about myself.. I also didn't notice until later that as we'd left straight after a show, my face was covered with streaks of fluorescent make up that we'd all plastered over our faces and hands!! We got home and not long after had a visit from a 'Social Worker' concerned that we weren't looking after our child properly, apparently it'd also made the local news as they loved to generate as much negative publicity as they could about the festival. Little did we know then that it'd be the last ever Stonehenge Free Festival....

THE HI'S & THE LOWES

After numerous smiles from across the street, we eventually met up with some 'neighbours' from a cottage across the road. They were a married couple called Kate and Brian and were originally from the North of England. Due to a sizeable insurance payout after a motorcycle accident, they were in the enviable position to able to buy one of a line of old cottages that were opposite our flats. They were originally from the old Bracknell when it was just a village and at the end of the row closest to us was the remains of a little cemetery which had originally been the size of the whole plot before the cottages were built... there were gravestones going back to the 1600's and Janey would often like to freak herself out by venturing onto the graveyard at night (with us all in view of course...), she liked freaking herself out our little Janey, so much so, that she now lives in a haunted 16th Century Somerset cottage of her own!

Brian and Kate were real 'old skool' rockers, they loved their AC/DC and Sabbaf and Iron Maiden and in a way it was kind of refreshing for me because in my quest for constant input of new musics I'd kinda forgotten about all the real classics, s'funny.. when you're into collecting obscure stuff you tend to pay less attention to the stuff that everyone else likes (except he who is Hendrix of course). Due to his accident Brian had one leg shorter than the other which gave him a pronounced limp (pronounced 'l-i-m-p'.. thankyou Spike Milligan!) and he would swagger to and from town in his fringed leather jacket with his more bohemian, ethnic looking missus Kate by his side. They too were musicians, Brian was the singer, guitarist and songwriter and Kate sang. They first came to our attention when they'd rehearse in their 'converted attic' with their band

'Deff Neighbours'(!) and like clockwork the supposedly deaf neighbours would be trying to bash their door down, but of course, they couldn't hear them because they were SO FUCKING LOUD!! The music was very loud, painfully so, even for me and the recordings from the practises would send the levels on my cassette deck so far into the red that the poor needles would be bashing at the side of the windows trying to escape.. On one occasion I can remember Brian and Kate coming 'round with their latest 'release' and Janey and newly found (playing synthesisers for Ozric Tentacles) boyfriend Joie were staying with us and got to share the experience. Joie, being one of the coolest dudes on the planet, gave nothing away while listening to the aural onslaught, but I could tell by the way his dreads were pinned back to the wall behind him that he too agreed that maybe it had been recorded a little over zealously!!!

Brian was (and probably still is) a keen collector of sci-fi memorabilia and his shelves would be stacked high and their ceilings dangling with figures, crafts and models from various cult sci-fi shows, some shop bought, some homemade, some dubiously so. He even gave us an old, black and white photograph of one of Dr Who's 'Cybermen' which we thanked him for, but didn't fully appreciate until he confessed that it was him in the suit... or was it?.. we'll probably never know... Kate was quite an accomplished painter I recall...

Another 'dubious' hobby of theirs was their dabblings with all things black magic and witchykrafty stuff. Ya know, widjii boards and devil mirrors and all that malarkey... that shit is something that I'd never have a truck with, but I was quite happy to hear about after the fact. I declined numerous offers to go over to the 'dark side' figuring that it gets dark enough on the light side, who'd want it darker?? But they'd have their sessions and basically report their findings to us, most of which seemed to suggest that since playing with the dark forces they'd never had such a run of bad luck, they had one disaster after the other... they also were convinced that their house was haunted (much to Janey's delight) and told tales of digging up human bones in their garden and of the ghost of a dog that would enter their cupboard under the stairs and piss into their vacuum cleaner (!) they swore that often there'd be times when they got their hoover out that it'd be leaking a smelly green liquid!! It got kinda weird getting stoned at their place as the hairs'd start raising on the backs of your arms and it was always devilishly cold everywhere and visits to the converted outside toilet were very swift by all involved... they were a lovely couple tho'.. nice and down to earth, something that we would get to appreciate over the years as we got better known and the 'hangers on' began to come creeping out of the woodwork, as they do...

It was also at their place that we'd met Steve, an up and coming poet and writer with an insatiable thirst for knowledge, who was lodging with them for a while. He fully embraced the scene that we were in and eagerly digested facts associated with all that was our 'alternative' lifestyle. He also became (with his brother Kelvin, another ex-Chopper Club member and custom bike builder extraordinaire) our first 'official roadie' and for a good while they were an excellent team affording us the luxury of not having to lug all the equipment around, set it all up and man our own 'merchandise' stall.

They did an excellent job and unfortunately the work load just got too much for them once the 'tours' started rolling in.. in my time I've seen a lot of roadies (and babysitters) come and go!!

Another character who we got to meet through Brian and Kate was this weird little dude called 'Duke'. He'd recently moved into the end cottage (nearest the graveyard) and resembled a short, northern english version of Elvis Presley. He'd have the high quiff, with the ol' shirt collar propped up and wear these high heel boots, but all they seemed to do was emphasise the fact that he was a shortarse. He'd just completed a rather tasty white Triumph chopper, but he was this dodgy greaser-type who was always getting himself into trouble (Jack Russell/little man syndrome). We didn't want trouble a knockin' at our door (any more than it was - we'd already had a couple of 'social' visits from the local constabulary, the reasons for the visits being quite unimportant and often obscure) so we didn't encourage visits from him and his special set of mates and he only made it over a couple of times.

Duke wasn't very subtle about his recreational habits which didn't impress us that much and one day it all just got a bit too weird. As was the norm at the time, we had a few people over and things were very relaxed and hazy when suddenly, late at night, there was a loud bash on our front door. "Fookinell! Let me in man!!!" I opened the door to find Duke, white as a ghost apart from numerous purple bruises and bloodstains.. he stumbled into our lounge and after composing himself started telling us about the events of that evening. He'd been down the local pub with his mates and decided to throw an impromptu party back at his place. They'd been without anything smokeable for some time and were celebrating finally finding some good weed. Not long after getting back, their door was suddenly smashed down and loads of police in riot gear had burst into his house, beat them around, ransacked the place and confiscated all his recently bought stash. He said he couldn't believe what had just happened as it seemed like such a planned exercise and he wasn't even a dealer.. but on leaving he did let it drop that they told him that they'd been sent 'round there to create merry hell... the creepiest thing was that he had the same house number as our flat and we shared the same street name.. we were pretty paranoid for a long time after that. Last we heard of Duke, he sold his house and was moving back up north to buy a chimpanzee.. I shit you not.

JOLLY ROGER

We started doing a few shows in Oxford, college gigs/benefits and the like and at one particular gig at the Jericho Tavern we were approached by this burly, Irish gentleman resplendant in business suit with that singing Irish lilt, a twinkle in his oiye and a saxophone in his hand. He was playing part time with a local band called the Particles, but wanted in on the fun with us. In his day job he worked in a bank, but I tell ya, he'd often turn up at gigs straight from work, still in his suit and all he'd do is don this funny little baseball cap with mushrooms stitched to the top, get his sax out of the case, leap on stage and proceed to strangle that fucker. He played like a demon wailing and we loved it, he also played a mean clarinet. Ironically, no matter how weirdly we, or indeed the audience were attired, he always came up trumps in the 'most bizarrely dressed' category!!

READING DOES YER HEAD IN

It was around that time that we first got to meet Reading activist and all 'round right on dude Pogle. With a couple of fellow students he'd issued a radical, anarchic magazine called 'Red Rag' and being equally right on we did a few benefit gigs on their behalf. We'd pretty much played every venue in Reading by then, including the University with Here & Now and the Majestic with a reformed Pink Fairies, but the favourite venue for us and the punters was a place that was then called 'The Paradise Club'. It had seen its heyday in some previous decade and was now relegated to holding the occasional disco, West Indian domino competitions and radical hippy events like ours.... It was large with a good sized stage, plenty of room for the lightshow and best of all it opened 'til very late.

It did get pretty out of it at times and there was always a chaotic vibe present but then great things can often come from scenes like that. I remember at one gig there, we'd finished our set, done all the encores but none of us wanted to finish, the audience were going crazy for more, so we started jamming. I don't know if it was what we had ingested that night but somehow the jam 'morphed into a crazy 12-bar rant about magic mushrooms ...not wanting to get into anything too complicated, like trying to think up words that rhymed on the spot, I just started shouting 'magic mushrooms!' very loudly down the mic and inviting the audience to join in, passing the mic around the front couple of rows. Only on listening to a recording of the show not long after, could we clearly hear Pogle and his friends also shouting in union from the mixing desk at the back of the hall (they had a mic too!).

Like I said, due to its location and late opening times, the Paradise club did attract all the dope fiends, most were great and fun and spacey, but you would get the occasional idiots. One such example springs to mind... Around that time, the 'new' generation of skinheads had taken the early punks' shock value tactic of sniffing glue and run with it. This resulted in groups of them appearing at venues really out of it and sometimes aggressive with it. One night we were playing there and we had a rare problem with stage divers... this didn't happen very often with us because a) most of the audience were too out of it, or b) couldn't be bothered to clamber up there in the first place. But this one particular skinhead had decided to have a go... he was that out of it that we could smell the glue up on stage, he stank real bad and kept trying to grab at Kim and Janey's legs, they weren't having any of it and we all got to witness the wondrous spectacle of Janey suddenly swinging her leg back and thrusting her black, shiny winkle-picker toed boot into the face of her assailant, jamming the pointy end of her boot right up his nose and literally flicking him off the stage. His girlfriend apparently tried to pick a fight with Kim and Janey after the show in the toilets because her boyfriend fancied them. I never got much of that myself... can't understand why....

I think the last event we did for Red Rag was at a free festival by Reading station's railway tracks. I think it was called 'On the Coals', a group of gypsies (pikeys) had set up camp there and after a few hasty discussions a makeshift stage was erected and a generator blagged. I remember the whole event being a bit chaotic and the pikey kids were complete bastards ripping off lots of things and it all got a bit nasty at the end. Pogle was to eventually become part of 'An Arc' lights who got in on the 'circuit', did a few most excellent lightshows for us and eventually wound up (with colleague Adie, another real nice chap) doing the lights for Hawkwind.

UNSUNG HEROES

Maybe a fitting epitaph for the Magic Mushroom Band?! We were approached by a video company (quite rare at the time!) to be part of a compilation video that was to be released featuring the best of the current Berkshire bands. They would put on a special night at Reading Town Hall, film all the bands and choose the best track from each set, with the sound recorded by a multitrack studio for premium quality. Some of the bigger local bands at the time like 'The Complaints' had a home grown video included as well... but we opted for just a track from the gig. It was a great night and all the bands played well, we chose our track 'Living in a Dream' because it featured a spacey bit, a rockin' bit and a free-form jazz cozmic jam bit.. pretty much summed us up all in one track. The video and sound recordings were excellent, everyone coming through loud and clear, even Roy(stone)'s blue afro wig which he bought 'specially for the occasion was evident!

When the video was all edited and ready for release there was a preview night at a club called 'Angies' on the outskirts of Wokingham, another favourite venue of ours. It was a long, thin venue and the stage was equally long and thin and due to there being eight of us in the band at the time, we'd often have to stagger our lineup so we were almost in single file in front of each other, but Porij very cleverly always put net curtains in front of each of us and when the projections were on us it produced an amazing effect (we were told)..
We sat around socialising and secretly sniggering about some of the other bands 'Eighties hairstyles, we even had a 'group' photo taken for the local paper! After our segment had shown, it was commented on that I looked really 'out of it' on the film, too kool for skool, eh? The truth is, I'd earlier that week bought a pair of old German jackboots down Portobello Road and

they'd rubbed a hole in the backs of my socks during the course of the day and by the time I got up on stage I was the proud owner of two of the biggest fuck off blisters known to man right on the back of each heel... so as I postured and preened around the stage, every step was met with a squish of blister being pressed onto red raw skin by a hard leather piece of German footwear.. not so kool for skool, eh? That was our first and last ever official piece of decent quality video though.. no matter how we tried in the future we just couldn't get it together.. sad really.

A CHANGE IN KEYS

Not long after the 'Unsung Heroes' video had been released, we decided it'd be mutually beneficial if Roy(stoned) departed the band. At the time he was very much in travelling mode and we needed a bit more commitment, plus his equipment wasn't really up to scratch and not designed for heavy duty gigging. With Roy gone, we muddled around for a bit without keyboards with me and Craig using spacey effects on the guitars to try to fill the gap, but it wasn't that long before we were offered the chance to bring local legend Mykl on board. Mykl was a resident of Windsor who played synthesiser and guitar and could sing a fair bit too (and he had his own transport!), he was diminutive of stature but had a very tall personality. He brought extra energy and stage presence to the shows and was an all round decent chap. His synthesiser set-up included the use of a computer screen, which was very 'hi-tech' for us and it looked great when his face was uplit by the monitor. He didn't mind dressing up a bit either, much to the delight of our girls in the dressing room and he'd often appear on stage dressed and made up like some kind of dishevelled Robert Smith of The Cure....

"Got our Magick Eye on you..."
Janey, Wayne, Craig, Kim, Jim, Moonboot and Mykl

LONDON CALLING!

As much as we'd played festivals and clubs all around the country by then, we really hadn't had much call to play in London itself, but in time the demand grew and a few venues started to show an interest in us.

Dingwalls was our first London venue, still attracting name bands due to its legendary status, but actually a real pain in the arse to play at.. especially on a Sunday. It was actually located right in the heart of Camden Lock Market of which Sundays were the biggest days and the only way to access the venue was to carry the equipment through the crowds of market shoppers. As you can imagine, with all our sound and lighting equipment it took a fair while. Kim was given the job of vehicle security while we carried the stuff in and as it was a hot day, she decided to have a rest, lay down on the back seat and stick her legs out the window to make the most of a cool breeze. It was at this point that she looked up to see Robert Plant standing there, he smiled at her and then went on his merry way.

Then there was the infamous 100 Club, as previously mentioned the original punk venue for the 'Pistols/Clash/Damned etc a good venue that attracted a fair crowd, the only shame was that the stage ran along the side of the wall as opposed to being at one end and once we'd set up our gear and the lights the audience was wide but not very deep, a very surreal experience from what I recall. We also played a small pub in Fulham quite a lot called the King's Head (aren't all pubs in Fulham called that?), it was a tiny stage but the audience was good, like a London equivalent of the Nag's Head in High Wycombe.

One shocking revelation for me was the fact that there I was treading the same boards at these legendary venues as my iconic predecessors, but the actual stages and dressing rooms were in fact real shit-holes.. the dressing rooms were still tiny and they still smelled like piss!!

BEANFIELD BATTLES & THATCHER'S DEATH RATTLE

Ok, things were looking up gigwise, we'd broken London and were getting out and about a bit and enjoying the ride and looking forward to the forthcoming festival season. Our van wanted to die and most of our equipment was held together by gaffa tape but we were well into it still... but there was unrest in the air and people had started talking about potential trouble with the powers that be who'd decided that last year's Stonehenge had just a been a leetle bit too much fun for everybody and that it was all to be stopped for good. A lot of people who'd bought a bus to live in for the previous year's festival had decided to adopt that lifestyle for good and a lot of other people saw it as a possible, viable alternative to living in the average shitbox in shit-town. This adopting of a lifestyle with far opposing ideals to what the government had in mind for its young generation scared the shit out of Mrs Thatcher and her minions and they sought to stop it dead in its tracks... by whatever means necessary.

As was usual every year the peace bus 'Convoy' trundled along the highways of England, holding impromptu free festivals at their chosen stopovers and we duly met them at Aldermaston airstrip, now deserted and did a show for them. I remember that night well as it pissed down incessantly all night not a minute of let up and our 'stage' was literally a tarp stretched across two buses.. the water was pouring onto my face and hands and onto my guitar and into my pedals on the floor, I really did wonder if I was going to get through that night... but we played on and it was fun, but after the conversation soon turned to the rumours of the cancellation of the Stonehenge festival and others like it and the disbanding of the Convoy. Of course, it didn't change anyone's plans, it was nothing to really worry about, after all, this was mid nineteen-eighties England and we just didn't do that sort of thing.. 1984 had come and gone and there were no signs of a police state or government-appointed hoodlums... or were there????

The next thing we heard was on the TV when the now infamous 'Battle of the Beanfield' had occurred. A huge force of police had surrounded and invaded the Convoys' buses and vans, beating them, smashing up their homes, women and children were crying and screaming. We couldn't believe our eyes, we were crying with them. Our good friends Simon (our lightshow man) and his girl Julie and their son Richard were right in the thick of it. That was it... show's over folks!!! Of course there was a huge uproar, not only about the treatment of the Convoy and how the police approached the whole situation but the sheer manpower costs involved in telling a minute percentage of the population's youth that they couldn't party for free in a field opposite Stonehenge anymore...

So there I was on the eve of the Summer Solstice 1985, like so many others blagging a lift to Stonehenge to show my support for the Convoy and to voice my defiance at the halting of the festival. You could have cut the air with a knife by the time we got there, you could taste the tension.. there were thousands of freaks converging around the stones which was guarded by a ring of police in riot gear complete with shields and batons at the ready, helicopters circled menacingly above shouting instructions for us to disperse.. it was like a really bad 50's sci-fi movie.. Quatermass or something... I soon lost my travelling companions in the crowd but managed to make my way to the 'front line'... I just couldn't believe what was happening... it was surreal. But sure enough, there they were, the riot police with arms tightly linked and shields and batons at the ready. They were pissed and getting pretty riled up at all these protesting hippies, but then to make matters worse, a few of the local 'yobboes' who'd heard about it all on the news had decided to come down and do a bit of agitating.. I actually saw some of them crouch down to pick up dirt from the ground and throw it in the cops' faces, I didn't think that was a particularly good idea...

Not surprisingly, when given the call to charge they did so with gusto and before I knew it I was caught in a stampede of panicking protestors and rampaging baton wielding cops, so I did what any sane person would have done and started running as fast as I could away from the craziness, narrowly missing a swinging baton and shield in the process.. I couldn't even bring myself to look back, I just kept running and running... and I wasn't alone.. I ran down to the A303 and just kept on running. Slowly but surely other people started ebbing away and before I knew it I was alone, in the early hours of the morning miles from anywhere, no money, mid-summer wearing a black vest and a donkey jacket. I carried on walking, sticking my thumb out at passing cars but they were either straights who'd heard about the 'riot' on their car radios and weren't in any hurry to pick up drug-crazed hippies... or they were full of refugees from the stones and just plain couldn't fit me in... so I walked.. and walked...

The solstice sun rose over the A303 casting a long shadow from this tired, freaked out, hot hippy. Still no lifts were forthcoming from the sparse traffic, I was hot and thirsty and my legs felt like lead. In the baking sun that followed I kept having a dilemma with what I was wearing... if I carried my donkey jacket and just had my vest I would be cooler but, not for long because the sun would burn my shoulders and arms, but if I wore the jacket I'd sweat like crazy.. I was in a right old mess. I hadn't seen anybody else walking from the festival for miles, although I did turn around at one point to see this scruffy little dog following me along the hard shoulder, the owner, if there was one, was nowhere to be seen. After numerous failed attempts to shoo him away (I couldn't take him home.. we weren't allowed to have a dog in our flat) he trotted alongside me for a while and we exchanged the occasional glance, grateful for the company until I turned around to see where he'd got to and he'd disappeared as quickly as he arrived. Most bizarre.

About a mile from the turn off to the M3 motorway I eventually got a lift from some dudes (cheers guys! eternally grateful) who updated me on what was happening back at the 'stones. It seemed that there was a lot of violence, women and kids were hurt and that it was a real nasty turn of events... no shit

Sherlock. Their car radio was blaring constant updates and the way it was reported didn't actually tally with what actually happened. Rioting, violent radical hippies? No wonder I had trouble getting a lift! By the time I got home I was absolutely knackered, burned to a crisp with a thumping head, I mumbled something incoherent to a very worried, but mostly relieved Kim and fell into bed and slept the longest sleep.

But that was it, the end of the Stonehenge people's free festival as we knew it.. the powers that be said "That's it" and were prepared to use any means to put a stop to it all. Of course, being the resilient types that festival goers tend (and need) to be, it didn't all stop there and against the nastiest, oppressive opposition a few hardy souls managed to keep the free festival scene going, ducking and diving around the countryside putting on impromptu festivals and trying to get it all going before the cops arrived. We tried to support them as much as we could and were often cited as 'sympathisers' to the free festival scene, not always in a good way either (During the Magic Mushroom Band's career there were more than a few events that got cancelled due to our inclusion on the bill). Of course, contrary to Mrs Thatcher's plans of total annihilation of the 'scene', she actually helped to create a new, better stronger version. Suddenly Thatcher's bastard children, her potential Falklands cannon fodder, were standing up and being counted, spurning her proposed society, dreading their hair and buying buses and caravans.

Well.... if we couldn't play at Stonehenge anymore then we would just have to keep on doing what we and an evergrowing roster of other bands of our ilk were doing, taking the spirit of Stonehenge to the people in clubs, halls and even the more commercial 'paid' festivals. We would never forget...

THE WAKING DREAM

As our Cassette e.p eventually found its way onto stereos

around the country, word was finally getting around about the band and the music, especially from the specialist/cult record shops that were popping up all over the land and doing very good business with mail order sales. Although psychedelic music was no longer 'hip' in the eyes of the music media there was a growing popularity underground and some of the '60's rarities were fetching big money, even then... creating a need for modern bands sympathetic to the music of the era...

And so it was that we got a call from such a store in Margate called 'Funhouse Records', who also happened to have their own label called 'Psycho Records' which specialised in re-releasing classic 'lost' psych albums and showcasing newer bands. They'd already released stuff by bands such as The Mood Six who specialised in the authentic Seeds/Misunderstood garage/psych vibe... we weren't quite that easy to pigeonhole, but nonetheless to their credit they offered us the chance to record two of our tracks for a forthcoming compilation of new bands like us, The Mood Six and The Green Telescope among others and it was to be called 'The Waking Dream'. They would put us into a top studio in London and the deal was that whoever got the best feedback from the punters when it was released would get an album out in their own right. This was very exciting news for us, not only were we going into a posh studio at someone else's expense but we were going to see two of our tracks released on vinyl for the first ever time...

We laid down our tracks fairly easily, as was to happen in the future, the engineer seemed most pleased to have a band in that he could have fun with as far as sound and textures went (and he could have a puff with us too) I think he'd had a lot of straight pop stuff going on at the time.. the two tracks we chose were..

Magick Eye - No surprises there, it was still our most popular track and with the addition of Mykl on keyboards and vocals the sound was really fattening out.

Wide Eyed & Electrick - Another live favourite, with a very driving beat, chugging rhythms and sci-fi lyrics this one was also good for audience participation!

We were so excited to get our copies of the album we almost burst. The mixes were great and all personal bias aside, I really thought that we shone out among the other bands on there. Our first major disappointment was that we never got a chance to do a full album with Funhouse, they were really nice people and had a good distribution network set up, but whenever we asked them about it they were evasive and non-commital. More fool them really because during one of our shows, Kim spotted John Peel in the audience and gave him a copy of the album. He thanked her and promised to give it a listen, which he duly did and played the tracks on his evening show and was full of nothing but praise for us and what we were doing. He was always very supportive of us, I think we took him back to his Radio Caroline 'Perfumed Garden' days... it was a great loss for the music scene when he died..

We also (shock, horror, probe!) got a good review in the music weekly 'Sounds' who said that we were the most promising of all the bands on the l.p... this gave us a real lift and we were beginning to think that all the hard work had been worth it....

IF YOU LIKE A LOT OF CHOCOLATE ON YOUR BISCUIT JOIN OUR CLUB

As previously mentioned, we'd 'broken' London and played at the usual suspects, but now there was a growing underground (pun intended) interest in the 'sixties/acid/festival vibe, and as had happened originally, suddenly there became a sprouting of psychedelic nightclubs with full-on cosmic lightshows, packed to the gills with 'groovy' people, hippies, psychedelic bikers, wheelers and dealers, TV monitors with old groovy sixties movies, incense burning, DJ jamming on the Electric Prunes, Sky Saxon etc. Far out!!... excellent!! I'd missed most of it first time around, but for a while there I really got a taste of what it must have been like, maybe minus the initial thrill of it never having been done before... but much fun none the less. As was the way with thrilling 'new' scenes in London, a lot of clubs came and went (and we played at most of them!), they all had great names like 'The Amazing Marshmallow Planet' (ok, I made that one up, but you get my drift...) and there was also a huge influx of hippy flavoured 'fanzines', a leftover from the old punk days, when hastily xeroxed A4 sheets of paper were stapled together and touted at suitable gigs, only instead of cut out newspaper print lettering a la 'ransom note' stylee (a popular punk font) there was poetry, new age noodlings, swirly, twirly acid laced illustrations and, great news for the bands, record and gig reviews. Any kind of 'press' coverage was pretty thin on the ground for us at that time, the music press just chose to ignore the scene.. ya see, they'd spent so much effort on searching for that elusive revolutionary new musical craze that was just around the corner that they virtually wrote off a lot of very good bands and pretty much the scene in general.. denying the inevitable onslaught of ageing will do that to a person... anyway, I digress....There were however three London clubs in particular that thrived, embraced the whole scene and managed to outlive many pretenders to the throne....

CLUB DOG

Run by the very amiable Bob and Michael Dog (I don't think that was their real surname... they didn't even look like brothers). Our first encounter with them was when they invited us to play at their first location in North London, Finchley way if I recall correctly.. Even at our first show with them we were introduced to and impressed by their army of helpers, luggers and sorter out-ers.. after numerous pub/club gigs with unhelpful promoters and disinterested landlords, we were pleasantly surprised with their powers of organisation.... a regular little troop of dog soldiers. The sound systems were always excellent and their in-house psychedelic lighting and hangings perfectly complimented our own.. we went on to do a few one-off special shows for them (we played at a squat for them once and in 'Smash Hits' magazine the following month, then rising 'acid house' star Adamski had said that he'd seen us perform there and found us 'interesting') and we were to become regulars at their most popular venue the 'George Robey' (I know, I know, duff name and the dressing room was a cupboard behind the stage that smelt of piss and stale beer, but the vibe there was fantastic and it was always packed), ironically located dead opposite the old 'Rainbow' theatre in Finsbury Park.. stuff of legends..

Club Dog also became a very good outlet for our music as they had a 'merchandise' stall at their shows selling all types of hippy paraphernalia, part of which was devoted to the music, favoured medium being the ever-growing inventory of home-produced cassettes of bands fresh to the scene, including ourselves, although at that time we'd been one of the few to actually have anything released on vinyl. They also developed a very successful mail-order service and eventually their own record label too...

In later years with the advent of the 'ambient/ethno/trance' club scene they were to blossom into the now infamous 'Mega-dog', doing huge tours around the UK and Europe featuring among others, Ozric Tentacles offshoot 'Eat Static' and Magic Mushroom Band offshoot 'Astralasia'... more about that later....

THE CRYPT

Whereas the Club Dog shows were pretty much held at 'regular' venues, nothing could have prepared us for our first show at 'The Crypt'. It was run by Andrew, the most unlikeliest of psychedelic promoters. He was a bulky, tough looking ex-cop (of all things!) and held his club in the crypt of a church in deepest, darkest Deptford. He'd picked up on the burgeoning scene and wanted in on it. I'd always assumed he saw it as potential cash cow, but I'll tell ya, for such a shady character, you know the type, Range Rover, sheepskin coat a la Arthur Daley and a bevy of heavies in tuxedos with broken noses and a complete pain in the arse at the end of the night when ya wanted to get paid and fuck off home, somehow he managed to put on some of the furthest out, space warped, cosmic mindfuck events that I've ever witnessed. He'd managed to persuade the church owners to let him run an all-night psychedelic club every friday night from 8:00 in the evening until 8:00 the next morning. Now, I ain't talking 'bout no deconsecrated ex-church here folks, this one was still 'live an' kicking', unlike the occupants on the other side of the ancient crypt's walls who were very much dead. Doesn't sound like the ideal place to do a trip does it? It was tho', the whole thing was always a trip.. good or bad.. fit to burst with the furthest out freaks, goths and just out and out weirdos.. cosmic chaos... we'd get so out of it...

Lacking though it often was on the organisational side of things, he always advertised well and brought many punters in. It was always full... very full... probably illegally full, what with there being only one way in and out through the old oak crypt door which was studiously guarded by his heavies, as much intent on keeping the cops out as the punters in. Also being a crypt there were no windows (read air) and it wasn't long before all we were breathing all night were dope, beer, vomit and B.O fumes. The stage lighting was minimal to say the least, at one point part of their lighting rig caught fire, luckily it was during our soundcheck before the punters had got in and we also had to provide our own p.a (not always the best idea... it was always dodgy as hell... often blowing up completely!!) which we did for many shows there, somehow cobbling it all together, until a member of the audience was caught leaving during one of our shows with one of our p.a speakers under his arm. He'd just disconnected it while we were playing and the space pilot at the mixing desk hadn't even noticed... from that point on we demanded that a p.a had to be provided!!
So many crazy occurrences there, but one particular night just

has to be recorded for posterity. So I think I'll call it....

THE ATTACK OF THE PSYCHEDELIC MUSHROOM VOMIT VAN

By this time, the dear ol' Luton van had given up the ghost and was retained for storage purposes only. From that point on, after numerous white knuckle journeys in said vehicle, we all agreed that we should at least have the privilege of hiring a decent van, seeing as how we were getting regular gigs by then and could just about cover its cost (most of the time!) and still have a bit left over for petrol money for the other vehicles involved. Fortunately for me, there was a van hire place exactly over the road from where I lived and once they learned that I was a musician they were quite happy to hire me any manner of van, which they did for many years to follow, as long as it was back in the yard by eight o' clock the following morning, relatively clean and preferably undamaged... this was the case most of the time...

Friday afternoon, the day of a Crypt gig and time to pick up the rest of the motley crew; band members, their girlfriends, lightshow, their girlfriends, various roadies/hangers on and, you guessed it, their girlfriends..... and Dave. Now this particular Dave (you know who you are and so do we) I've known since the Farnham Close years (see previous story) and as party animals went, he was right up there with the best of them... Never one to say no, to anything, he would consume all and sundry and get as out of it as was (sub)humanly possible, then he'd get drunk. Always fun at parties/weddings/bar mitzvahs etc. craziness was always guaranteed when Dave was in the house.. He'd started early that day and continued going for it as it progressed, I remember us all thinking that he was going to be pretty crazy later.

It was a particularly good night, I remember that much. The crowd was great, vibe was good, nothing got stolen and occasional sightings of Dave confirmed that he was truly getting into the spirit of things, a large spliff in one hand and a beer in the other.. he did disappear for a while but we discovered that he'd just wobbled down to a local kebab shop to sate his growing munchie pangs... Come time to leave, about six in the morning, the crowd had all gone home, I'd finally managed to prise some money out of the promoter's tight little fist, and we wearily packed our gear and assorted bodies into the van and set off for the long road home... By that time, Dave's face had turned a distinct shade of green and due to the amount of passengers in the back and assorted equipment, I deemed it wise to not fully pull the shutter down all the way, leaving a gap of about two feet for a bit of air circulation.

The deal with the fuel situation for the hire van was that I should return it to the yard empty, and as usual I had totally miscalculated the mileage and was in need of an urgent fuel stop. In those days (God I sound old!) all night petrol stations were few and far between and it was getting a bit hairy for a while before I eventually found one open. I swung into the forecourt and found a suitable pump, but before I could get the nozzle into the van a voice boomed out over the tannoy in finest Hindu English "You cannot be filling up there, the pump is inactive, use the one further back sir, please". So, I checked the mirrors, started to reverse back and suddenly there was a loud CLUNNNKK!!! followed by shouts and screams. As I stepped out of the van, it was like stepping into 'Chaos-World', my semi-sleepy casual drive back through sleepy London town suddenly became the stuff of nightmares with a bit of Cheech & Chong thrown in for good measure!

It seems that in the time it took for me to get back into the van and start reversing, a mini cab driver had pulled in behind me and I'd reversed right into him. I was first greeted by the sight of one pissed off Greek taxi driver ranting and raving and pointing out the smashed front indicator on his car, while at the same time trying to blame me for the rusty scratches on his bumper, threatening to call the police and trying to get the petrol pump attendant's attention. I tried to offer him some money to replace the indicator lens but he wanted us arrested and hung at least.. That was bad enough, but I then noticed a severely green Dave fall out of the back of the van, lunge past us and onto the forecourt, throwing up everywhere as he did so. Apparently he'd spent most of that journey hanging out of the back of the van, spewing as we went and he was quickly followed out of the van by all the other grossed out passengers. So there we were, the angry cabbie, the panicking petrol station employee and the spaced out mushroom freaks. As the cabbie called once more for the police to be contacted, a patrol car happened by. My heart sank as I saw the cop almost drive past, stop and reverse back and into the petrol station with a somewhat bemused look upon his face. As I looked around at us raggle-taggle hairy bunch of misfits (and our girlfriends), I remembered that we'd been having fun earlier with fluorescent fingernail paint and we all sported various fluorescent shades, no point trying to pretend we were normal citizens then... shit.. we were fucked!! As the cop car approached, the cabbie and I both made a bee line over to him, trying to get our side of the story to him first. Being an angry Greek, the cabbie got there first, almost pulling the cop out of his car. "You, poliss! Arrest thiss pipple!! Look wha they do to my cab?!" The cop, obviously coming to the end of a long nightshift, didn't seem too impressed with the pushiness of the cab driver and raised his hand to shut him up. "Tell me" the cop said "Did this chap here offer to pay for the damage to the lens??" "Yes" replied the cabbie "But I wouldn't accept it!" "Why not?" said the cop "Seems like the logical thing to do to me.." and with that the cabbie put his face right up to him and said "Well mite, how do I know thass liggal???". For some reason unknown to me, but I wasn't complaining, this seemed to really piss the cop off. Suddenly he's got the cabbie sprawled over his bonnet, searching him, everyone's freaking out, Dave meantime had been vomiting constantly in the background while all this was occurring, and just when I thought the moment couldn't get any more surreal, the cop turned to me and said "It's ok sir, I've got the situation under control. You tried to do the right thing by offering to cover his damages and more fool him for turning it down. Gather up your friends and head home... I'll take it from here" and as we pulled away, I glanced back in the mirror and saw him tearing into the cabbie, checking the tyre treads, tax disc etc. I drove that van from the scene as quick as legally possible, only this time the back shutter was firmly secured.....

GO ASK ALICE

Not long after the Crypt gigs started up, we were contacted by another London club that was growing in popularity. Called (appropriately enough) Alice in Wonderland, it was held every week at a (usually) trendy nightclub in Soho called 'Gossips' (weren't those 'eighties nightclub names just horrendous??). Run by the very affable Christian (his name, not his denomination!) and partner in crime Clive, who apart from being resident DJ, was better known as the doctor in Doctor and the Medics, who were pretty much the house band there. They were always a good fun band live and like us they had two girlie singers and we always got on well when we played together.

If I had to compare the Crypt and Alice in Wonderland to their 'sixties counterparts then the Crypt had the squalid element of the Roundhouse, while Alice in Wonderland was more like the UFO. This was where the beautiful people hung out and if you went there, you dressed up for the part. The music had more of a garage punk vibe, so we'd ditch the reggae tunes to keep more into the spirit of things. The club was always decked out real nice, with lots of ultra violet lighting, projections and movie screens on the go. We always really enjoyed playing at Alice in Wonderland, but getting there and finding a parking space was something else tho'!!!

MYSTERY TRIPPIN'

As word got around about the club, they decided that there

was enough interest to embark on a very ambitious, but hugely successful venture called 'The Mystery Trip'. As the name suggests, they would sell tickets to an unknown (to the punters) destination, which included a train ticket, arrange a convenient meeting point and the rest would become apparent as the day unfolded. I didn't go to the first one, for reasons which escape me now, but it was a huge success and a sequel was well on the cards. Of course, the second one had to be bigger and better and they really pulled the stops out. When the call came inviting us to play, we jumped at the chance!! The venue was such a well-guarded secret that none of the bands playing were told of its location until a couple of nights before the event! The call eventually came through and we were informed that the venue was to be a disused 'Butlins' holiday camp in Clacton (of all places, not exactly the centre of the rock n' roll universe... or so we thought...). In hindsight it actually made really good sense... those sort of holiday places had had their hey-day in the 50's/60's/70's (as I can attest!) and with the cheap bargain-bucket flights becoming available to far more exotic locations such as Spain, Ibiza etc. they just couldn't compete. Hence these huge, sprawling derelict sites like the Clacton one, with bars, concert hall etc. sitting there gathering dust and in the case of the Clacton one it was occasionally hired for the odd 'Rock n' roll Revival' shows and that was about it.

Come the day of action, we set about gathering the entourage and set sails for Clacton. We had to get there early as we were one of the last bands on and as was often the case, we had to be one of the first bands to soundcheck. It's a cruel system, especially for an all-nighter, but we suffer for our art... We arrived in sunny(ish) Clacton mid-morning and after a bit of searching found the holiday camp. We pulled into the entrance past the rusting gates hanging limp from their hinges faded from neglect and headed for the loading area of the hall. Christian and Clive were both there to greet us, as were a (most welcome) army of helpers and humpers. As we entered the main hall we were blown away by the decor. These guys had indeed pulled all the stops out and there were hangings

The Moonboot and the Oz
circa 1986

and projection and TV screens and a multitude of lightshows, including our own. It looked like we were in for a fun time!

The line up for the day/night was also very impressive, by this time a lot more bands had sprung up playing music that was complimentary to ours and the Ozrics, most of them had played with us already either at the Crypt, Alice in Wonderland or festivals. There was 'The Treatment' from London, a wacky band of drug-crazed minstrels who played a wild selection of punky/festival/psychedelic/garage surf music. I loved their stuff, them was some wild and crazy guys!! From Cornwall we had trippy/trancy riffola courtesy of 'Webcore' and their ambient off-shoot 'Another Green World'. There were many more bands and acts/performing artists etc. but it's all a bit of a blur to me now. Head ('scuse the pun) band for the night though had to be Dr and the Medics who were on their meteoric rise to fame (eventually reaching number one in the singles charts with their version of 'Spirit in the Sky') and after all the effort Clive et al had put into this event, we certainly weren't grumbling.

After a most painless soundcheck, we decided to head on down to the beach while the crew got on with the rest of the organising. It was really nice just strolling around the promenade and a really nice way to wind down before the event began. When we got back though, we couldn't believe the transformation! By now the (many) punters had arrived and the lights were on and globulating over the backdrops and there was a real buzz in the air. As the day wore on (and normality wore off!), we'd dug a few bands and had many wanders around the venue, including one to where the old swimming pool lie dormant and empty apart from the lone figure of Clive, frontman for The Treatment sitting on a statue at its edge blowing on a bugle to nobody in particular! The face painters were doing good trade and there was a lot of dressing up which really added to the surrealism of the event. At one point, Kim and I were approached by a space girl with a green face and alien clothes trying to convince us that her husband was this jelly which she carried around in a plastic bucket.

When we said that we weren't convinced that she would have married a jelly, she merely replied that it was the shape he took when in contact with our planet's atmosphere!! I think, no, hope, that she was one of the entertainers.... but who can say????

THE POLITICS OF ECSTASY

What with the excitement of the reaction to our tracks on the 'Waking Dream' compilation and the ensuing disappointment when the chance of an album of our own with Psycho records didn't materialise, we were itching to get back into a studio and lay down tracks for our debut release. I sent numerous demos to umpteen record companies but didn't get one positive reaction, like the music press they were so far up their own bums they couldn't see our potential, being far too busy trying to create 'new' scenes of their own. It was a very frustrating time for us, but eventually we got to hear about a company in Reading who had expressed an interest in releasing an album. This was music to our ears! Not only had they contacted us, thus showing some level of enthusiasm, but they were just up the road from us. The company was called 'Pagan Records' and ours was to be their first ever release at their 'newly installed'/'state of the art' eight-track recording studio. The head honcho had regaled us with tales of his workings with Kate Bush and Peter Gabriel among others, plus they had just taken delivery of an Ensonique Mirage, one of the first ever studio quality 'sampling' machines. We'd heard about such a machine, but never in our wildest dreams did we ever imagine getting the use of one for our own recordings. The deal was that they would put up all the money to cover recording, pressing, cover art etc. and once those expenses were covered the remainder of the profits would go to us!

Sounds almost too good to be true, eh? Read on....

We were so excited at the prospect of getting into the studio, we had numerous meetings and organised what tracks to lay down. Come our first day, we packed up our gear and headed off to sunny Reading with a hastily drawn map of the studio's location in our hot, sweaty little hands. When we eventually found it, we were a little taken aback.. sure, it was a big, old victorian town house in the heart of Reading, but it was in a residential street, but we assumed that with such hi-tech credentials, they would have spared no expense in sound proofing the joint. Upon entering through the large, oak front door, we were greeted by Steve and Mike Pagan and ushered through to the 'recording area'. Our first impression was that although it was a pretty big, posh house it was more than a little dilapidated and the inside was full of junk and shit, everywhere we looked. There was dust and cobwebs everywhere, now I'm not the most house-proud of people, but this was a supposedly 'hi-tech' studio remember... the further we ventured in, the more the alarm bells were beginning to ring... but, all the expenses were being covered, it was all there on a plate, we just had to get the tracks down and let the record company do their thing.

The 'recording room' turned out to be an empty bedroom at the back of the house, with a hole knocked through to the dining room and a picture window put in. The recording console itself was situated in the dining room on an old dining table. You know how when you're really looking forward to something and you can't help but visualise what it'll be like (this happened to me with gigs always) and it somehow doesn't turn out how you imagined? This was turning into a prime example of that... the eight-track machine was covered in dust, with plates of old food and dirty coffee cups all around it, full to the brim ashtrays resting on the mixing desk... the place was a pig sty. But, like I say, we were in no position to be picky so we decided to go for it and duly unpacked our equipment.

The arrangement was that we had total control over the content, Steve Pagan himself would record the tracks and we would be in charge of the mixing (seems like a good idea, but think about the prospect of letting a bunch of inexperienced stoners loose at the mixing desk). As is the norm, bass and drums were to be laid down first, so as Jim and Wayne were setting up, our 'recording engineer' busied himself moving ashtrays and dinner plates out of the way to gain access to the equipment. Right from the start we were questioning the attendant hiss that, even to our untrained ears, seemed more than a little noticeable as the recordings commenced. That was the first time we were to hear those immortal words 'Don't worry, we'll lose all that in the mix!', trust me, if a recording engineer utters those words, get the hell out of there! We didn't.

The Pagans were strange characters themselves, the lanky, gangly, scruffy Steve bearing more than a passing resemblance to Shaggy from Scooby Doo and his partner Mike a rather rotund, greasy, beardy oik who laughed a lot at his own jokes, which was good because we couldn't understand him through his large greasy beard. There were no time limits put on us, but it soon became apparent that late night sessions were to be avoided at all costs, as on numerous occasions we'd be listening back to tracks with Steve at the helm, only to be greeted by the scary sight of Mike bursting through the door naked, having just stomped down the stairs from his bedroom unable to sleep due to the excessive noise emanating from the dining room (I guess the sound-proofing wasn't that hi-tech after all). It wasn't a pretty sight as he'd stand there stark bollock naked, layers of greasy fat shading his diminutive manhood hanging around just a bit too long after he'd made his point, scary stuff for us guys but potentially damaging for the girls!!

As the sessions wore on, it became more and more chaotic. The frustration was beginning to set in, sound levels of the individual recordings were all over the place, that ever present hiss seemed to get louder with every overdub and we began to notice an ever present whining sound that came and went during the tracks. We were told (after the recordings were finished) that it was due to their washing machine (?!) being on at the time and not to worry as... you guessed it.... he'd lose it in the mix. We were getting well out of our depth and even we knew that these weren't going to end up as crystal clear representations of our works, so we decided what the hell, we'd psychedelicise the recordings, in a way similar to how the reggae dub masters did it, and add lots of echo and sound effects, also the sampler got used a lot, maybe on reflection a little too much, but we were desperately trying to salvage the mess into some kind of listenable material. We eventually managed to (somehow) get a halfway decent mix of the tracks together and were happy to leave it at that, all agreeing that it was the best we could do considering the circumstances. The Pagans agreed, but when we next came back to the studio we discovered that Steve had run the whole thing through an 'aural exciter' to 'give it a bit more pep' according to him, but what it did in fact was make everything really toppy and tinny, but he insisted that it was needed and so we left it at that.

The next revelation was that we were going to have the master cut at Abbey Road studios! Now, for most bands that would be the ultimate accolade, in fact most people would have given their left nut (or whatever) to be in that situation. We, however, were more than a little apprehensive about the prospect, but hey ho, can't look a gift horse in the mouth. After looning about on the zebra crossing outside the studios for some time we entered the hallowed halls and after wiping off any food stains/cigarette ash from its cover, presented the engineer with the master tape. I forget the engineer's name, but he was intrigued by our name and style of music and impressed us with tales of how he'd produced and cut all the Pink Floyd albums etc. but any interest he showed in us soon waned as he played the master tape. 'What the hell is all that hiss?' we explained that our engineer had promised it would be lost in the mix - it wasn't. 'What the hell is that whining sound?' we again explained that it was their washing machine, much to his surprise! But worst of all, he turned to us and said 'Wait a minute, has an Aural Exciter been used on this?' we confirmed his fears to which he replied 'with everything put through that, by the time it's cut it's going to sound like shit!' but, we were in too deep to turn back and we spent the rest of the session cringing and blushing every time he picked up on one of the many sound 'discrepancies'. We left that place with our tails between our legs, not impressed with our record company at all and smarting from all of the hurtful criticisms....

But, there it was, our first album 'in the can' as it were... the next time we'd hear it would be on a test pressing of the vinyl. Being the democratic bunch that we were, it was put to the vote as to the design of the album sleeve. The end result (an anatomical diagram of a man and some obscure far eastern symbols - I think some members of the camp thought a more modern design would bring us screaming into the '80's) wouldn't have been my first choice, I was hoping for something more along the lines of a Grateful Dead style cover, we'd had a young chap that we named 'Dan the Man' draw up some amazing posters for us, featuring some superb psychedelic art work, but like I say, it was put to the vote and I lost. At least we all agreed on the title.. a familiar phrase to those that we hoped would appreciate our stuff... We did however, include a poster featuring Dan's art with the album.

After a few disasters with the vinyl pressings, we then discovered that there wasn't actually any kind of distribution arranged by the Pagans, all the boxes of albums were stored in one of the bedrooms in their house, so we took some and did the rounds of the local 'indie' record shops (the big stores wouldn't touch 'em) and also sold them at our gigs and festivals. After many a heated discussion with the record company, we agreed to part company and so all that were ever pressed were the first batch of 1000, about 200 of which were either warped or had the label stuck halfway across the tracks, so in reality there's probably only about 800 copies out there somewhere, if that.... making it highly collectable... although that wasn't the original intention!!

THE PIT & THE PANDEMONIUM

By the early-mid 'Eighties, Punk's influence was still abound but by then it had mutated into many variations. There were the poppier, spiky-haired , new-wave commercial acts on 'Top of the Pops', hell, even the mainstream had punks in TV commercials or comedy sketches (don't even mention 'The Young Ones'!! I used to have kids shouting 'Hey Neil!!' at me and then running away...) and then there were the more hardcore punks. Bands like the Exploited, New Model Army and Crass were at the forefront of the radical, anarchistic scene (boy, they really took the 'Anarchy in the U.K' message to the max, eh?). By then it had aligned itself with the more radically inclined hippy/freak faction via Stonehenge and various squatted venues around London. One such venue was a cinema in Westbourne Park, just down the road from Notting Hill Gate and we were invited to do a gig there by the Crass organisation who were its current squatters.

As previously mentioned, we were using 'hire-vans' for every gig. I'd gotten too paranoid about driving around in a clapped-out old Luton van with no MOT and an old beer mat for a tax disc. As was to be expected, the show was a 'benefit' gig and so we all agreed to swallow the expenses and just have a good time. I'll tell ya, as much as I loved playing in London, I always used to dread travelling there, because we'd always have to try to get there right during rush hour. It was even harder when we didn't know where the venue was. As usual the A-Z was about as useful as a parchment covered in Egyptian hieroglyphics and it was more by chance than anything else that we actually found the place. Lucky for us that we arrived late that night, as the police had just busted the cinema and taken away its occupants. We were just about to turn around and drive home, when this freak who recognised us came over and said that although the place had been raided, the whole gig was moving to an area under the Westway flyover at Paddington. He gave us directions and off we headed, we figured that what the hell, we'd already committed ourselves to the hire van, why not have some fun?

The place was pretty easy to find, we just followed the lines of punters as they walked from the cinema to the new location. As was usually the case in those kind of situations, the spirit of the venture was formidable but the organisation often seemed to delegate itself out of existence, too many chiefs methinx. And so, when we arrived we were met by a large amount of eager punters standing around in what looked like a large concrete bunker underneath the Westway flyover. Standing around in darkness and an eerie silence unfortunately, as the generators and p.a were still to be 'organised'. By this time, we'd all been travelling for a long time, cramped up in the van during rush hour traffic, so we couldn't wait to get out and stretch our legs. I swung the van 'round to the perimeter of the bunker and parked up. The long journey and subsequent waiting had taken its toll on my bladder and I was seriously desperate for a piss. Not wanting to be seen pissing in the only available light which was populated by lots of eager punters wondering what the hell was going on, I opted to find my way in the darkness in search of a suitable, private place to piss.

Off I wandered, into the darkness, the murmur of the expectant crowd and dim lights fading as I wandered ever on into the inky blackness that awaited me. I'd decided to look for the nearest vertical surface 'pon which to piss against as it would help me keep my 'bearings' and up ahead I could just make out the faint outline of one of the large concrete columns that supported the flyover. Upon reaching for my zipper I remembered that as it was the middle of winter, I'd decided to wear my Black plastic imitation leatherette 'stage' jeans (very popular at the time, honest judge!) under my army surplus 'boiler' suit, so I could change into my stage gear without having to reveal too much flesh to the cold London air. A nice idea in theory, very practical. Unless you happen to be fumbling around in the dark with the multitude of buttons and zippers that presented themselves, stumbling along until suddenly, nothing... no ground... gone beneath my feet! One minute I was walking along, the next I was falling, falling, deep and deeper into this dark pit.

Suddenly there was a large, painful jolt as I realised that I was falling down a large hole and I had just bashed my coccyx on the edge of said hole as I fell. The next thing I knew I came to at the bottom of the hole, which turned out to be a large moat-type structure that surrounded the column. My legs seemed to be all wrapped and twisted around some sort of piping that was at the bottom of the pit and the pain coming from the base of my spine was unbearable. Somehow (read: not wanting to be stuck in a hole under the Westway flyover for the rest of my life) I managed to summon the strength to drag my broken body up to the surface and crawl toward the light. I was beginning to phase in and out with the pain, but I could just make out in the distance the unmistakable silhouettes of roadies Kelvin and Steve. With a few feeble cries of "heeelllpppp mmeeee..." I managed to attract their attention and they came running over to get me. The guys carried me over to the van and lifted me into the back, there was no way I could have performed that night and so we decided to cut our losses and get the hell out of there before anything else happened.

Before long we were on the M4 headed for home. Although I knew I needed to go directly to a hospital, I didn't want to go one in London, I wanted to be closer to home, so we headed for Ascot's Heatherwood hospital which was just down the road from where we lived.... The van pulled up outside the emergency entrance and the guys went into find some porters with a trolley for me. Apparently, because we'd arrived at the emergency department in our own vehicle and not an ambulance, the porters weren't covered and so they wouldn't take the responsibility of taking me out of the van. The guys carried me in and I was put into a temporary cubicle. Kim and I told the rest of the guys to take the van home, as it looked like we'd be in for a long night. Kim stayed right by me, she was worried about me and was good company and a welcome distraction from the pain. Of course, I still hadn't got to have my pee and when a nurse eventually poked her head around the curtain to see if there was anything I needed, I urgently requested some kind of pot to pee in before I added to my physical discomfort.. she came back not long after with a small polystyrene container rather like an egg carton but with a large funnel-type shape at the top. Nice invention I thought, but I soon realised that there was more to my predicament than I'd originally thought. After finally discovering the right sequence of buttons and zippers that released my long-suffering dick into the fresh air, I came upon the realisation that my back felt paralysed.. it was jarred and there was no way that I was going to be able to sit up and pee into that little polystyrene container. So, with a little shuffling and some pretty impressive dexterity on my part, I lay there on my back, pissing up into the air and catching the stream of urine as gravity got the better of it and it started heading back down towards me again... Somehow I managed to get it all in without spilling a drop! I impressed myself!...

Next up was a visit to the X-Ray room. Kim followed me in as I was wheeled on my trolley through some corridors into the X-Ray department. As I lay there they took many X-Rays, but then a doctor said for me to sit up so they could take further shots. I told them that I was flat on my back because the pain was too intense for me to move, but he insisted that I do it. I tried my hardest to get upright but the pain was just too much and the next thing I knew, I came to on the floor looking up at Kim as she leaned over me in a state of panic.. I'd just blacked out with the pain and as Kim helped me up, we could hear the doctor getting a bollocking from one of his superiors. I was taken into the 'back injury' ward and told that I'd have to stay in for the night and be kept under observation. Unfortunately, the 'bad back' ward also happened to be the 'geriatric' ward and I had to spend the night with all the very eldery patients... coughing and wheezing and dying all around me.. there was one old git in the bed opposite me, who was snoring so loudly all night that at one point I shouted out "Fer Chrissakes, will ya shaddup?!?!" He stopped suddenly and I was then greeted by an eerie silence.. nothing... nary a whistling nostril.. "Ohmighod!" I thought.. maybe I'd killed him by shouting at him.. but, with a cough and a fart he kickstarted himself back into the land of the living and once the drugs kicked in I eventually dropped off into a deep slumber... I was sent home the following day, but was laid out for weeks unable to move. I even had to miss a couple of gigs, some were cancelled but the others showcased a very make-shift Magic Mushroom Band featuring Mykl on vocals with the girls and some good impromptu jamming. It was very brave of the guys and gals to do those gigs, but the show must go on!!! As I improved I got back into it but had to walk with a stick for a month...

NOT NECESSARILY STONED, BUT BEAUTIFUL

Ok, so our first album was 'released'. Not quite the blockbuster we'd (naively) hoped it would be, but we had an album out nonetheless. Things fared a lot better with our gigs, the venues were getting larger and the audiences growing to suit. Promoters were getting wise to the fact that this motley bunch of musicians and other bands of a similar vein were actually puling in decent-sized crowds. None more than wily entrepreneur Andrew of The Crypt, who decided it was time to take his roster of bands out on tour. The first I heard of it was when I got an excited call from him...

"Garry, I've booked a nationwide tour and I thought that what with all the trouble at Stonehenge, I'd make them 'benefit' shows. I've called it the 'Stoned Out of Your Head' tour... geddit?"

I couldn't believe it... especially from the mouth of an ex-cop!! Jeez, we weren't exactly a low-profile act at the best of times and this would be about as subtle as a brick between the eyes.. but the tour was booked and advertised (something I have to give credit to the promoter for, he did a great job on that side of things) and there it was, in print in all the music papers the next week. The venues were all of a decent size and together with bands like the Ozric Tentacles, Webcore, The Treatment among others as well as our accumulated lightshows we played some great shows mostly to capacity, appreciative audiences..

Luckily dramas were kept to a minimum during the tour, give or take the odd crowd of angry christians waving placards and complaining vigorously outside the venue at some of our shows... Actually there was one place we played at in the East End of London, another big, old church. It was a huge, sprawling gothic building with a multitude of large halls and once we'd set up and soundchecked, we decided to go and have a look around. We left the legion of lighting riggers, sound engineers and the seemingly endless army of 'lock, stock and two barrels' bouncers in monkey suits that accompanied Andrew wherever he roamed and set off down a dark, dusty corridor.. We eventually came to a large doorway and as we entered we discovered yet another large hall with gilded woodwork and huge stained glass windows adorned with godly motifs... it was truly beautiful, but totally empty and best of all there was at one end probably the biggest, badass pipe organ I'd ever seen, it was huuuuge!!! A real 'phantom of the opera' job with pipes that reached up to the sky almost touching God himself.. So of course a few of us jumped straight on it in a vain attempt to merge some great gospel jazz with maybe a little bit of 'chopsticks' and as fingers hit keys it suddenly struck out with this huge sound, followed by more huge sound as the keys had stuck together and it was now howling at a million zegawatts (real loud) and we couldn't release the keys as by that time we'd hauled ass out of there quicksmart and were wandering around backstage trying to look like we'd been there all the time...

But no, the real dramas were saving themselves for the big finale show at the Clarendon Hotel in Hammersmith, London....

This was gonna be one huge affair, it was very well advertised and the Clarendon was an excellent venue for size and location. It got even better when I got a phone call from John Peel of all people who asked me if he and a photographer could come down and interview us and take a few photos for the Observer newspaper! That was great news, John was good to us and I'm honoured to have met him..

All the bands that had done the tour were on the bill with the addition of new kids on the block Zodiac Mindwarp & The Love Reaction. They'd got a break through their Alice In Wonderland and Miles Copeland connection and were getting good press. They looked and sounded pretty cool in a kinda Groovy Acid Biker style and I thought it'd be nice to meet 'em. Well, they weren't that cool when they turned up, in fact they were pretty cold, snotty and more than a little precious, so I wasn't surprised when I heard that they were throwing a tantrum because we were headlining and they wanted to go on at that time.. ah, what the hell... we jiggled it about a bit. Come opening time, the queue was stretched right around the block, it was an amazing turn out, made even more amazing by the fact that all day it had been absolutely pissing it down, I mean real big time cats and dogs, constant. We had a little merchandise stall and our roadies Steve and Kelvin were selling albums, badges and posters by the bucketload...

After wandering around and digging the scene for a while we set up camp in our surprisingly spacious dressing room in readiness for the impending arrival of the esteemed Mr Peel. The Observer's photographer had arrived already and taken some great shots of us, all professional like... so we waited... and waited.. and waited, until it was time for us to go on. We played a great set that night, the audience was fantastic and judging by the amount of 'Magick Eye!!' chants that were emanating from the crowd, it began to dawn on me that all our hard work over the past few years had not been in vain and that there were people out there really digging us.. that felt great! We did a few encores and made our way sweaty but happy back to the dressing room. Still no Mr Peel! He phoned me a couple of days later to apologise, saying that all the heavy rain that night had flooded his farmhouse in Oxfordshire and he physically couldn't drive anywhere, bummer!! It wasn't his fault, you could only blame it on the elements but, fuck!! Why'd it have to happen then??

Not to worry though, we'd heard from a reliable source that a journalist from 'Sounds' magazine was at the show and so we looked forward to a good review of the event. Anybody who was there couldn't have failed to have been impressed by all the bands and the presentation of the whole thing.. unless you're a 'Sounds' reporter who sits through a whole set by the avant-garde psycho/punkers The Treatment absolutely hating it and thinking it's the Magic Mushroom Band. Yep, I know our performance times were changed around a bit, but it wouldn't have taken a lot of investigative journalism to find out who the band currently playing were... really! So, as we eagerly opened our 'Sounds' magazine later that week, we were greeted with probably our worst ever live review.. ooh it was scathing, he hated it! He said we were tuneless and grating to the ears.. just the sort of review we needed! I couldn't believe it... I was stunned.. we'd played great that night and the people loved it, I felt like king of the world.. As it turned out, I got a very apologetic call from Sounds, explaining what had happened and the following week they printed an apology, blaming it on something that was slipped into the reporters drink...

GUDBUY T' JANE, ROGER & OUT

As is the way in life and in the music world in particular, people come and go and our forever changing line-up was testament to that. For reasons personal and professional, Jane Reaction departed the band. This was a particularly sad thing for me and Kim as by then Jane was family, she had virtually lived with us over the past few years and was (and is) a very dear friend. Happily though, Janey didn't disappear into obscurity, rather she reinvented herself as Nana Obscuri and through then boyfriend Joie met and performed with the Ullulators, Cheap Suit O'Roonies and released her personal 'Evil Edna's Horror Toilet' concept (!) album which Kim and I guested on. In later years she would go on to be one of the key stage organisers at the Glastonbury Festival. We decided not to replace Janey as Mykl was keen to sing and he had a high voice anyway (he wasn't as pretty though).

Not long after, Roger too left the fold. He worked long hours at his job and as the band got busier he struggled to keep a balance. Also, it must be said, he'd made numerous complaints about our onstage guitar volumes (guilty as charged) and just decided to quit while he still had some semblance of hearing... understandable really... eh? Wot?

Both were excellent contributors to the band and were key players in its success...

BOMSHAMKAR!!

Through our association with the London clubs we'd come to the attention of one Dave Loader, owner of Aftermath Records a small independent label based in (of all places) Acton, West London. He'd been involved with other record labels and Aftermath was his own personal project. He'd previously released an album by Voodoo Child, a Hendrix tribute band who we'd shared the bill with at numerous shows in London and he wanted us to be the next release. After the nightmare of the last record company, we held a couple of 'pre-contract' meetings with Dave to discuss the process. The whole set up seemed a lot better though, Aftermath actually had an office for a start, which was shelved out to the max with various albums from numerous bands that Dave had been involved with. He had the knowledge and, it seemed, he had the contacts too. We discussed the terms and duly signed with him.

It didn't take us long to agree on a title for the next album...'Bomshamkar!!' it was a phrase often heard uttered at the festivals, not by ancient sufi mystics but by chillum-toting freaks as they inhaled the sweet smoke through a damp, sweaty bandana that was wrapped around the mouthpiece of said pipe. I'm still not sure of the spelling to this day but as it was something that was always shouted out, I hadn't actually seen it written down anywhere. In the end I asked Ed Ozric, so if it's wrong blame him...!

We'd decided to return to the recording studio at Bracknell's South Hill Park where we'd done our demo. Marcus the engineer had been replaced by a Marc (aka Swordfish) who had vastly improved the place acoustically and equipment wise. We got on well and after thrashing out how to meet the meager budget allocated to us, we calculated that we could get it all done in 33 hours, which we did!! We recorded all of the backing tracks live, which allowed us the luxury of being able to spend time on multi layering the vocals. The sound quality was great (considering) and we confidently handed over the final mix to Dave at Aftermath.

Next up was the cover artwork. After the last album cover disaster, I finally got my way and chose an old black and white photo I'd found in an old OZ or IT magazine of a London bobby sucking on a chillum. It was obviously a staged photo, but it'd be nice to think it wasn't. eh? Together with the album designer we weaved in psychedelic optical shapes and patterns and lettering and due to our equally limiting 'two colour only' artwork budget, we'd decided on vivid red and blue, which actually worked out great as the clash between the two colours was a trip in itself. This was, I think, the start of many fine, creative album covers that we were to produce which was something that we got quite a reputation for over the years.

GOODBYE PORIJ, HELLO FRUIT SALAD!

Due to a severely limited maintenance budget (read trying to keep it all together on a wing and a prayer), Porij elected to put his Electrick Gypsy lightshow on ice for a while. It was a struggle for him alone as his partner in crime Simon had been involved in the Battle of the Beanfield as mentioned previously and had retired to Ireland with his lovely lady Julie and son Richard. Obviously, finding a replacement was going to prove to be a challenge but we limped on, doing a few shows with

limited lighting and, like the audience, noticing the difference...
it just wasn't the same.

Luckily for us, not long after we were approached after a
particularly rockin' but severely underlit show at the Nag's
Head in High Wycombe by a young, bright eyed and bushy
tailed, enthusiastic chap who introduced himself as Jasper and
together with good friend Terri and dog Bob (a huge, crazy but
lovable hound who was to have many gigs and festivals under
his belt (if dogs wore belts) before his sad demise many years
later), had put together their own lightshow called Fruit Salad.
He'd noticed our lack of lighting and promptly offered their
services and from that point on and for most of the band's
career they were to be our resident lightshow. They started off
with modest but very creative lighting and in my opinion went
on to produce one of the most amazing full-on lightshows I've
ever seen.

GONE WITH THE WIND

As time went on, we eyed the progress of Bomshamkar! The
mainstream press weren't playing, but more importantly for
us, all the independent acid/psychedelic fanzines and
magazines that had sprung up were giving us glowing reviews
and spreading the word to their ever expanding readership.. i.e
those that mattered. The independent shops and mail order
companies were ordering copies and all seemed well with the
world. We did feel a little like we were always second fiddle to
labelmates Voodoo Child though and after a while, meetings
with Dave at Aftermath were akin to hearing one of your
parents telling you how good your brother was. I understood
that they were with him first, but really, how far could he have
got with a band that just did Hendrix covers? They were great
live of course, and the nearest I ever got to seeing Hendrix live,
but why buy an album of it when you can just get the real
thing?? But no, they were his babies and we were for some

The Magic Mushroom Band live at the legendary Marquee
Club in London's Wardour Street

reason fast becoming an afterthought to Aftermath. But we soldiered on regardless...

Then we got the news that were going to be filmed live at London's famous Marquee club for a television show, which was to be directed by legendary pop producer Mike Mansfield..... supporting Voodoo Child! Bums! But, breaks like that don't come along very often so we swallowed our pride and eagerly accepted...

We'd at that point had no previous TV coverage, apart from a brief glimpse of Kim's elbow and my guitar amplifier in a short piece about the Crypt on some late night news bulletin, so this was most welcome news and they didn't come much more influential than Mike Mansfield. The date for the show was in October 1987. October 1987... sound familiar to you? It should do, it's a date which still strikes fear and dread to some of the UK's populace..

We woke up to a typical autumn day, a bit damp and grey, nothing unusual about that, with a bit of a gusty breeze about. That breeze was soon to escalate though as (contrary to that day's weather report) by the afternoon it had become of hurricane-like proportions. Trees were uprooting, branches snapping under the force of the gales and visibility was becoming difficult. At the time Jasper was ferrying us and his equipment in his large Mercedes van but as we approached the M3 into London the warnings were being broadcast on the radio. 'This is a severe hurricane warning, many houses and vehicles have been damaged... on no account go out tonight, stay in your homes!!'

Stay in your homes? No!! We were doing probably one of the most important gigs of the band's career and they were telling people to stay at home? What was it about the weather and the Magic Mushroom Band? Was it divine Intervention?? Who knows? It took hours for us to get to the Marquee to set up. There were cars and trucks strewn across the motorway and trees and branches blocking the roads where they fell. It was raining too. When we entered the venue we had our first experience of live TV crews and the amount of people (and cabling) required to make the whole thing work..We did our soundcheck and waited for the audience to arrive.. and waited.. and waited until we could wait no longer and we clambered on stage and did a cracking set to an audience of three or four punters and a whole crew of luvvy darling TV technicians. Still, with a bit of creative editing I guess they could have dubbed a crowd onto the soundtrack.

Was this to be our big break? TV coverage at last? Was it fuck! We never heard another thing about it and somewhere in Mike Mansfield's archives there lies a top quality video recording of us live at the Marquee.

KEVIN THOMAS, HE'S ON THE RADIO

As we aspired to the status of 'local legends' we were beginning to become faces 'around town' and strolling one day through the car park of Mount Pleasant flats where a lot of our friends and band members past and present of the band were living, we met a chap called Kevin. He introduced himself as a DJ (pre house music) and at the time he very much looked the part, blonde curly hair, 'palm tree' Hawaiian shirt, medallion, he looked like he'd just stepped off the set of a disco at 'The Blue Lagoon'. But as time went on, there developed a cosmic side and depth to this disco boy from Cornwall and more than a little mischief. For example, he had remarked that he often used to marvel at our old van that was still parked in the corner of the car park, now resplendent in a cloak of ivy and in return showed us his old, green transit that he used for ferrying his disco equipment about that was parked at the opposite end of the car park. His van, like ours, was held together with duct tape and a prayer but when we looked at where his tax disc was supposed to be I instead saw the circular design of our band logo that he'd cut out from one of our letterheads! We politely suggested that maybe that wasn't such a good idea...

As was often the case, once we'd met Kevin he started coming 'round to the flat on a regular basis, sometimes bringing friends 'round to meet us. We didn't mind as he was a decent chap and our place was a regular drop in centre anyway.. and of course, because we were so laid back (man) we just let people turn up unannounced, after all... plans are for squares man..

Now, as we got to know Kevin, we were amazed to discover that he'd actually been in the RAF during the Falklands war and had seen some action. It was hard to imagine him as a soldier, he was just too laid back, but I think it was a family tradition thing, not for us to judge, ya do what ya do.. and on this particular day he'd chosen to pay us a visit with one of his old soldier buddies. Trouble was it turned out to be the same day that myself and a willing roadie had just dropped some acid that was new on the scene. It's hard enough trying to hold a conversation down with anyone who's straight when you're in that sort of headspace and Kevin wasn't a struggle but his friend, a thick-set Welshman with short back and sides and military regulation moustache, didn't know what the fuck was going on and as we giggled and drooled and pointed at imaginary things he just sat there fuming at his lack of control over the situation and eventually stormed out of the flat. Luckily he was a one off and we got to meet some great people through Kevin, especially his bizarre cousins from Carnwhall who were brothers and both called Den.

In time Kevin got a gig doing pirate radio where he often played Magic Mushroom Band tunes and he later went on to become a very in demand 'House' DJ, while at the same time developing his own 'Solar' lightshow which we actually used for some of our later gigs when Jasper was unavailable to us. He remains to this day a very dear and good friend and we keep in touch often.

MYKL O'VERITT

Gigs were very plentiful at this stage, great news for the band and the fans, but the pressures and lack of money coming in was beginning to take its toll, especially on those in the band who were working at the same time. This was to prove too much for Mykl who had to move on, it was totally understandable and amicable, in fact we worked on a few projects in the future together, but he just couldn't commit to us anymore. He went on to eventually form a really sweet ambient duo called TUU with his friend Martin.

'ELLO 'ELLO... SPLIFF ON THE DASHBOARD??

On one particular night we were playing at Birmingham University, we loved playing there.. the drive up was a pain but always worth it because the crowd was always enthusiastic and the 'Freak Brothers' who promoted the show always looked after us really well. As was the case at most shows, the 'private dressing room' was party central and as things were lit and passed around we were presented with a large, and I mean huge, perfectly rolled spliff by these two young chicks. Not being the types to turn that sort of thing down, we stashed it away for later on and duly went on stage and performed.

The gig was great and as was usually the case we got back to Berkshire in the early hours of the morning, I'd dropped off most of the band and all that was left was me, Steve the roadie and young Jason, a friend of ours who'd come along for the ride. As we approached the main roundabout in Bracknell, lo and behold, a patrol car appeared out of nowhere (as they were wont to do), lights a flashin', siren a whooping. As you can imagine, this wasn't the first time this sort of thing had happened and we pretty much had our emergency stashing system well worked out. I pulled the van over and got out to see them and we got the usual "Where ya been?' 'Where ya goin'?" "What ya got?". I explained that we were musicians just back from a gig in Birmingham, on our way home to bed. Obviously that wasn't enough, so everybody out the van. "There's no point looking" I said "You won't find anything.." just as I said that one of the cops pulled out the huge spliff we'd been handed at the gig, which someone had been admiring earlier and absentmindedly placed on the dashboard for all to see... bollocks... then the other cop found a blim that Jason had stashed under the seat... that was it... down to the station we all went.

We were put in separate cells (so we couldn't collaborate our stories) and as was often the case, I got the 'nice' cop who was full of apology about having to do what he was doing and that he used to smoke a bit of weed at college and liked Pink Floyd.. I tell ya.. I used to get that so often... if they were that sympathetic, why not just let us go and catch some murderers instead? He left me on my own for a while to contemplate my navel, wanting me to admit that it was my spliff on the dashboard... yeah, right... When he returned he said that Jason had admitted to owning the blim that was found under the seat and that both him and Steve the roadie had just been subjected to a strip search including the ol' rubber glove trick. Now, I don't profess to having many skills, but for some reason if my back's against the wall I can pretty much talk my way out of anything.. and I ain't ever had no rubberised finger up my jacksy and wasn't about to change that. Somehow through a torrent of verbal diarrohea I managed to persuade the cop that it really wasn't necessary and that a turn out of the pockets would suffice... whew! We were released later that morning tired, wired and looking forward to a good sleep. Jason was eventually charged for the blim and as for the giant spliff that caused all the trouble in the first place??? It was just tobacco..

EYES OF THE ANGEL

Although 'Bomshamkar' hadn't been the huge success we'd hoped it would be, thwart with distribution troubles as it was, it had been well received critically and was selling well at gigs and the specialist shops. With this in mind (and because there weren't any better offers forthcoming) we opted to do our next album with Aftermath Records again. This time though, as the band's reputation was growing at an encouraging rate, we said to Dave that we wanted a bigger budget on the next one... no more 'half live' rush jobs. We thrashed it out back at Marc's studio and came to an agreeable (ish) budget. This was our first chance to go into a studio and really spend some time being creative without watching the clock too much... luxury!

The main cover artwork was to be of a multi-armed Hindu deity superimposed over a swirling mandala... deftly executed by our new resident artist the gushingly flamboyant Beladine Diva. On the back of the cover we had some photos of us with our faces whited out and Jasper's Fruit Salad projections on them. We decided to call it 'Eyes of the Angel' after a track of the same name written by Jimbo the drummer.

I have to say that it was during the making of this album that Marc really came into his own and I was really impressed with his production skills, it was a real challenge for him and he really got some sweet sounds in there. We got all the basic tracks of the songs down and then spent lots of studio 'dead time' and late nights working on the production/effects etc, we did this when and where we could so's to keep to the budget (ish - again). Luckily, as I mentioned before, the recording studio was situated in an Arts Centre which meant that there were many musicians from all walks of life passing through the building, whether performing there or recording at the studio and as we really wanted to make a statement with this album we weren't too proud to allow other musicians to come and lay a few extra textures to the tunes.

First up were a violinist and cellist from the visiting Kreisler Orchestra, who laid down some really amazing stuff and seemed quite happy with the freedom that our sort of stuff allowed as opposed to the rigidity of classical music. We had local slide guitar legend Mike Messer pop in to do a few bits with his wailing Dobro and a chap called Jerry Andrews who played some sweet dulcimer. Also, due to our lack of keyboards at the time, the roles were perfectly filled by Chris Haynes on keyboards and Rod Mansell on swoopy synthesisers. By this time I felt like we had some kind of Sgt Pepper on the go here. But it was great, it seemed like all these talented musicians were queuing up to have a go! The possibilities were endless and I was honoured to have such talent playing on songs that I'd written! Ok, it all took a bit longer than expected, but on listening to the album today, it still stands up really well and the quality of the musicianship is astounding...

So there it was, in the can. A long time coming but well worth the wait we thought... we excitedly dragged Dave from Aftermath along to the studio to hear the final mix of our latest opus and were met with.... mild enthusiam. Godammit! What's wrong with these people? Anyway, it was duly pressed and released and once again sold well at gigs and with the specialist shops but suffered more distribution hassles. As of the time of writing both the previous album 'Bomshamkar!' and 'Eyes Of The Angel' have never been released on CD which is a real shame..

The reviews however were fantastic! We got a rave review in the Melody Maker (of all places!) who thought it was the best thing around and seemed to appreciate the time and effort that had gone into it, even at one point comparing us to Abba (!?), I tell ya, I don't know what they were on but I'll have half... and of course, some of the 'purists' knocked our cover version of Hendrix's 'Are You Experienced?' saying that the sexual overtones cheapened what THE MAN was trying to convey... get over yaself ya self-righteous nerds! Hey, drugs can be fun, but sex is pretty good too... a lot of people are doing it.... man.

ENCYCLOPEDIAS & RAINBOWS

Around about this time, I came into contact with a character called Fraser Clark, he introduced himself as the creator of a magazine called 'Encyclopedia Psychedelica'. A little older than us, he'd been around in the '60's and had somehow managed to survive relatively unscathed with most of his hippy ideals intact. He was a very educated man and his magazine covered a broad spectrum of issues relevant to the psychedelic way. It was classily put together, unlike a lot of fanzines of the time and he showed me a review he'd done of 'Bomshamkar!'. We hit it off right away and kept in regular contact, I even sent him a poem for inclusion in some book or other.. I forget now.

Through Fraser I met another equally intriguing character called George Weiss, a name probably unfamiliar to most, but in political circles he was seen as someone to keep an eye on. He was older than Fraser with a sound mind and a mischievous twinkle in his eye. He'd been trying to get ahead in politics but was deemed far too 'radical' to be taken seriously, he had an idea for the introduction of electronic remote voting but was met with a wall of indifference, probably because it would have been too accurate a reflection of the peoples' beliefs.. too many fat cats on the easy ride saw that as a threat to their lifestyles so he could make no progress. I personally thought he would have made a great Prime Minister!

The next thing I know, I get a call from Fraser asking me to get in touch with George about a possible 'benefit' gig. By then we were having to pick and choose our benefits, we couldn't afford to do them all... but for George and country... well. It turned out that this would be well worth the effort! The local M.P for Kensington had died recently and a by-election was to be held at Kensington Town Hall. All of the major parties were going to be there vying for votes, as well as George with his Rainbow Alliance Party (RAP), Screaming Lord Sutch & his Monster Raving Loony Party, Cynthia Payne & her Payne & Pleasure Party, The Prince Charles Appreciation Party and one called The Raffles Party, where the person with the winning raffle ticket on the night would be the candidate. Completely farcical of course (as indeed were the major parties) but George asked me to be a candidate for a party myself, so I formed the Magic

Mushroom Ganja Party! We were also slotted to play a set half way through the proceedings..

When we turned up on the night, it was chaos.. there were a lot of people and press/media there.. Chris Tarrant blanked me on numerous occasions as I tried to get his attention.. he was too busy chatting up the hookers who accompanied Cynthia Payne. But we had lots of photos taken, Kim especially as she vamped it up with the best of them... the performance that night was great, as they usually were when things went a little left of centre and a great time was had by all, much to the chagrin of the 'proper' M.P's.. We had the pleasure of meeting Atomic Rooster's Vincent Crane in the dressing room and I even got my name on the front page of The Times newspaper!!

Suspiciously, not long after that event George was busted in his home and sent to prison where he was safely tucked away...

HE-MAN & THE SCOOTER TRASH CRASH

Due to a continuing lack of funds, I decided in a rare fit of responsibility to go out and find a job to somehow squeeze in among all the madness. As luck would have it, Royston(ed) and a few other guys I knew had got labouring work on a local building site via an agency called 'He-Man'. I hastily signed up and had a site assigned to me on the other side of town. It didn't dawn on me at the time that I didn't have any transport (all I had was a Triumph chopper in incomplete pieces in the storage room of my flat) and buses in Bracknell were about as reliable as a very unreliable thing. Luckily (sorta), Royston(ed) offered to lend me his recently acquired moped. He'd got some other transport and said I was welcome to use it. Hmmmm... it was free..... but a moped... it'd get me to work and be cheap to run... but it's a moped. Oh well, beggars can't be choosers and so it was that I strode the beast one fine Monday morning and putt-putted my way to the building site. As I entered the site aboard my iron stallion sporting an overlarge, white crash helmet that resembled a large ostrich egg, it suddenly dawned on me that I'd have to make my way to the site office, slide my visor open and introduce myself as the guy from 'He-Man'. Once the laughter subsided I was handed a shovel and directed to the nearest ditch. The work was as okay as far as pushing wheelbarrows of wet cement and digging holes was concerned, but they'd teamed me up with this old yokel labourer from Reading who insisted on whipping his dick out and waving it after passing women, I tell ya, if he'd spent as much time with his hands on the shovel as he'd spent with 'em on his old fella, the work would've been done a lot quicker! I think I lasted about a month before it all just got a bit too much for me...

Not long after, Royston(ed) decided to sell the moped and gave me first 'dibs', I thanked him kindly but declined, offering instead to find a buyer for him. Of all people, our artist friend Beladine expressed an interest in checking it out, a bicycle being his only mode of transport at the time. I invited him to pedal over that evening and check it out. As usual, by the time he arrived there was already a decent sized gathering in the flat and when I took him down to the car park to check out the moped many decided to come and watch the show. When quizzed about his motorbike riding experience he admitted that it was zero but if I showed him he'd soon pick it up. In front of the expectant crowd I directed him to start 'er up and slooooowwwlllyy pull on the throttle. Well, I didn't even get to the 'y' in sloooowwwllyyy' because in a fit of excitement he ripped the throttle open and a flash of peroxide blonde screaming banshee went like a bat out of hell across the car park heading straight for a large parked truck in the corner . As I started to chase him in true seventies 'slo-mo' stylee all the while shouting "Nnnooooo!!!!", the attended throng gasped as in true Steve McQueen style he suddenly yanked the little bike over and travelled the rest of the journey on his side with the bike on top of him until they skidded to a halt under the aforementioned truck. When I reached him, he was one tangled mess of hair, legs, clothes and small motorbike.

I dragged them both out and he was checked for any damage, but apart from his pride all was just shaken but not broken. The same couldn't be said for the moped tho' as it had a fair few scrapes and scratches on one side, but worst of all the kickstand had been totally bent out of shape. Politely requesting everyone to stand back, in true 'He-Man' style, I removed the bent stand from the bike and looked for a suitably strong enough object for me to straighten it out on. Finding a drainage grate in the car park, I jammed one end of the stand in between the bars and tugged with all my might. I thought I could feel it slowly bending back into shape, but that sensation turned out to be the stand slowly loosening itself from its mooring and with an almighty claannnggg!!!! it popped out of the grate and whacked me straight in the head. I stumbled around for a bit admiring all the stars that had decided to come and orbit my head, cursing all the while and trying to ignore the chortles and guffaws coming from our spectators who'd had a most enjoyable show! When we all went back up to the flat and Kim and the girls saw Beladine limping in with road rash all up one side, ripped plastic jeans, hair like a tortured Barbie doll and me clutching my head and rubbing a big lump of real 'Tom & Jerry' proportions on my head, they all wondered what the hell had gone on in the car park. The truth of course was much more entertaining and devoid of any exaggeration.....

ACID MONKEYS AT SIR HENRY'S ABODE

By now, Janey and Joie had moved out of their squat in Clapham and were temporarily staying at a huge manor house in its own grounds just outside of Brighton. The top half of the house was owned by the parents of the then Ozrics drummer Tig (after Ozrics he played with the first line-up of Jamiraqui) they weren't living there at the time so it was ok for them to stay there, while the bottom half of the house was owned by some old military colonial gent who fought in Indiah! in the war. Janey and Joie referred to him as 'Sir Henry' after a similar

Proud Father with Jasmine Childperson

character played by ex-Bonzo's Vivian Stanshall and we often visualised his house being full of stuffed tigers and blunderbusses.. It was an amazing old house, absolutely huuuge and Janey and Joie were surrounded by antiques and I do believe there was even an original Picasso on one of the walls. As is the way of most musicians though, first to be set up was the music room and Kim, Jas and I were invited over for a session or two.. we were well overdue for a little break and eagerly accepted..

As was to be expected the weather was pretty naff, but in a place like that, who needs to go out? Actually we did go out at one point because we thought it'd be nice to see Brighton beach as we were so close, we had a quick scurry around in the driving rain and then dived back into Joie's van and headed back to the house. Not long before we arrived, Joie had got a new battery for his van, trouble was it was the wrong one and it was too tall but being about as practical as me, Joie put it on anyway. The notion that maybe it was a bad idea came to us on the way back from the beach as the van just kept cutting out at the most inopportune moments. We got out in the rain and stuck our heads under the bonnet and scratched our collective beards eventually coming to the (obvious) conclusion that the battery was actually shorting out because it was pressing against the wet, metal bonnet of the van. Aha! Stoned logic came to the fore and some nice, dry cardboard was wedged between the top of the battery and the bonnet, thus isolating them. Hmmm.. seemed ok for a coupla miles until we saw plumes of thick smoke coming out... yep, the cardboard had caught fire and now we were stuck on the side of the road in the pouring rain in a smouldering van (Janey in a fit of panic had leapt out of the van and managed to successfully blow out the flames!). Luckily Joie had a breakdown service so we weren't stuck there for too many hours.

Back at the Manor and after a major bout of mellowing out (and table soccer.. Joie loves his football!) we hazily sauntered forth into the music room. Of course, me being the spongebrain that I am, I'd forgotten to bring my guitar but there was a fretless bass, Janey's shenai, Joie's usual bank of synthesisers, a sampler and some superb Manali hashish which made for an interesting session indeed... Joie set up a 'portastudio' and away we went..... Our first brainstorm was to record some 'jingles' for our DJ friend Kevin who'd recently started doing shows on pirate radio... very funny... and what with the combination of the strong hash and Joie's infamous weird sample library, pretty soon we were laying down some weeeiiirrrdd shit, man... and after Joie and I entered further into 'alternative states' it proceeded to get even more out there.. at one point we were recording phrases, playing them backwards and memorising how the words sounded that way, recording us saying them backwards and then flipping the tapes over again... the end result being rather like listening to a Russian-accented alien on the set of the movie Eraserhead. After the session we retired to the lounge and played inventive variations of table soccer, stared at the many stars through the huge skylight and giggled incessantly as Joie, for no apparent reason, slowly began to regress into an ape-like creature, proving Darwin's theory once and for all... some of the music we recorded there ended up on Janey's 'Evil Edna's Horror Toilet' album.

MERRY OLD LAND OF OZ

Although Kim's years in England had been very fruitful to say the least, quite understandably she yearned to go back to Australia to see her family who she hadn't seen since just after our daughter Jasmine was born. I too had always wanted to go there, ever since my Uncle Brian emigrated there in the '60's. There was no way we could have afforded it on our own, I'd never been and it was beginning to look unlikely that I'd ever get to see the place, then just before Xmas 1988 we got a call from Kim's parents saying that the family had all chipped in and they'd bought us tickets to go over, much joy!! The family lived in the Adelaide hills in a big house in the country, so accommodation wasn't a problem and we'd already mastered the art of living on a shoestring budget so... no worries mate! A good friend of ours (and chief babysitter) Tiff offered to look after our flat and cat for us and Marc said he'd take us to the airport.. sorted. Kim was very excited and I wasn't far behind her.. the furthest abroad I'd ever gone was France and I'd never been on a plane before! I duly got my passport sorted and we got the tickets.. all systems go...

After a particularly good 'send-off' party the night before, we gave Tiff the keys to the flat and climbed into Marc's van and off we went to Heathrow airport. We said our goodbyes to Marc and queued up to check our luggage in. Kim was fine, Jasmine was fine and then it came to me..."Ticket?" said the sour faced check-in clerk "Yes, here you are" "Passport?" "Yup, here ya go" "Visa?" "Wot?" "Visa. You need a visa to enter Australia.." Holy Sheeit!! Nobody told me that! Kim wasn't even aware of it.. so there we were, stuck at the airport, cases and all, plane leaving in thirty minutes and no visa! "What can I do?" I asked the clerk... "There's nothing you can do... you can't go.." Oh jeez... by now Kim was crying, Jasmine was crying and I was standing there pulling my hair out when all of a sudden this official looking guy wanders over and asks what all the commotion is about. After much explaining and gesticulating he asked us to follow him into his office where he promptly called the Australian embassy and caught the secretary just as she was preparing to go home (it was 4:45pm on a Friday!) he explained the situation to her and she faxed a visa through for me there and then... I couldn't believe it, what a stroke of luck and what a lovely guy... my hero. Before I knew it, we'd ran to the departure gate got on the plane and were up in the air before I had time to realise that it was my first time on a plane and that I was supposed to be a bit apprehensive... I didn't care tho', I was just happy to be on my way..

After what seemed like an eternity on the plane, we finally landed in Adelaide to be met by most of Kim's family, which was great... we felt like royalty. It was a cold December day when we left England and the first thing that hit me as I stepped off the plane was a 'Whoompphh!!' of hot Summer air.... mm... I love the sun... this felt good. On the journey to the family home my head was turning like that girl in 'The Exorcist'.. it looked kinda the same, but the trees were different, the cars were different, the sky was different.. we went past some beaches and they were different too... clean, white sand and empty.. never seen that before! We spent the next six weeks with Kim's family and had a great time, lots of beach, barbies and that all prevailant 'no worries' attitude to life, it took a lot of getting used to.. all those happy go lucky people... no wonder my Uncle hadn't gone back to the UK. Kim has a big family so there was no shortage of things to do, one of her brothers Hadley is a radio DJ and he invited us onto his late night show for an interview (he was the only person in Australia with a copy of the newly released 'Eyes of the Angel'!) he also let us choose a few songs from their vaults to be played on the show.. my first choice was 'Dynamo Hum' by Frank Zappa which promptly jammed the station's switchboard with irate, outraged listeners!

Having a Summer Xmas and New Year took a bit of getting used to (as it still does) but one of the nicest Xmas events was when Kim's family clubbed together and bought me my first didgeridoo... I was gobsmacked.. and very grateful. Ya see, I'd been strolling down Rundle Mall in Adelaide when I heard the strains of my first ever 'live' didgeridoo playing.. I fought my way through the crowd to see a white Dutch guy sitting there puffing away... that was it... that would be my new challenge.. and after a few farty indiscretions I pretty much got the hang of it and have played them ever since..

If it wasn't for the band and other family commitments, I would have loved to have just not gone back.. but of course duty called... we did decide then and there though that Australia would eventually be our home of choice.. not so much fun on the way back, tears at the airport, arriving back to a cold, wintry January Heathrow Airport and after all that wide open space, suddenly our big, spacious flat wasn't so big and spacious anymore.. Tiff did a good job of looking after our flat, although she did have some band turn up and stay for a while as they said we'd be ok about it.. first we knew of it!

As for the band, the first bit of news we got was that while we were away Craig had decided that he'd had enough and had left the band. It was a shame that he went, as apart from his guitar playing which was very different from mine (although just as loud!) him and Wayne were very visually striking on stage being identical twins. But, he wanted to try different things so fair play to him... I didn't bother replacing him, I just turned my guitar up. Over the course of years we'd gone from an eight-piece band to a four piece.. oh well... mutate and survive, eh?

A HOUSE FOR THE USE OF

The flat we were living in had served us well over the years, but when a brand new council house was offered to us, we jumped at the chance. Jasmine had never had a garden and the childrens' play area at the flats was out of view from our place so we couldn't let her play on her own. The location of our new abode was in a newly finished estate in Bracknell called Forest Park, it was a three bedroomed(ish) house in a quiet cul-de-sac. We went and had a look at it and decided there and then to go for it... after all, a brand new house on a brand new estate? What could possibly go wrong??

It wasn't until we started moving our stuff over and unpacking it that we realised that it wasn't all going to fit in. Yes, our three bedroomed(ish) house had less space than our two bedroomed flat... go figure. Of course it was the start of a trend of fitting as many houses in as small a space as possible thus maximising the profits.. a small inconvenience to us at the time, we weren't ungrateful... but it would eventually become a recipe for disaster... Because we were in the middle of a three house terrace, we had the smallest garden and we also worked out that we had nineteen(!) other houses overlooking our garden. Not really a problem until Summer kicked in and then we were treated to the sound of numerous stereos pumping out their music and numerous barbecues wafting their burnt offerings into our house. In no time at all most of the neighbours were at each other's throats and in the end we'd spend most Summer weekends packing up our tent and moving into the nearby woods for a couple of days of peace and quiet!

To make matters worse, we had postmen living either side of us and obviously the sound of numerous drunken/stoned freaks piling out of a van to unload the gear at some unearthly time of the morning didn't go down too well with them.. plus, horror of horrors, we didn't have the same matching lace curtains as the others... we were like The Addams Family of the block! The walls were paper thin too and often me and Kim would lay awake in bed with the neighbour's headboard bashing against our wall.. thinking "Fer chrissakes... hurry up and shag her!!!"

But, for all that. Jas loved it, she made some good friends (although she did tell them her name was Sarah.. to try and fit in.. poor love) and we made the best of a naff situation...

KEYNESTONED KOPS

As was the norm around that time, I'd got a call from some types informing me of an impromptu free festival being set up, this time in sunny Milton Keynes.. I was a bit apprehensive about it, we'd once got hideously lost trying to find a venue there and eventually made it just in time to go straight on and perform, but Wango Riley was providing the stage and we loved working with those guys.. So we agreed.
Now, Milton Keynes is a very surreal place... we thought Bracknell new town was bad, but it seemed that the whole of Milton Keynes had been designed by a guy with a ruler and a compass... and he wasn't afraid to use either. EVERYTHING LOOKS THE SAME!! Even the trees were all at the same height and as was bound to happen we got lost again. We found the original site for the festival but the farmer who owned the land

blocked all the entrances with his tractors.. so now it was a case of driving around playing 'spot the freak'.. we did eventually find the site... actually it was in the car park of the Milton Keynes bowl, a huge, grassy area now covered with a stage, buses and numerous hairy types. As usual Wango Riley were right on it and had us set up and playing in no time.. which was good because time was running out... more and more cop cars were pulling up and before I knew it half the audience were wearing blue uniforms.. a familiar sight for us at the time.. I knew we'd be cut off soon, so after a quick discussion with the band we went into a blistering rendition of Pink Fairy Larry Wallis' 'Police Car' which we continued until the power was shut off..

KOPS AT THE DOOR!!

So, life in suburban Forest Park was as to be expected.. the neighbours hated us (and each other), all the new trees had been vandalised by bored kids and we discovered that our garden was, in fact, made from pure clay. More of a problem for the neighbours on one side, for whenever it rained their garden would flood, it just wouldn't soak in!! What more could be sent to this troubled neighbourhood to add to its teething troubles? I know, how about cops??

There I was, in between gigs, chilling out, righteously stoned and quite pleased with myself when I suddenly get a phone call. "Hello there.. this is Reading CID we'd like to come down and talk to you about a murder, we'll be there in twenty minutes, don't go anywhere.. " YAARRRGGHHH!!!! Me? CID? Murder? What th'??? I went from being a couch potato to a whirling dervish... emptying all the ashtrays and (pointlessly) hiding all paraphernalia.. just finishing in time for a 'tappity tap tap' on the front door. I opened the door to be greeted by the sight of two burly plain clothed detectives and I showed them in. They told me straight away that I wasn't an actual suspect in the murder case (phew... that helped) but the guy who'd

The Magic Mushroom Band circa 1989 now down to a
four-piece but the groove remains

Garry, Kim, Wayne and Jim gear up for the impending
Treworgey Tree Fayre

been murdered was a notorious dealer in Reading and he'd been killed when a deal went wrong and as I probably knew him and bought dope off him, if I would confess to that in writing they would go through the money found back at his flat and check for my fingerprints... yeah right. Confess to buying dope off someone in writing... yeah right!

I honestly didn't know the guy, had never met him and didn't know how the bloody hell they got my phone number from him! That was driving me crazy.. crazier than the fact that I had two detectives in my house and a not-so-plain clothed police car parked outside... Then they let slip that my phone number had been found on the dead guy's bedside cabinet scribbled on a notepad. That didn't help clear things up at all... but then, as fate would have it I had a call from a girl friend of our acquaintance and I said to her that I couldn't speak due to a murder enquiry currently underway at my house.. she asked if it was about the murder in Reading and I confirmed that, telling her my phone number was on his bedside cabinet... "Oh, that!'" she said.. "I've known him since college and I was around there the other day and needed to phone you and called a mutual friend from there for your number.. " Wouldja believe it? I told her right there and then to come 'round to my place as fast as she could and tell my visitors exactly that... which she promptly did.. whew.. whodathunkit? Case solved.

TREWORGEY (DAWN OF THE CRUSTY)

Whew, where do I start on this one? It could be a book all on its own, although many people have a story of their own when it comes to the infamous Treworgey Fayre..

It all started for me with the usual phone call from a bunch of guys putting together a festival in Treworgey, Cornwall. As Glastonbury had become so successful as a paid festival and free festivals were rapidly becoming a thing of the past, this would be a paid event with the 'spirit' of a free festival but with flushing toilets, showers, on-site security and, even better, payment for the bands! Sharing the bill with us over two large 'main' stages were Hawkwind, The Ullulators (featuring ex-Mushroomette Janey), RDF, Back to the Planet.. all the usual suspects and more.. The 'scene' that had rapidly grown around us was getting of quite sizeable proportions, to the point of us and other 'likeminded' bands pretty much doing the same tour circuit around the country and we were even starting to get a bit of press, verging on the positive too... it had to happen sooner or later, the scene was growing so fast you couldn't ignore it, especially if you wanted to sell music papers...

We received our passes and site/performance info through the post and packed our tents and equipment into the Fruit Salad tour bus. Although we discovered that our allocated time slot was in the afternoon, Jasper had been hired separately to do the lights for the duration. So, sensing a good time for all and the fact that we could stay for the duration of the festival (away from the housing estate) we cadged a lift with Jasper and crew and off we headed to sunny Cornwall... Funnily enough, that wasn't an ironic statement, as it had been a particularly hot summer, especially for Cornwall and the land was very arid, dry and dusty... as we were to discover.... crusty dust.

As we approached the festival site it was all looking quite professional, a lot of punters had turned up already and others were forming an orderly queue and the performers had their own entry gate... luxury!! It was all very colourful, lots of rainbow coloured ethnic banners, numerous 'alternative' trade stalls and the stages looked very impressive. We excitedly unpacked our gear and wrestled the tents into position before heading out to take in some of the atmosphere.. we checked out both main stages, very nice... we had Wango Riley's stage again... excellent, happy with that.

There were tents and buses as far as the eye could see in any direction, except one... that was a dark, dank field way up behind the performers' camping area flanked by a large, dark structure that seemed to be made of a material not known to this planet.... there were weird sounds emanating from the structure... kinda punky, kinda techno and a strange smell was wafting down to where we camped, kinda like a blend of stale Special Brew, strong Sensi and old, smelly army socks... that, we were to discover, was the 'Crusty' field. What is a Crusty? One may well ask.. well at the time, with the infamous Battle of the Beanfield still on a lot of people's minds... the idea of moving out of home and buying a bus and getting constantly hassled by the law and ostracized by society seemed very attractive to the more radical factions who were running out of ideas of how to fuck the system. There were a lot of ex-punks who got in on the act, bored with their tired old scene.. and of course the remainder of the original Convoy were at once honoured and yet hindered by this new wave of New age Travellers. For most, their intentions were good, live off the land, fuck the system, yeah.. but at some point it entered the realms of 'style', you know... 'style'.. when all the individualists start wearing the same thing...

And so it was at Treworgey that the 'designer' Crusty was born - Dreads, army surplus clothing, dog on a string.. the music press loved it, they had a novelty image to play with.. but at the same time it did bring the scene to the masses and many came to check it all out... army fatigues an' all...

We settled in and had a fun time catching up with friends and chatting to the other bands, checking out the stalls and chewing the shit and it was looking like being a cool scene... not for long though, because a dark cloud was looming, the bubble was about to burst... it became a game of rumours at first...

"Did ya hear? All the toilets are locked and they don't know how to unlock them.. people are starting to piss and shit all over the place!"
OH..

"Did ya hear? There was a dead sheep found in one of the water tanks!"
REALLY? YUK..

"Did ya hear? loads of people had the stuff from their tents ripped off!"
BASTARDS!

"Did ya hear? Some girl got raped by a security guard!'"
NO SHIT..

"Did ya hear? It's been declared a free festival!"
ER... RIGHT ON!

And best of all..

"Did ya hear? The security guards were all sacked and they marched into the office and stole all the money!"
YAAAGGGHHH!!!

'Did ya hear? The promoters have all disappeared... they've done a runner!'
DOUBLE YAAAGGGHHH!!!

Fuck! It was all going so well.... luckily some people we knew got it together to try and get some money for the bands at least.. it was really nice of them to do that and we weren't completely out of pocket...

After a few days, the dry Cornish dust had adhered itself to most people at the festival.. because so many people were trudging around (mostly in army boots) the dust had become very fine and was now permanently attached to our clothes, hair and lungs.. it set a very nice contrast against the unaffected parts of the skin that were just plain sunburnt... but on one particular morning I literally witnessed the 'Dawn of the Crusty' as in true 'Zombie flick' style I actually saw the ground moving up at the Crusty field... but it was actually all the bodies rising from a particularly good night of Special Brew imbibing ceremonies.. By that time there was no difference between the colour of them and the earth from which they rose...

Anyway, come the day of our performance and I was looking pretty crusty myself... I didn't care though.. I was itching to get up on stage and take our Mushroom music to the masses.. it was by far the biggest crowd we'd ever played to... by that point it was down to just me on guitar and vocals, Kim on vocals, Wayne on bass and Jimbo on drums... my Echoplex had shit itself prior to the show and Craig very kindly lent me his Copycat echo unit, I needed it to fatten my sound out... I couldn't turn it up any more!! Once up on stage and after a quick welcome we blasted our way through a high-energy set and were cookin' on gas, baby! Just the sight of all those people out there, fired us right up and we gave our all. I've actually seen video footage of our show there and we even get a guest appearance by Bob, Jasper's dog, during one of my guitar solos.. well, with it too light for a lightshow, between Jasper's smoke machines (which were really cool actually) and a performing dog what more could you possibly need?

After the show I was really buzzing... I felt like I had rays of light coming out of my eyes.. my feet weren't contacting the ground... people were coming up to me and congratulating me, smiles and cuddles and spliffs all 'round, I shared some special times with some great people. I was tripping for the rest of my time there.. I know some people have horrendous tales of what happened to them and I count myself lucky that not only did I not have a bum trip, I really had a blast..

Strangely enough, as was often the case... after such a successful show we had another departure from the band.. this time we were shocked to hear that Jimbo wanted to leave.. he was becoming disillusioned about it all and as his singer brother had scored some kind of management deal for his white soul pop band, he decided to join them as the drummer in pursuit of pop happiness. We were devastated, Jim was such a great guy to have around, his zany, warped humour and effervescence would be sorely missed. He was probably the best drummer I have ever had the pleasure to share a stage with.. he'd been with us from the start.. but he felt he had to do it though.. so it was completely amicable. The shame was that the band he joined never got anywhere apart from into debt, but.. hey ho.. ya makes ya choices...

STUDIO TAN

Due to my employment situation (or lack thereof), I was instructed to go and do some 'work experience'.. luckily I was able to wangle it so that my experience would be at Marc's recording studio.. nice one. I really learnt a lot of stuff while helping Marc and watching him engineer, listening in on the mixes etc. He tried in vain to show me the ropes but my capacity to understand anything technical is limited to say the least... but I really enjoyed being in on the mixing sessions.. one down side for me was that, as I spent more time analysing each mix we were working on.. I began to find it very hard to go home and listen to some of my favourite records! The bass might be too loud, or the drums too thin.. it drove me crazy... we also spent a lot of time cooped up in that little room and I was beginning to resemble Johnny Winter.. pink eyes an' all! A 'studio tan' is a genuine condition.. I know, I had one..

Again, because the studio was in an Arts Centre we'd have all manner of bands in to record: From the geographically obvious (near Reading, home of the Heavy Metal festivals) local rock bands, who were all computer programmers by day and at the weekends they'd don their Levi's and white baseball boots, muss up their mullets, roll up their shirtsleeves and 'rock out', to obscure 'modern' jazz bands, with percussionists who played bits of wire and kitchen utensils, local 'legends' trying yet another demo in their relentless pursuit of more rejection letters from record companies and best of all a small, wiry, gay chap who sang nothing but Barbara Streisand songs in a falsetto voice!! We saw it all there.. and Marc had seen a lot more than me..

The whole thing was actually a lot harder work then I'd ever imagined and very long hours too.. I'm surprised more engineers and producers don't lose the plot.. although the best ones are all slightly touched, eh?

FRANTIC MUSHROOMS

A fun, although mind warping experience I had while helping out at the recording studio was the contract that Marc had with Link Records. They were a top 'Psychobilly' label and were churning out albums by these, wild,crazy dudes all looking like day-glo psycho-punk teddy boys. The music was like Stray Cats on acid, with the obligatory foot-high quiffs, slap double-bass and twangy guitars. The whole scene fascinated me, and most of them were real characters.. we'd all get pretty out of it right from the off.. then hold on!

There were bands with names like The Sugar Puff Demons, Demented Are Go and local favourites The Frantic Flintstones. It was with the latter that we got on the best with and in fact we had so much fun during their album session that we decided to make the time to do an album with The Magic Mushroom Band and The Frantic Flintstones together.. 'Psycho-Rockabilly meets Acid Troubadors'!!! The session was a real blast and the mix of ideas and styles had the tunes going in all directions... this was real 'jazz fusion' man!!! Most of the tracks were basic songs written by lead Flintstone and all-round larrakin Chuck, whos broad west-country accent gave some of those old R&B gospel type tunes a very surreal slant and we just psyched the whole thing out. We were all very pleased with the end result.. but Link Records didn't want to release it, they saw it as too much a departure (no shit?) to their usual fare. Fortunately, it was rescued from the vaults in 2007 and finally released as 'Date with the Devil' by The Magic Frantic Mushrooms on Voiceprint Records. This album was a lot of fun to do.. we laughed our bellies off during most of the 'sessions'.. we did it in 'dead' time so we didn't have to rush it all too much and it was fun for me to step outside of my usual musical spectrum as varied as it was...

MEET THE NEW 'SHROOMS

Best of all, through meeting and playing with new musicians on the Frantic Mushrooms album, we'd found the next recruits for the ongoing saga that was the Magic Mushroom Band!

Sam the violinist we'd already met when her band Harrold Juana played with us at a gig in Windsor. I've always had a soft spot for a good bit of violin, I always thought Simon House's contribution to Hawkwind's 'classic' sound has been sorely underestimated, Sam was a good player and after seeing her play with her band and in the studio on the Frantic Mushrooms sessions, we gingerly asked her if she would fancy playing in our band on a sort of 'time share' with Harrold Juana, fortunately she agreed and the Harrolds were cool about it too.

Ed (Bones - because of his striking resemblance to Dr McCoy from Star Trek) was playing slide and rhythm guitar with slide guitarist Mike Messer and he too played some great slide guitar on that album. We got on really well and I have the utmost respect for his guitar playing. Like Craig before him, his style was a lot different to mine and we played together well. He too eagerly accepted the mission, the band was slowly filling out again! Kim too had locked herself away in our music room with some newly acquired synthesisers and before long was playing them live and in the studio bringing back that much missed spacey, synthi vibe..

And on drums? Well, the answer was under my (rather generous) nose all the time! Marc the Swordfish proved himself to be a rather formidable drummer during those sessions, he had a much heavier beat than Jimbo but that too gave the whole thing a real fresh outlook.. plus Marc already knew the songs and what we were about so the whole thing just sort of fell into place..

The line-up was again complete, with a fuller, different sound and suddenly I had a whole lot of tunes forming in my head... now where was that pencil???

The Magic Mushroom Band Mark 3
Sam, Kim, Swordfish, Wayne, Garry, Ed (Bones)

ASTRALASIA

At the same time as all that was happening, Marc had been toying around with some deep, ambient synthesised soundscapes and I'd added some spacey guitar and didgeridoo into the mix and Kim contributed some ethereal vocals.. the tracks turned out really well and before long there was an album's worth of material. Marc wanted to name the project and as Kim and I had recently returned from Australia and had been banging on about it ever since, the name Astralasia eventually came to mind.. there were eastern musical instruments and sounds in the mix as well as the Australian didgeridoo so the name kind of summed it all up quite well. I'd introduced Marc to the album 'Revenge of the Mozabites' by the Suns of Arqa, we loved its eclectic mix of deep, stoner dub and ethnic instruments and it was fun taking sounds out of their natural surroundings and mixing them all together.. who was to know that that in itself would eventually grow to be a huge scene all of its own??

Due to the musical climate at the time, house/rave music being all the rage... the 'chill out' scene was still at the embryonic stage, the chances of getting this kind of stuff released through a record company was slim, but we 'released' it anyway. Kim knocked up some suitable cover artwork and the 'album' was released as 'ASTRALASIA' on cassette only via gigs and mail order. That's how the whole Astralasia trip started.

PROCESS OF ILLUMINATION

With fresh members and ideas aplenty, it wasn't too long before material started coming together for the next Magic Mushroom Band album. It was like I'd got a fresh shot in the arm and song ideas were popping out of my head at a rapid rate, I felt like this was going to be a great album and by the time we got to the final mixes we'd established the new Magic Mushroom Band sound. The title came to me in a flash of inspiration... 'Process of Illumination'! Of course! That was exactly what the band had been through since its inception..

As for its release as an album.. we were having no more truck with bastard, untogether record companies.. Psycho never came through with our promised first album, Pagan had been useless, period and Aftermath just never got the distribution to the record shops sorted, so our albums just sat collecting dust in some warehouse. We decided that if we wanted more control over our album releases, we'd just have to do it ourselves until the right company came along.. thus 'Fungus Records' was born....

Marc and myself were both avid record collectors, specifically late sixties/early seventies space rock stuff. We loved the elaborate album covers of the time and the whole way they were put together. With that in mind we decided we'd release 'Process' as a special limited edition album, a thousand copies only, all numbered and signed by the band. Kim and an excellent artist friend Kam(aeleon) got to work on the panels for the cover, which became a huge, fold-out poster and we threw in a few posters etc. and put it all in a printed plastic cover a la the 'Revelations' Glastonbury Fayre album, my most prized record(s) of all. Due to financial reasons (we had very little money!) we decided to stick to the two-colour printing process but this time we chose a violent pink and green which made the artwork and words really leap out at you.. it looked great, if I'd seen it in a record shop, I'd have bought it!

The whole package looked and sounded great and once they were numbered and signed we started selling them at gigs, to specialist shops and via mail order. The response was phenomenal, especially through the mail order as not only were there urgent requests for the album (limited edition ya see) but every piece of mail had a really nice letter attached, saying how much the band meant to them.. we'd never really been contactable before.. and it was great to get such positive feedback! We got just as much mail again from people who'd received the album and enjoyed it so much they had to tell us..

we even had mail from soldiers in the front line during the first Gulf War, they were listening to it on their 'Walkmans'!

COME ON SWEET CAROLINE!!

The success of 'Process' had generated a lot of interest from various parties, not quite the likes of Richard Branson, but funnily enough someone from one of his subsidiaries Caroline Records. We received a letter from a chap called Brian from Caroline informing us that he'd like to re-release it in a cheaper, standard format, keeping the production costs down for him, but more importantly for us, keeping our limited edition copies special. Due to certain music industry politics beyond our comprehension, he couldn't release it in the UK but was more than happy to cover the European distribution. This was very good news for us and took our music out there to the continentals who embraced it with open arms, especially in Italy where we discovered that there was a huge appreciation of all things psychedelic and progressive... He also released the first Astralasia album which was basically the first two cassettes put together...

SPACED OUT

With the new line-up well bedded in by now, it wasn't long before enough material surfaced to justify doing another album. This time we were ably abetted by the saxophones and flutes of David Jackson (ex Van Der Graaf Generator) who gave the tunes a whole extra dimension. We were very grateful for his help and repaid the debt by appearing on his solo album 'Tonewall Stands'.

As our Fungus Records experiment proved to be such a success we decided to bite the bullet and do another album in a similar way. Once again it would be a signed and numbered limited edition with a fold-out sleeve and extra goodies. The cover turned out excellent with a (tastefully) computer generated portrait of a mushroom infested landscape with a real tripped-out sky courtesy of our photographer Jonathan's computer whizz friend Paul the Pencil. We shamelessly modelled this one on Hawkwind's 'In Search of Space' album cover complete with fold-out wings and added various photos and trippy lettering courtesy of Kim's formidable pen work...

One of the goodies we slipped inside, and something I'd always wanted to do was a comic book featuring the band. At the time 'Star Trek the Next Generation' was a huge hit on the TV and we'd all gather around each others' homes to watch the latest episode with an almost religious fervour.. so I decided to call the comic 'Spaced Out - The Next De-Generation'. It told the story of our crew's intergalactic journeys and somehow (by coincidence rather than actual planning) I managed to interlace the tracks and lyrics with the thread of the plot. It was an epic undertaking for me. I drew and drew for days on end, but I was pleased with how it all turned out.

This album was also to be released on CD, but instead of shrinking all that lovely art down to fit a typical jewel-box type case, we opted to house the disc in a smaller version of the album cover, around the size of a 7" single. We thought that not only was it a really revolutionary and different idea, the artwork and writing still being very readable, but it would stand out more when displayed in the record stores. Boy, were we wrong! Although the fans loved it, the record shops and distribution companies didn't like it. Apparently it didn't fit in with the 'normal' CD covers of other albums and therefore they didn't know what to do with it! Ah well...

All in all, we were very pleased with how this album turned out. It can be seen now as the point where the crossover to the ambient/dance side began.. It wasn't a pre-determined thing, but that whole side of it was fresh and new and all around us. We saw it as an added dimension to our sound and a way of getting all these new, younger space cadets to dig our music too... which they did. The limited edition copies sold very quickly and subsequent re-releases by Caroline, Magick Eye and Voiceprint Records have sold well too..

THE ROAD TO UTOPIA

The recording studio at South Hill Park Arts Centre was an integral part of its activities and led to an involvement with the yearly Bracknell Festival. It'd started out as first a Jazz festival, then a Folk festival, then both, then Womad and eventually (after a few financial disasters) settling into just a nice, laidback mixture of all of the above. Apart from the outdoor festival stages, the centre's new Wilde Theatre was incorporated too. A really well thought out venue, the sound was always excellent as was the whole set-up visually.

With the success of the recording studio and a newly set-up shop that we'd put in under the stairs by the terrace bar, selling new and second-hand records/CD's etc. (including ours of course!), Marc found that the staff at the Arts Centre were beginning to give us a bit of a free reign to organise a few events. This was nothing short of amazing as they were a bit stuffy, pompous and arty farty usually but they began to listen to our ideas...

And so it was that with the initial success of the Astralasia recordings and the general buzz that was going around about us, we managed to talk the Arts Centre into letting us hold Bracknell's (Maybe Berkshire's?) first ever all-night rave.... UTOPIA.

We decided on that name for our event due to a mutual admiration for Todd Rundgren and his band Utopia... maybe it was unconsciously one of our first attempts at building the bridge between our old-school acid rock and the new generation of bleepers and acid casualties..

The vibe building up to that first Utopia was fantastic.. we were keeping it all in-house and very much a community event so we rounded up all of our artists, photographers, face painters, jugglers and assorted humpers and dumpers and secured their services in exchange for a free ticket on the night. Before long we had a veritable army of helpers and doers, other bands booked, lighting and sound sorted and the main DJ for the night would of course have to be our own Kevin Thomas (or Dr Love as he called himself back then!).

We put a plan together for promoting the event, Kim designed a poster around a large, spaced-out head (kinda 'borrowed' from a Spirit album cover) and we printed up flyers too and we hit all of the independent record stores near and far. All of the music papers and magazines were notified (not that they held the front page or anything!) but the most important thing was the buzz on the grapevine.. it was all that people would talk about and although being such a relatively new experience to promote, we could feel the excitement building...

Come the day of that first Utopia, we were primed and ready and it looked fantastic. The stage there was massive and we had two lightshows working it (Fruit Salad Lights and AnArc Lights), everywhere you looked there were hangings or bizarre sculptures that we'd picked up along the way. We even bought a large weather balloon which was inflated and hung above the stage and projected onto. The Chill Out room had an underwater theme, so all of the murals and hangings had fish and other sealife painted on them and lots of ultra-violet lighting and ambient sounds. As soon as you walked in there you felt immediately at 'one with the universe'!

As opening time approached, everyone assumed their allocated positions and in they came, and they came, and they came.. the turnout was unbelievable! We expected a few hundred there, quite a few of them out of curiosity, the theatre had a legal limit of eight hundred, but within a few hours the place was heaving and way, way more than that got in. The security guards eventually started turning people away and there were even people climbing the building trying to find a way in.

The buzz inside the venue was magical, as you entered past the (frazzled) security guards there were bodies everywhere you looked, and it looked like everyone was there to party and get into the spirit of it all... a huge queue formed for the face-painting (which made for some surreal conversations as the evening wore on) and there were already crashed-out bodies in the chill out area and others dancing, whirling dervishes as the DJ pumped the heavy, acid sounds on the main stage. It was so full that wherever you went you were either walking past someone or stepping over them...

As darkness fell, the jugglers and fire-eaters outside did their thing wowing the spectators many of whom were either wide-eyed from the sheer spectacle of the event or from some 'alternative' stimulant (or both).. in fact that same expression, coupled with one of sheer joy and happiness was shared with pretty much everyone there.. it was a huge success and all the hard work had been worthwhile..

As I strolled around the venue, I felt a huge, communal, good-feeling vibe, people were getting really loved up and it was a feeling I hadn't felt since the good ol' daze of the Stonehenge festivals, yet it seemed to even surpass that as at Stonehenge, as great as it was, there always seemed an element of danger around, people were beaten and robbed, tents caught fire (!), cops busting people, stuff ripped off.. but at the Utopia, there were no cops (they were blissfully unaware that just down the road there were over a thousand ravers tripping the light fantastic.. in fact they were probably wondering why it was so quiet....) and the whole vibe seemed to be one of pure, unadulterated love and togetherness. To give you an example, at one point I saw this huge motherfucker of a guy hurtling towards me intent on getting right up into my face and I thought to myself "Oh well, here we go.. there was bound to be a bit of aggro.." and when he got up to me he threw his arms open and said "Oh man, I love you! This is fuckin' great!" and with that he disappeared back into the crowd.

Dr Love spun some great tunes and had the crowd heaving and the first band Salt Tank performed a great set (the main guy was a friend of Marc's, his dentist in fact, pass the Novocain!). As we prepared to go on we donned our white, hooded suits (the kind used by tradesmen - ideal for us as they could be projected on by the lightshow) plastered our faces with white make-up and Kaz, Jade and Mary our dancing girls donned their white, ballet tutus, with Kim adding an extra dimension with a cloak and crown looking like some kind of mythical Snow Queen. A hush fell over the crowd as we went onstage and as soon as the first beats began, they erupted into a huge, seething mass of dancing, smiling, party people..

Once we'd done our bit, we spent the rest of the night doing the rounds and meeting and greeting everybody. The Chill Out room was packed to the gills and there were more than just acquaintances being made there, Nick, a friend of ours had made a large wooden 'video booth' which he'd painted in all manner of psychedelic swirls and people could go in there and talk about whatever they liked. As you can imagine, as the evening wore on the conversations and situations became more and more abstract, a lot of them forgetting completely about there being a camera in there and just getting it on, making friends, making out, and making love! (When we saw the footage not long after it was amazing... hours of really far out stuff.. unfortunately the tape got accidentally wiped.. that was a real shame..).

Come closing time, everybody left in an orderly fashion and considering the sheer amount of people there the damage was minimal and the cleaners had it back up to spec in no time. We couldn't have wished for a better event if we'd tried and it could only have happened there and then. Although the whole thing had cost us a fair bit of money to put together, we managed to cover our costs and anyway it wasn't intended as a money-making exercise and I really believe the punters felt that. Unfortunately, not everybody felt that way...

We were floating on air for the next few days following the event, already talking about getting the next one together, until we got a call from the Director of the Arts Centre. It turned out that he'd received a visit from the local mobster and a few assorted heavies. His gripe was that he alleged that his son had attended the show and someone had spiked his drink and he'd arrived home really out of it. He was insisting that if there was to be another Utopia put on, then his people were to provide the 'security' and if that wasn't forthcoming then they'd do their best to ruin the show and cause a few casualties.. this was obviously a thinly-veiled attempt by them to get in on what they assumed to be a huge money-making venture. There was no way that that would happen, like I said, it wasn't about the money, in fact it was all about everyone putting in their energies and talents and giving the punters more bang for their buck. so... what to do? We could either cancel the Utopias, which none of us wanted to do or.. wait a minute? For the mobster it was all about the money.. so what if there wasn't any money? We decided to do the next one as a charity event with all proceeds (after expenses) going to the Arts Centre's disability centre. The mob would no way garner any positive publicity for smashing up a charity event, we'd get our expenses covered and a really good charity would benefit out of the deal.. problem solved!

Utopia 2 was put on not long after and again was a resounding success and unlike the previous one had attracted a reporter from the music paper 'Sounds'. He got so loved up (we helped him a little there...) he wrote a raving ('scuse the pun) review of the event and even went off and formed a band himself!

The theme for the Chill Out area this time was to be the 'Trap Door' a claymation kid's TV show voiced by Willie Rushden which was popular at the time (for kids of all ages) and Kim and her team of artists did a great job, painting the large hangings. Aside from Astralasia, bands that performed included Salt Tank and Armatage (weird name, always reminded me of a urinal...) featuring a young Jason Relf (son of the Yardbirds' Keith) on keyboards. For the Astralasia set a 'space' theme was decided upon and the girls lucked out on getting sexy space costumes from the movie 'Spaceballs'.

Once again the vibe was fantastic, coupled with the relief that there'd been no trouble as threatened, we were all extremely pleased with the outcome. We covered our expenses, the Arts Centre got their cut and best of all the Disability Centre got a fat cheque towards their facility.

MAGICK EYE ON U

The success we'd achieved releasing our own albums brought a few interested parties into the mix, each with their own theories for world mushroom domination. A lot of them turned out to be complete wasters and legends in their own lunchtimes, but one good man came through. Chris was an old friend of Marc's who was working at the time for Zomba records, a huge corporate affair that dealt with the biggest high rollers of the music scene. Of course, they weren't interested in us, but Chris had always had a hankering for forming his own record company and with a wealth of contacts at his fingertips and a genuine liking for the band he seemed like the perfect person to get it all together. He called it Magick Eye records after our tune of the same name. For the first time in our career, here was someone who not only enthused about what we did, but he put his money where his mouth was and made good on every promise. He set up excellent distribution deals, paid for advertising, sorted out the publishing and over the years has been a real pleasure to deal with. I think it's safe to say that Chris took us to the next level as far as Mushroom Band awareness went.

We tentatively started it all with two 12" releases, one each for the Magic Mushroom Band and Astralasia. The success of each being a good gauge as to how future releases would be received...

The Magic Mushroom Band release would be the tracks 'Pictures in my Mind' and a re-mix of 'Squatter in the House', both from our 'Spaced Out' album and a previously unreleased (very spaced-out in itself) version of Pink Floyd's 'Set the Controls for the Heart of the Sun'. The cover featured my painted face super imposed over a dawn solstice photo of Stonehenge.

We decided that for a hoot (and a bit of scandal/hype), for the 'promotional' copies that we were sending to the media we'd slip in a small plastic baggie of dried mushrooms. Plans for the real 'magic' ones were soon scuppered as a wave of paranoia and visions of 'live from Wormwood Scrubs' albums being released took effect. Instead we popped down to the local Safeways and purchased lots of packets of dried field mushrooms. Once the records arrived back from the pressers we got a posse together and slipped the mushrooms into the respective sleeves... Well, the hype didn't quite cause the stir we expected, some must have ignored them, not noticed them, but there were a few who wondered what the hell was going on and in fact one record store owner thought they were real ones and went off big time...

The Astralasia 12" featured two tracks 'Celestial Ocean' and 'Rhythm of Life' both excellent tracks, my personal favourite being the kool jazzete-style of 'Rhythm of Life' which was the first Astralasia track to be played on the radio. That was a real buzz to hear as we knew when it was going to be played and we all gathered together for the event.

Both releases did well, not quite elevating us to tax-exile status but getting our names out there nonetheless and receiving many positive reviews. Enough so at least for Chris to want to devote his record company to the furtherment of both bands. Which he did and continues to this day to do. Good onya Chris!

REHASH

Around about this time, Kim and I had a chance to get over to Australia to catch up with family and have a bit of a break (although a three-week trip over Xmas was hardly chill-out time!). It was great to catch up with everyone and grab a bit of well needed sunshine. Upon our return, Marc had been working with Jason Relf (son of Yardbird Keith) who lived locally and had been recording some keyboard-based dance tracks. He had some good, fresh ideas to bring into the mix so we invited him to join the band. It was good to have some new blood, but also just as important that he would provide valuable input for the next phase of the band.

The Acid House/Dance scene was growing like wildfire and with the growing success of Astralasia and the positive comments we got with regard to our initial toe-dipping into that genre with the Magic Mushroom Band prompted us to have a go at releasing a whole album with a modern, dance vibe. We titled the album 'Rehash' because we'd decided to re-record our most popular tunes with dance grooves and also to throw in a couple of cover versions of our favourite tunes also done in that style. It was a brave attempt on our part, admittedly some of it worked better than others, but we weren't afraid to take chances! Reaction to it was very mixed with some people admiring our merging the two scenes and others feeling we'd created the utmost sin and sold out (man)! (This was kinda ironic as by the mid-nineties most freaks could be found at one 'chill out/trance' event or other!). Regardless of the mixed opinions about ReHash, it became one of our best selling albums and even reared its pointy little head in various indie charts.

R U SPACED OUT 2

The success of ReHash prompted us to get back in the studio and work on a new album while the iron was hot. Taking in all

The Spaced Out Process...

sides of the digital versus live recording aspects, we decided to make a more concentrated effort to blend the two more successfully.

I'd had a few tunes knocking around in my head and the band was in a good place so recording this one was a breeze. We decided to include a cover of Hawkwind's 'Hurry on Sundown' as we'd jammed it a few times and the slide guitar and fiddle really gave it some extra flavour. As hoped, the album did really well, topping some indie charts and receiving really positive reviews. We were riding high and finally it felt like all the hard work was paying off. The quality of the venues we were invited to play were improving too, Brixton Academy, The Rocket, Marquee and numerous Sports Centres and Universities around the country and we were playing with some great (and my favourite) bands including Hawkwind, The Pink Fairies and Gong.. whodathunkit??

ALL ABOARD FOR CRAZY TOWN!

Finally, after three and a half years of being 'The Munsters' in our new-town suburbian hell that was Forest Park, a postcard that we'd put in a newsagent's window had prompted someone to contact Kim and I with regard to a possible house swap. We were so desperate to get out of that place we would have taken anything.. but as it turned out, she was offering an old, three bedroom house with a huge garden in the nearby picturesque village of Crowthorne. She said the rooms were too big for her and the garden too much to deal with so she was looking to swap for something smaller and more modern.. result!! We obviously agreed right away and within a couple of weeks we were in there, contracts signed and records unpacked.

Crowthorne itself is a beautiful village, surrounded by pine forests and steeped in history. Part of the forest is called 'Caesar's Camp' as he'd once stopped around there with his army and the area had a very spooky feel about it, with numerous sightings of Romans on horseback and various hootings and hollerings. The village itself has a real High Street as opposed to Bracknell's modern 'mall', lots of second-hand shops and felt a lot more homelier all round.

Of course, Crowthorne is known for more than it's rural pleasantness as it sites the infamous Broadmoor Maximum Security Facility. Yep, where all the REAL psychos are sent! Among the crazies was a Kray Twin and the infamous Yorkshire Ripper, Phil Sutcliffe who, not long after we moved into the area had been stabbed in the eye with a pen by a disgruntled fellow inmate.. yeesh! A lot of the locals worked at Broadmoor and it became a bit of a joke when you saw a huge guy who was obviously a warden and a lot of them would have bite-sized chunks out of their ears or other scars and afflictions.. and in fact the whole village had a bit of a slightly mad edge to it.. One contributing factor to the crazy air could have been something that we weren't warned about until we'd moved in. We found out the hard way that every Monday morning at 10 o' clock the siren at Broadmoor was tested and if we thought it was tucked away far enough not to be a problem we were sorely mistaken! We were working in the garden and when this noise started, if you didn't run for cover with your hands firmly clamped over your ears, by the time the 'all clear' had finished you would have been eligible for a spell there yourself, with or without pen..

The house itself was amazing as was the garden. The reason that such a large property was let by the council was because it was a 'pre-fab' as in a pre-fabricated house, one of many that was built in the 1950's by German prisoners of war to recompense for bombing us during the war. The upside was indeed the huge size of the rooms and lovely well-established (private) garden and brick out-buildings. Downside was that the prefabs weren't brick houses, they were built from layers of concrete slats to save on expense and although the size made up for it, it was virtually impossible to heat sufficiently. It was bloody freezing there! Especially when the snows came, we'd often go to bed fully dressed, not daring to bare any flesh for fear of frostbite.. but the summers were glorious and we had many a crazy party there.

The street we lived in had a real community, almost Bohemian feel to it, there were lots of families that had been there for years and they were all very accepting of us and we felt very comfortable there. It had its fair share of 'characters' in the street, the neighbour on one side was a horror story writer and the little old lady (who loved us 'veggies') on the other side was the local (unofficial) animal rescuer, she had lots of cats and recouping birds and was always campaigning and going on marches for animal rights. Because we now had the space, we decided to finally get some chickens and when we told her about it she said that she could get hold of some ex-battery farm chickens that need a good home. We keenly expressed our interest until she confessed that as they were ex-battery they'd had their beaks cut off and were very light on feathers. We said we'd think about it..

I mentioned the downside being the cold in the house, but as it turned out, a much larger problem was looming.. to be fair, the lady who we'd exchanged with had warned us about the pre-fab houses being eventually demolished and replaced with modern housing, but they were only supposed to have been up for ten years and they'd survived forty years so far.. Of course, we weren't even there for a year before we got a notice from the Council saying that our house was unfit to live in and a 'health risk' (read taking up too much valuable land) and that they would be consulting with a Housing Association with regard to either fixing up the current homes or preferably knocking down the entire street (40 houses) and instead building 75 modern 'compact' homes and 'easy maintenance' gardens and a block of flats! The deal was that they'd interview each household in the street and it would be put to the vote..

We loved our new home and weren't going to give it up without a fight and so we hastily called a meeting with the other residents on the green outside our house and explained to them that we'd just come from a new, easy-maintenance house and that it was the stuff of nightmares and would destroy and decimate the community. We had a good response from the neighbours, most of them wanting to go the option of having our existing houses renovated. Then came the fateful day of our interview with the Housing Association representative.. There was a tappity-tap on our door which opened to reveal a swarthy dude with an equally swarthy moustache and a large briefcase. We invited him in and he proceeded to slither and sleaze as he offered us all the modern conveniences of living in a smaller, modern property. When we explained that we'd just left screaming from such an estate and that we wouldn't be voting for his option, he hurriedly gathered his glossy brochures and moustache and left the house. Thus began our campaign to save our beautiful house and indeed the whole street.

We wrote constantly to the local papers about our plight and harassed the council on a regular basis, saying that we wouldn't leave our place unless they could provide us with something of equal proportions in a similar area (something we knew they'd have trouble finding). We were dug in and giving them hell. Unfortunately, as the swarthy salesman worked his way along the street he eventually managed to sway a lot of the residents with promises of luxurious central heating and the easy maintenance of it all. Inevitably the Council sent us all a memo announcing that the decision had been made and the houses were coming down.

MAGIC

With all the crazy antics going on at home, a welcome distraction was the making of the next Magic Mushroom Band album 'Magic'. We were still riding high on the success of the previous album and although we'd since lost Jay Relf to solo projects and had to shift to a smaller studio, we'd accumulated a few good, new tunes that were ripe for recording. Due to the ongoing negative reactions (from those that didn't matter I hasten to add) about the band's name, we thought we'd try just calling ourselves The Mushroom Band and calling the album 'Magic'. As it turned out, it made no real difference at all, but I guess you have to try these things!

Kim had the idea of doing a collage for the cover and seeing as she was the only person we knew that even came close to having that kind of patience, she soon set to armed with lots of old photographs and magazine cuttings. The end result looked great, although the vinyl version was much easier to see. This album again got good chart action, but we were beginning to notice the shift in 'the scene' toward the more 'Ambient/Techno' vibe, something I believe we were partly responsible for ourselves, but which didn't bode well for the bands as much as it did the DJ's....

RADIO ONE YOU'RE IN MY HEAD

With the release of 'Magic' we finally got the call we'd been waiting for. BBC Radio One's Mark Radcliffe had called and wanted us to do a live session and interview for his evening show. We were a bit tentative because we'd lost out previously on a John Peel session, but he was good for his word and the session was booked for a Thursday night at BBC Manchester. And thus began one of the most bizarre evenings of my life...

Upon arriving we were ushered into the 'green room' where we would hang out until the show was underway. Live radio sessions are a bit of a daunting task at the best of times, let alone for the BBC, you knew you'd have a large listening audience, but how many thousands?? To ease the tension, I'd brought along a great game called 'UFO Attack' that I'd been hopelessly addicted to since I found it at a car boot fair. It was set up like a small pinball, but the ball took out little UFOs and the first to wipe them all out was the winner and ruled the Universe.

Mark Radcliffe eventually poked his head through the door (peering quizzically at what we were playing), introduced himself and said good luck.. oh, and that he'd be talking to us from a studio on the floor above and all communication would be through our headphones.. wow, interviewed by someone who wasn't there in front of you! So off we went to the studio, set up our gear, donned our headphones and waited for our cue. We all assumed the position and listened intently as the show started. After a while I got kinda used to it and it just felt like I was listening to the radio on my 'phones (which I was!) but suddenly the radio said "...And now, I'm going to speak to the Magic Mushroom Band who are going to play live for us tonight, hello Garry??" Fortunately I pulled myself together in time and after a chat about the album and an introduction to the members of the band we proceed to do our tunes. We did 'When Dreams Collide' from 'Magic', 'Hubbly Bubbly' and an acoustic 'Life is so Strange' from 'RU Spaced Out 2'. We all played really well with good energy (although due to nerves a coupla tunes were super-speedy!). We got on really well with Mark, who seemed a true fan and he came down after to thank us..

BYE BYE MUSHROOM

As much as the release of the album 'Magic' showed promising sales and the radio session had given the band a much higher profile, the live scene for us was in a sorry state. The free festivals were a thing of the past and the 'official' ones weren't too keen to add us to the bill, in fact, we'd just had a festival cancelled (one of many) with Back to the Planet among others because the police objected to our name on the bill.. they said we promoted drug taking..?!?!

At the same time we had the 'popular' music press making a fashion statement out of our scene (best way to make something unpopular is to make it popular first!) and had heralded the birth of 'Crusty', a generic term for those of the festival/traveller/pothead persuasion and all that surrounded it. Apart from the ridicule, the image of the straggly ragtaggle with a dog on the string which permeated most reviews of bands in our scene at the time, some people actually bought into it and almost became a parody of themselves and sales of dogs, string and stripey jumpers went through the roof. It seems rather comical now, but at the time, although I knew a band called The Magic Mushroom Band would never get on Top of the Pops, I thought that after twelve years of hard slog, the numerous albums and our huge fanbase that the press would at least give us some credit as musicians... silly me..

Due also to the bourgening 'Ethno-Ambient/Trance' scene, our other project Astralasia had itself become a monster in its own right. Album sales were doing very well and the quality of gigs were improving immensely with regular appearances at Whirly-Gig, Megadog, WOMAD, even Empire Pool, Wembley! As we put more and more energy into feeding that demand, so less could be spent on the Magic Mushroom Band shows where the venues were definitely diminishing as more and more clubs turned themselves over to the dance scene..

The final nail in the coffin for me was what turned out to be the last Magic Mushroom Band gig ever. It was in a tiny club just outside Cardiff, Wales. The promoter had been hassling me for a while to play there, it was quite a journey for us and we were still hiring vans for gigs and as we'd lost Jasper (Fruit Salad Lights) to an Ozric Tentacles tour, we also had to hire a lightshow and pay eight musicians and crew.. I suggested a suitable fee to the promoter, one which I thought would just about cover everything and he agreed by contract to cover it. We had the typical long, cold, rainy drive to South Wales and arrived at the club in time for the soundcheck. We were a bit suspicious about the lack of people hovering around outside waiting to get in, but the promoter assured us that there was a good scene there, he'd done lots of advertising and it'd do well. Of course, it didn't.. there was but a handful of people who turned up, but we soldiered on and gave a good show to those that were there, content at least that we had our expenses covered. At the end of the night, I looked over to the promoter and saw an expression that filled me with dread, I'd seen that look too many times before! He shuffled up to me all sheepishly and said "Oh man.. that was great, thanks a lot for coming.. (here it comes...) unfortunately there weren't as many people as I'd expected but I managed to scrape some money together for you...". What he offered was nothing short of an insult and wouldn't even have covered the van hire and petrol. The whole band and crew threw their arms up in the air and left me to deal with it. After explaining to the promoter that I actually had a contract with the agreed fee on it, signed by him and that he had to come up with that amount, his attitude suddenly changed. He started calling me all the names under the sun and that he was just trying to get a scene together and we were nothing but a bunch of breadheads....

Breadheads.. now that hurt.. after twelve years of innumerable free festivals, countless benefit gigs, struggling just to pay the bills at home. I, in turn, laid into him and got him to get more money together and mail the balance to me. I was devastated for a while after that.. it had got that stupid.. so I decided there and then that it was best to put the Magic Mushroom Band to rest while it still had some dignity, the last real high being the Radio One session... that was where we would leave it.

Looking back on it now.. I still think I would have done the same thing. The band had seen twelve years of absolute craziness, but people are still talking about it all even now.. and many of our old fans have become dear friends..

DEPARTING ASTRALASIA

As mentioned previously, Astralasia had really taken off and all the hard work we'd put into it had paid off. The albums and singles were selling well and we'd gained a good reputation as a live act worth checking out. Kim and the girls' choreography combined with their outrageous outfits helped us to stand out from the crowd and the live sets were stomping with some really good tunes, especially 'Sul-e-Stomp' a track we'd done with Suns of Arqa which never failed to get the kids going..

By this time we were regulars at the 'Whirly-Gig' shows at Shoreditch Town Hall and at Mega-Dog events and countless festivals and events around the country and abroad. It sounds like the stuff of dreams, but I was beginning to have a problem with it all. I felt empty... vacuous. As great as the tunes were, I often felt like a spare wheel and I wasn't writing anything towards it and a guitarist's lot in the digital dance scene is a slim one! We'd do some great full-on shows but I'd wake up the next morning wondering if I'd done it yet.. something had to give!

I eventually had to speak to Kim about it and she told me she'd been feeling the same way as the music was slipping more and more into the Trance vibe, which although great listening, didn't really give much scope for live choreographed performances.

After our next show with Astralasia, I approached Swordfish and told him that me and Kim were jumping ship. It certainly wasn't an easy decision to make and it was a really hard thing to do. We'd all been through so much together, but the band would carry on without us and we'd be free to pursue something more challenging.

So, after all those years and all the craziness, seeing the rise, against seemingly unsurmountable odds, with both the Magic Mushroom Band and Astralasia, the crazy shows, all those albums, I suddenly had nothing! No music, not even a secure home! If I felt empty in Astralasia, it was nothing compared to how I felt after letting go of it all. I was in a deep funk for a very long time after that and it took a lot of work, and a lot of support and comfort from loved ones and good friends to get me through it...

So.. whatcha gonna do now, eh??

The all-acoustic Moonboot Oz circa 1996

Let the fun begin!

MOONBOOT OZ

After a while (and much analysing of my situation) I got to thinking about what I should do next, bearing in mind that I really needed to satisfy my songwriting urges and to get playing again. In a flash of inspiration, I had a cunning plan.. If I'd felt limited by playing with digital dance music then I'd go completely the opposite way and go acoustic, and nothing but, just me on acoustic guitar and vocals, a percussionist and Kim on vocals and her recently acquired Indian Harmonium. If I had any doubts about this project, they were soon dispelled once I sat down to write a few suitable tunes.

For the first time in a long while, I suddenly had no limits, I could write any style, whatever took my fancy (or, more often as not, fell out of my head at that time) and it felt like the floodgates had opened.. song after song flowed out of my head, ballads, reggae, world fusion, if I could play it on my acoustic then it was in. I'd mentioned what I was doing to ex-Mushroom drummer Jim and he said he'd be more than happy to come in on percussion. We had some great jams at home and the new project was born. Taking mine and Kim's stage surnames, we decided to christen it Moonboot Oz.

ORGANIC MUSHROOMS

After not very long, we had a full set of original, acoustic Moonboot Oz material and after our first live appearances, the first one funnily enough at Windsor Arts Centre where the Magic Mushroom Band had debuted, we sorted out four of our favourite songs for our first recording venture. Vince, a good friend of ours, had got a little recording studio together at his home and offered to record for us and we laid down a rhythmic (already live favourite) tune called 'Adjust Yourself', 'Is Anybody there?'(a song about UFO's, not audience numbers!) a ballad 'When Will that Be?' and a jaunty little number called 'Red Sea Blue'. We'd decided to start simple with just a four track e.p to introduce us and fortunately, Chris from Magick Eye Records saw fit to release it on a subsidiary label especially set up for us called 'Chameleon Records'. It took a while for word to get about who we were (no Facebook then!), but the more we played the better the crowds got and we started to get a few good reviews for the e.p. Although not a 'million seller', it was proof enough for me that I was doing the right thing...

SACHA BARON COHEN & THE MOONBOOT MAN

Not long after the e.p's release, I got a call from Chris from Magick Eye saying that there was a Cable music, art and current affairs TV show called 'Pump TV' who'd heard the Moonboot Oz e.p and would like us to play and be interviewed live on their show. Amazingly enough, after all those years of the Magic Mushroom Band and Astralasia, apart from Kim's elbow being shown in a short clip about Deptford's The Crypt club and a few short clips of my campaign at the Kensington By-Election on the BBC Nine O' Clock News, we'd never had any TV exposure, cable or otherwise.. so we jumped at the chance. The show's host was called Sacha, who we'd meet upon arrival at the studio. The show was being broadcast from their studio in Slough, so there wasn't much travelling to get there and upon arrival we were ushered into place. The TV studio was actually just one huge room, but each corner was arranged as its own individual set, so as each segment finished another camera would start filming a different corner.

After taking all of five minutes to set up (I can't stress enough how luxurious that was for us!), the doors swung open and in waltzes this dude in a shiny silver suit, all teeth and hair and looking very much the show's compare. From the moment his teeth entered the room we knew that this guy was destined to be a star, he really had it going on. This was Sacha Baron Cohen, just pre 'Ali G' and the ensuing stardom and it couldn't have happened to a funnier guy!

The only bummer was that upon setting up, we were informed that we couldn't actually play live as they didn't have the facilities to do it, so we would have to mime! We did two songs from the e.p and the interview and the whole experience was a real blast. You can find the clips on Youtube I do believe..

THE GREEN MACHINE

As word of our little act got about, the offers of live work started to come in. The beauty of our setup was that there were only three of us with acoustic instruments, so we'd just travel to shows in our car and for festivals it was a real boon as there'd be no hire van involved and we could stay longer. Having such a small, easy to set up act helped us to get slots on some great All Dayers as we could set up and play in between the main bands' sets and we did some great shows with our old compadres Gong, Ozric Tentacles and Here and Now as well as club gigs and festival appearances in our own right.

At one point we met up with a guy called Nick from Reading who had pioneered a 'Bicycle-Powered' stage and the way it worked was that there would be a row of tandem bicycles which audience members would take turns to pedal, and these in turn would power the stage p.a and lights. It was a great, albeit surreal, idea in that he could set up anywhere, anytime and the stage would be up and running in no time at all. The surreal part was actually playing on this stage looking out to a sea of pedalling audience members, I remember wondering whether if they tired, would our music slow down????

As our reputation grew we got more and more festival offers, in particular the Green Fayres which were just coming into their own at the time. They tended to be more sedate affairs, with the emphasis more on the green-ness of the event, so no loud, banging techno then, and they seemed to attract more family-based, laid-back orientated people, which actually made them a pleasure to do as there just weren't any crazy vibes around..

THE PSYCHEDELIC CAFE

One of our favourite shows during that period was in a coffee
shop in Glastonbury. It was amazing for me how this little band
was able to do things that I hadn't been able to do previously,
for after all those years with the Magic Mushroom Band and
Astralasia we had never, ever played at Glastonbury, festival or
otherwise! We had such a blast on that night, it inspired me for
how the upcoming Moonboot Oz album might be themed.

We decided to call the album 'Music from the Psychedelic Café'
and the track listing would be like a menu, with a description
of each 'dish' and I would design a cartoon picture for the
cover, only the second time I'd ever done that, the first was an
Astralasia cover for the single 'MAD'. Rod Mansell, a good
friend of ours who had previously contributed sounds for the
Magic Mushroom Band album 'Eyes of the Angel', was keen to
record the album for us, so armed with acoustic guitars, a
harmonium, bongos and assorted percussive instruments we
laid down the tracks/dishes.

It was a great atmosphere in Rod's studio, good humoured
with a laid back vibe and I think it shows in the recording! We
did relent a bit with the 'acoustic only' rule (because we could!)
and I added some electric bass and we had keyboard player
Quiller (ex 'Moksha') lay down some warm sounds and piano.
As a special treat we had our old friend and ex-mushroom
Janey come down to lay some vocal tracks with Kim. Aside
from the All About Eve comparisons and the 'What the Hell are
they Doing?' type reviews, we got some good feedback about
the album and I felt like a songwriter again.. and it was good.

ELECTRIC MOONBOOTS!

As is the norm for most musicians, as you go along in life, you meet other musicians who you would really like to add to your sound and such was the case with Quiller on keyboards and a bass player we'd recently met called Andy. Andy was (and still is) an amazing bass player, wired with energy, the type of guy you could jam with endlessly (and I did!). He brought to the mix his Rickenbacker bass (a sound I'd always loved) and his Chapman 'stick', a weird instrument, favoured by bassists, with many more strings, that he would tap and pluck and had a unique sound of its own.. sweet! He'd played with various bands over the years (including, amazingly, Sham 69!) and picked up the Moonboot Oz vibe very quickly.. so combined with the urge I was getting to have a full band behind me again, we expanded the lineup with Quiller on keyboards, Andy on bass and our daughter Jasmine on backing vocals.

Rehearsals with the full band went well and most of the songs easily lent themselves to being 'electrified'! Jasmine and Quiller's partner Gabi had been studying Egyptian Belly Dancing and we worked out a percussive segment for them to shake their shimmies to. Well, here we go again! Back to a full band once more, but we kept the fun angle to the fore and it all had a good vibe to it. We only did a few standard clubs and concentrated mainly on the upcoming festivals for that year.

Apart from the Greens, Guildford, Bracknell festivals and other suitable gatherings we were particularly looking forward to our first ever live appearance proper at that year's Glastonbury Festival which went down really well and we met many old friends and faces, even having our lights done by our old friend Jasper of Fruit Salad Lights and our sound by regular Mushroom Band engineer, the formidable Rat. The whole event was a real blast, even the fact that it rained constantly all weekend (and anyone who's ever been to the Glastonbury Festival will know the hell on earth that it becomes!) couldn't dampen our spirits that weekend!

But the festival experience to beat them all that year was soon to follow. We'd been invited to play at a New Age festival being held at the Ascot Racecourse, which was great for us as it was just down the road from where we lived! It was a very posh affair, being Ascot, where even Her Majesty the Queen was known to have a flutter and there was a fairground and countless New Age stalls selling everything from crystals to new personalities. It had a nice atmosphere and it was a family event so all cool and laid back, smiley cops, the lot....

It was only just as we were about to go onstage that a passing comment suddenly transformed my day into yet another one of those surreal moments in my life...

It was one of the sound engineers who'd said it just as I was strapping on my guitar.. "Jus' fort oi'd let ya know that Jimmy Page is in the audience and he's looking forward to hearing you".. he said it to me in pretty much the same manner as if he'd said to me "Ere, moind yer 'ead on the way out". As I digested what he'd just said, the sheer enormity of what I was about to subject myself to suddenly hit me like a ton of bricks. I had no doubt about the abilities of my bandmates, they'd be great, but I'd just had a large Jamaican Woodbine backstage and as I looked at my hands, they suddenly didn't feel like my own.. not a good time to be Mr Wobbly Head! But, being the consumate professional that I was (ahem!) I took a deep breath and went onstage. Of course my plan was just to forget who was in the audience and just go for it, but one nervous eye just would not stop peering out to try and find him, luckily I couldn't see him, that would have just made it worse!

As we worked our way through the set I began to relax and get into it, in fact, I'd gone way past the caring factor and was actually getting some sweet sounds from my guitar and playing it with gusto. This is great from a performing side of things but my ol' Fender Stratocaster can only handle so much gusto before things start to go 'ping!' And so it was, that during the lead guitar solo on a new number called 'Breathe' which was the last one of the set, I didst bend the string just a bit too much and 'ker-doinnnggg!' I managed to snap a string. Bollocks! It had all been going really well and I really felt like I'd conquered my (admittedly rare) stage nerves and was cooking on gas and then that had to happen. But, hey, this is Rock and Roll baby and I just got to thinking 'What would Jimmy do?'. So, upon hearing said string ping (and the guitar tuning drop down a tone!) while still twiddly-diddling with my left hand, I managed to reach into my equipment bag with my right hand and change the string, tuning it up as near as dammit and finishing the song with as much dignity as I could muster.. Wow! That was almost a Cheech and Chong moment, but the show must go on, eh? Jimmy did send a message backstage after, saying that he'd enjoyed the show, although I don't know what he enjoyed the most, the band's performance, or the sight of a freaked out Chong type wrestling to get a string out of its packet while still playing a lead guitar solo...

That turned out to be the last ever live show for Moonboot Oz, not through any disappointment, but we'd done some great gigs and we were all getting involved in other projects and none of us at the time wanted it to get too 'full on' again..

We did go back into Rod's studio to record an e.p called 'Lost in Space' which pretty much summed up how we were at the time, but up until now it has never been released...

EARTHLIGHT AT YOGA NIGHT

Throughout the nineties, Kim had been studying to be a Yoga Teacher under The British Wheel of Yoga and her Swami, Satchidananda Ma had a trust set up to provide funds for a planned Yoga Centre. There'd been numerous fundraising events but nothing that brought in any kind of substantial amounts of much needed cash. Always thinking one step ahead, Kim suggested a gala performance at the Wilde Theatre in Bracknell and set about organising acts from across the spectrum of 'alternative' practices including a Tai Chi demonstration, a Cello recital, a Native Drum workshop, a Tibetan throat singer, a Yoga dance troupe and a beaming, yogic motivational speaker and singer who was once, would you believe, lead singer with the band The Rubettes (!). Not quite our usual affair then, but a show is a show, and we'd had plenty of practise with all that.

One more act added to the bill was our new project for the night, an 'ethno/ambient' act that we called 'Earthlight', featuring myself on didgeridoo, Kim and Jasmine on vocals and dance, Quiller on keyboards, Andy on his Stick and Martin (previously with ambient outfit TUU) on ethnic percussion. We recorded an ambient piece on our home studio and decided to perform it live on the night.

Against insurmountable odds, Kim managed to pull it off and the show was a real success, selling out within a couple of weeks. The place was decorated really nicely on the night and our old friend Jon was providing the light show and it all looked really impressive. Kim was a sight to see, as she hurried around talking into her headpiece as she set about organising the acts, the lights, the sets and appearing onstage at various times during the night with various performances. The whole thing went off without a hitch, the audience loved it and it earned a huge amount of money for the Yoga Centre.

I JUS' WANNA RIDE ON MA MOTORSICKLE!

While taking a (well earned) break from all the music craziness, I decided to fulfill another lifelong dream of mine and finally get around to getting a motorcycle of my own. Over the years I'd seen many friends getting motorbikes but through a (constant) severe lack of funds and the risk of damaging myself and being unable to do gigs or recording, I'd never had the pleasure of owning my own. I'd bought an old Triumph T110 engine with the aim of building a chopper and had begged and borrowed (but not stole) a hardtailed frame and various other custom parts for it, but I had no money (or skills, or time) to finish it and I got so frustrated one day I swapped it all for a mountain bike!

Of course the 'custom' motorcyles were what attracted me the most, like most guys my age I'd spent many a pubescent moment thumbing through an Easyriders magazine and occasionally glancing away from the women just long enough to notice the shiny, kool motorcycles they were draped over. I'd always loved the custom scene, many bikers were friends of ours and the bands we played in.

Fate stepped in relatively soon, in the shape of a friend of our roadie Spiney (himself a biker who'd been a member of the local 'Lepers' motorcycle club) called Spotty who worked at the local Council Dump and had picked up a motorbike that had been left there. I know, I know, 'beggars can't be choosers', but it wasn't as bad as I'd thought it would be, when for the sum of fifty pounds he produced a Jawa 350cc in suprisingly good condition. I had a bike! Of course, ya gets what ya pay for and it never was reliable enough to get out on the road but I managed to sell it for a decent sum and most importantly of all, it had introduced me to a new friend Steve, who not only had a nice bike of his own, but was a good bike mechanic and would help me realise my two wheeled dreams over the coming years.

I was still a long way from the custom bike of my dreams, but I always operate best when I have goals and fate does seem to smile on those who dare to dream, eh?

In no time at all, I'd found a Yamaha XS Custom in the local paper for the immense sum of a hundred and fifty pounds (!). A Harley it wasn't, but it looked cooler than the average jap bike and it gave me the chance to learn how to customise, so with the help of Steve, we lowered the seat, got a teardrop tank for it and plopped on some 'ape-hanger' bars, Kim had even made me a leather tool-roll for my birthday. For not a lot of money, I was suddenly 'out there', knees in the breeze, 'In The Wind' as it were... I hung on to that bike for years and it was still running when I eventually sold it..

By that point, I'd really got the taste for it all and wanted a bigger bike to customise, I wanted to make a real chopper as opposed to a factory custom. Of course, my budget was literally what I got for the Yamaha, which wasn't much but back into the local trade papers I dived anyway and it wasn't long before I came across a Honda 550 'streetfighter' (a term in the UK for a basically stock bike that's been hardtailed, giving that long, low stance but providing the stability in the front end of a standard bike.. well... stability be damned!). I picked it up from nearby Camberley in Surrey for the princely sum of two hundred pounds. Of course, for that kind of money, it was rough as fuck. It had been under a tarpaulin for a few years in all weathers, but it was all there, an ideal basis for the project I had in mind and the owner had even managed to get it started.. bonus! Especially as we didn't have a trailer and I had to ride it home... of course I was only ten minutes down the road when it decided to conk out but after much kicking and cursing I eventually got it back home.

Off came the stock petrol tank, bars, indicators, ratty old cables and shitty seat to be replaced by a mustang tank (tastefully customised with metallic purple and silver ghost flames courtesy of my old mate/roadie and customiser Kelvin), a shiny new set of apehangers, tiny custom indicators, braided steel cables and Kim re-made and upholstered a new seat and we added an 'old school' sissy bar and coated the frame with more metallic purple. By the time we'd finished it was looking most kool! Unfortunately, the engine never really got over the trauma of being stuck out in all the elements for all that time and when we did eventually get it going I was followed everywhere by huge plumes of white smoke! Subtle it wasn't! It was a great learning curve for me, but I wanted something equally as cool but a bit more reliable, so I eventually sold it for considerably more than I paid for it, I wonder if it's still out there smokin'?

Of course, like most custom bike afficianados my dream was

always to own a Harley Davidson, but up until then there weren't many on the road in the UK as they were just plain out of reach pricewise for most custom bike riders, plus the 'Shovelhead' motors that Harley were putting out through the seventies were unreliable to the point where you had to be a qualified mechanic just to keep the things on the road. The introduction of the much more reliable 'Evolution' engine in the mid-eighties had resolved all that and due to the popularity (and reliability!) of the new Harleys people were more than willing to take the gamble, hence more Harleys than ever out there on the roads.

It was when Steve sold his Kawasaki chopper and bought a Harley Sportster for a reasonable price that I realised it could be possible for me to get one too. I'd managed to pick up a bit of work at that time and with a bit of financial juggling, I found myself in the unlikely position of being able to get one! So, at the grand ol' age of forty, amid cries of 'mid-life crisis!' I set about finding a Harley of my own and in no time at all I found myself in a Harley shop in North London. I'd seen a cheap Sportster advertised there but upon inspection by the time I'd fixed it up and got it into decent shape it would have cost a lot more. It was then that Kim said to me 'Well, how about that one?' and over in the corner of the shop was a beautiful, shiny red Sportster, four years old at the time and it looked like it had hardly been ridden. The shop had got it as a trade-in and after some serious haggling I did the deed and with a "See ya back at home!" to Kim, on came the helmet and I was off! There's very little that comes close to the feeling of getting your first Harley if that's what you have a hankering for and I couldn't wipe the grin off my face all the way home, that beautiful throb of the Harley engine, the reflection of the chrome and throughout the journey people would turn their heads to marvel at this grinning idiot on his new toy!

I hadn't told Steve that I'd bought it, so I casually invited him around that evening and his jaw hit the floor when he arrived. Of course, what's the point of having a biker buddy if you're not constantly trying to have the cooler bike? So not long after,

Steve traded his Sportster for a larger Heritage Softail.. I had a
good, fun couple of years on that Sportster taking in
Harley/Custom bike shows and checking out all the Harley
shops which were springing up around London or just going
for rides with Steve and a few other local riding buddies. It also
made it a lot easier to get up in the mornings and go to work!
There was a bike shed there and it shone out like a jewel
among the Jap racers and BMWs.

JASMINE BLOOMS

Naturally I hadn't totally given up with the music, I was still
writing songs and jamming around, I just didn't want to get
into anything too serious. I'd been lent an eight-track home
recording studio and got loads of stuff down on there. But
there was another burgeoning star in our household who was
preparing to let her star shine...

Having spent her childhood surrounded by musicians and all
that goes along with that lifestyle, my now-teenaged daughter
Jasmine was playing guitar and keyboards and had begun
writing her own stuff. She'd developed an amazing voice honed
over the years of listening to all the varied types of music in
our household as well as soaking up all the vocal acrobatics of
the soul/R&B that she was listening to at the time. I'd already
snuck her into my local pub where at the age of sixteen (!) she
won the karaoke contest and after receiving the fifty pounds
prize money she very quickly got the taste for performing! She
was also studying Performing Arts at the local College at the
time..

We'd recorded a few songs of Jasmine's on the eight-track and
started putting it around as a demo, not only getting her a huge
article in the local paper, but securing her live appearances at
the Bracknell Festival and eventually Glastonbury! Because all
of her tunes were in a funk/R&B style, I'd managed to work all
the music out on one digital keyboard, so I was the 'band' and

Kim helped out on backing vocals. The shows were very well received, especially Glastonbury and it gave Jasmine a real boost and helped immensely to get her to the point of being the amazing performer that she is today.

FAREWELL TO THE OLD COUNTRY

So, the Millennium had come and gone with a bang and a whimper. I'd got a good job earning good money and after being relocated by the council to a great new home, we'd decided to buy our house and all was good with the world. The only problem was that after a while, we were starting to feel 'comfortably numb', we were beginning to feel like we'd achieved everything that we'd set out to do (and more!) and new challenges were very much needed. Kim had gone back to her native Australia over Xmas for our friends Mandy and Tim's wedding in Brisbane and to visit her family in Adelaide, I'd spent my money on the Harley and stayed at home!

Not only did I miss Kim over Xmas more than I can explain, but when she came back all healthy and tanned with tales of amazing adventures and shitloads of photos of her in the sun, in the sea and to be honest, the happiest I'd seen her in a long time, we got to thinking that maybe it was the perfect time to think about making the big move to the other side of the planet! It had always been in our plans, we were just waiting for the right moment. All three of us sat down and had a good, long talk about it and we made the decision there and then to go for it, but we would all go over first for a visit to check it all out, house prices etc.

It'd been ten years since me and Jasmine had been back to Australia, but it was exactly how we'd hoped it would be, we all had a ball and couldn't wait to get back to the UK to start packing. Obviously, it wasn't as cut and dried as that seems, it was a huge decision as I would be leaving my family and all of our good friends that we'd made over the years, but in the end it was all about quality of life for me and Kim, but more importantly for Jasmine. She was eighteen by this time, finished with school and college and ready to start a new phase in her life. We were initially worried that she might not want to go but after the preliminary visit she was packed before we were!

I'm a firm believer in the ol' adage that 'if it's meant to be, it's meant to be' and in a relatively short space of time we'd sold the house (and the Harley!) at a great price, jacked in our jobs and had a twenty-foot container delivered to our door. Luckily, Kim's brother in Australia was owed a favour by a guy who owned a shipping company and the whole transition was all as smooth as smooth can be. Luck was also on our side as at the time the English pound was very strong against the Aussie dollar so once the money got transferred we made a few bob in the process with which to start our new life. We had a huge farewell 'do' at our local pub and after many kisses and hugs, and a few tears, we were off......... Destination Australia!

Garry Moonboot and Kim Oz now reside on eleven acres in the Adelaide Hills of South Australia. Garry divides his time between demonstrating and selling didgeridoos and other aboriginal artifacts (!), riding his beloved Harley Davidson Heritage Softail and supplying articles and cartoons for 'OZBIKE' the Australian custom motorcycle magazine. He has also recently been coaxed out of musical retirement to perform, along with Kim and Jasmine with local band 'Elwood Road' and a recently reformed Moonboot Oz....

A Few Thanx:

Thanx to my lovely Kim for her never ending inspiration and love, my beautiful daughter Jasmine just for making me so proud and also Michael for providing me with much needed technical assistance! A big shout out to Christian (Alice in Wonderland) for his invaluable advice, thanks and respect to Steve 'Speed Machine' for getting me into doing this book in the first place, all the fellow deviants and miscreants (alive and dead/male and female/good, bad and ugly) that I've met over the years and all the amazing musicians that I've played with. Lemmy, Dave Brock, Daevid Allen, The Pinks et al, the music that you played with your bands provided the soundtrack to my youth and beyond and was an inspiration to me, live long and prosper.... Big luv to all who sailed the good ships Magic Mushroom Band/Astralasia/Moonboot Oz whether playing, lighting, mixing or just plain humping the gear about and especially those that dug the bands, bought the music, played the music and came to the shows......

Garry 'Moonboot' Masters

*Cover portrait by Ed Neef (aka Beladene Deva)
*Cover photography by Mark Hamilton Photography

Garry 'Moonboot' Masters

BAND FILE

Speed Machine (1977-78)

Garry 'Moonboot' Masters - Guitar/Vocals
Steve 'Speed Machine' - Bass/Vocals
Caetano 'Deso' Desouza - Drums/Percussion

The Magic Mushroom Band - Mark 1 (1978-79)

Garry 'Moonboot' Masters - Guitar/Vocals
Steve 'Scruff' Gilder - Bass
Caetano 'Deso' Desouza - Drums/Percussion
Jacqui Miller - Vocals/Whispers
Paul the Chef - Synthesiser (1978)
Thamby - Synthesisers (1979)

The You Band (1979-81)

Garry 'Moonboot' Masters - Guitar/Vocals
Thamby - Synthesisers
Gary 'Bap Bap' Pearson - Bass (1979)
Colin the Weightlifter - Bass (1979)
Wayne Twining - Bass (1980-81)
Alan Hitt - Drums/Percussion

Ali Katt & His Baghdad Boogie Band/Psychic Attack (1981-82)

Garry 'Moonboot' Masters - Guitar/Vocals
Adrian Androgyny - Wasp Synthesisers
Wayne Twining - Bass (1981)
Ormond – Bass (1982)
Steve 'Speed Machine' - Bass (1982)
Clive - Bass (1982)
Alan Hitt - Drums/Percussion (1981)
Nigel Tubb - Drums/Percussion (1982)

The Magic Mushroom Band Mark 2 (1982-89)

Garry 'Moonboot' Masters - Guitar/Vocals
Kim Oz - Vocals/Synthesisers
Wayne Twining - Bass
Craig Twining - Guitar (1982-1988)
Jim 'Max' Lacey - Drums/Percussion (1982-89)
Royston(ed) Burghall - Synthesiser (1983-84)
Jane 'Reaction' Bradfield - Vocals (1984-87)
Roger Lewis - Saxaphonium/Clarinet (1984-87)
Mykl O' Dempsey - Keyboards/Guitar (1985-88)
Jethro - 2nd Drummer (1983-84)

The Magic Mushroom Band Mark 3 (1990-94)

Garry 'Moonboot' Masters - Guitar/Vocals
Kim Oz - Vocals/Synthesisers
Wayne Twining - Bass
Marc 'Swordfish' Hunt - Drums/Percussion/Production
Ed 'Bones' Genis - Slide/Rhythm Guitar
Sam Turner - Eclectic Violin
Jason Relf - Keyboards (1992-93)

Astralasia (1990-94)

Marc 'Swordfish' Hunt -
Drums/Percussion/Programming/Production
Garry 'Moonboot' Masters - Guitar/Vocals
Kim Oz - Vocals/Synthesisers
Chris Haines - Keyboards/Samples
Wayne Twining - Bass
Ed 'Bones' Genis - Slide/Rhythm Guitar
Sam Turner - Eclectic Violin
Jason Relf - Keyboards (1992-93)

Moonboot Oz-Acoustic (1995-97)

Garry 'Moonboot' Masters - Acoustic Guitars/Vocals
Kim Oz - Vocals/Harmonium
Jim 'Lim Bim Sim' Lacey - Percussion

Moonboot Oz-Electric (1998-99)

Garry 'Moonboot' Masters - Guitar/Vocals
Kim Oz - Vocals/Synthesisers
Jim 'Lim Bim Sim' Lacey - Drums/Percussion
Andy Prince - Bass/Stick Bass
Mykl O' Dempsey - Keyboards (1998)
Quiller Rees - Synthesiser/Keyboards (1999)
Jasmine Masters - Vocals/Belly Dancer
Gabi Rees - Belly Dancer

Earthlight (1999)

Garry 'Moonboot' Masters - Guitar/Vocals/Didgeridoo
Kim Oz - Vocals/Dance
Andy Prince - Stick Bass
Quiller Rees - Synthesiser/Keyboards
Jasmine Masters - Vocals/Dance
Gabi Rees - Vocals/Dance

Garry 'Moonboot' Masters

DISCOGRAPHY

The Magic Mushroom Band

1984 - Cassette e.p - three tracks 'Magick Eye', 'Astral Action' & 'Redemption Time'

1984 - Unsung Heroes (compilation)- one live track 'Living in a Dream' (Video only)

1985 - The Waking Dream (compilation)- two tracks 'Magick Eye' and 'Wide Eyed & Electrick' (Psycho)

1986 - The Politics of Ecstasy (Pagan)

1987 - Bomshamkar! (Aftermath)

1987 - Feed Your Head - live 1982 - 1986 (cassette only)

1988 - Eyes of the Angel (Aftermath)

1989 - Live '89 (Cassette only)

1990 - Process of Illumination (Fungus/Caroline/Magick Eye/Voiceprint)

1991 - A Psychedelic Psauna (compilation)- 'Don't Be Afraid' (Delerium)

1991 - Spaced Out (Fungus/Caroline/Magick Eye/Voiceprint)

1992 - Pictures in my Mind 12" (Magick Eye)

1992 - Magick Eye 12" (Magick Eye)

1992 - Re-Hash (Magick Eye/Voiceprint)

1993 - R U Spaced Out 2 (Magick Eye/Voiceprint)

1993 - Freshly Picked e.p (Magick Eye)

1994 - The Fungus Among Us e.p (Magick Eye)

1994 - Magic (Magick Eye/Voiceprint)

1997 - Archives Of Space (compilation) - 'Hubbly Bubbly' (Purple Pyramid USA)

1997 - The Spaced Collection (Purple Pyramid USA)

2003 - Singles & Rarities (Voiceprint)

2006 - Spaced Out III (Voiceprint)

2006 - Magic Frantic Mushrooms - Date With The Devil - studio collaboration with The Frantic Flintstones (Voiceprint)

2007 - Feed Your Head - live 1982 - 1986 (Voiceprint CD re-release)

2007 –Live '89 (Voiceprint CD re-release)

Astralasia

1991 - Astralasia (Fungus/Caroline)

1991 - Rhythm Of Life 12" (Magick Eye)

1992 - Shamanarchy In The UK (compilation) - one track 'Squatter In The House' (Evolution)

1992 - The Politics Of Ecstasy (Magick Eye)

1992 - Sul-E-Stomp 12" (Magick Eye)

1993 - Mad 12" (Magick Eye)

1993 - Unveria Zekt 12" (Magick Eye)

1993 - Pitched Up At The Edge Of Reality (Magick Eye)

1994 - Hashishin (Magick Eye)

1994 - Realise Your Purpose 12" (Magick Eye)

1995 - Mother Durga (Change The World) 12" (Magick Eye)

1995 - Axis Mundi (Magick Eye)

1995 - What Ever Happened To Utopia? (Magick Eye)

1995 - Astralogy (Magick Eye)

2004 - Volume 1 & 2 (Voiceprint CD release of two cassette only albums)

Moonboot Oz

1995 - Organic Mushrooms e.p (Chameleon)

1997 - Psychedelic Cafe (Chameleon)

1999 - Lost In Space e.p (Unreleased)

With Other Artists

1992 - David Jackson - Tonewall Stands (Voiceprint)

1995 - UVX - Rays - guitar sample - one track 'It Just Takes Time' (Magick Eye)

BIBLIOGRAPHY

2000AD Comic issue 112 - Cartoon - 'The Real Judge Dredd'

Back Street Heroes Magazine no 24 - Cartoon - ' Aw Dad...'

Ozbike Magazine no 257 - Article - 'Coming to Australia'
Ozbike Magazine no 263 - Article - 'Tattoo You'
Ozbike Magazine no 264 - Article - 'Talk The Talk'
Ozbike Magazine no 267 - Article - 'Going the Whole Hog'
Ozbike Magazine no 272 - Article - 'Groovy Movies'
Ozbike Magazine no 277 - Article - 'Moonboot's Stool Sample'
Ozbike Magazine no 279 - Article - 'Cruisin' fer a Bruisin'
Ozbike Magazine no 283 - Article - 'Show us your Tits!'
Ozbike Magazine no 286 - Article - 'USD Forks..'
Ozbike Magazine no 302 - Article - 'On One Knee'
Ozbike Magazine no 307 - Article - 'The Patch upon his Back'

Printed in Great Britain
by Amazon.co.uk, Ltd.,
Marston Gate.